Economic Environment of International Business

RAYMOND VERNON

LOUIS T. WELLS, JR.

Harvard University

ECONOMIC ENVIRONMENT OF INTERNATIONAL BUSINESS

Second Edition

PRENTICE-HALL, INC., Englewood Cliffs, New Jersey

Library of Congress Cataloging in Publication Data

Vernon, Raymond (date)
    Economic environment of international business.

    Includes bibliographies and index.
    1. International business enterprises. 2. International economic relations. I. Wells,
Louis T., joint author. II. Title.
HD2755.5.V47 1976   338.8'8   75-37752
ISBN 0-13-224311-3

Printed in the United States of America

10 9 8 7 6 5 4 3 2

PRENTICE-HALL INTERNATIONAL, INC., London
PRENTICE-HALL OF AUSTRALIA PTY. LIMITED, Sydney
PRENTICE-HALL OF CANADA, LTD., Toronto
PRENTICE-HALL OF INDIA PRIVATE LIMITED, New Delhi
PRENTICE-HALL OF JAPAN, INC., Tokyo
PRENTICE-HALL OF SOUTHEAST ASIA PTE. LTD., Singapore

Contents

Part One

The Firm from Within

v

List of Illustrations

Preface

This is the second edition of a book that is intended to introduce the reader to the fields of international payments, international trade, and international investment. These problems are introduced from a very special viewpoint, for our aim is to illuminate these subjects as seen through the eyes of enterprises operating in an international environment.

Though nominally a second edition, most of the text is wholly new. One reason for the extensive revisions has been the change in the international economic environment itself. As the reader hardly needs to be told, the changes over the past five years have been profound. Old institutions have been swept away; old assumptions have been altered. We were determined to try to capture some of the dimensions of that shift in the present edition.

Another factor has generated the extensive revisions. About a decade has passed since scholars at Harvard and other institutions began to study in detail the multinational spread of large enterprises. In that period of intensive study, a stream of materials and concepts has emerged which illuminate the strategies, structures, practices, and effects of such enterprises. This edition introduces many of these concepts for the first time in textbook form.

Although we have borrowed frequently from the concepts of economic theory, this book is different in both purpose and content from a standard textbook in international economics. Such texts must discharge an obligation that this book has not assumed; here we must face some issues that standard texts can quite properly disregard.

Any discipline, such as economics, is concerned with the development of a system of mutually consistent and interrelated principles that, in the aggregate, "explain" a field. A textbook in a given discipline has the task of presenting the principles that make up the discipline. However, many of the propositions that are indispensable to fill out the rational structure of the discipline have no obvious relevance for understanding the international environment or for analyzing the problems encountered in it. Accordingly, we have chosen the uninhibited course of presenting principles and concepts from the economic discipline (and other disciplines, for that matter) when we thought the ideas useful, while disregarding the contributions of the disciplines when we thought them irrelevant in this context.

On the other hand, enterprises cannot hope to solve their problems solely by the application of well-articulated principles; they must take their problems as they come. And many of those that arise in the international economy can derive little help from the familiar precepts of the disciplines. As a rule, the problems encountered in the international economy are shrouded in uncertainty and risk, and the disciplines are still in their infancy in the development of propositions in which uncertainty or risk are involved. At other times, as in the case of problems involving foreign exchange risk, the coupling of propositions from various disciplines, such as economics and political science, is required in ways that may not be satisfying to either. Accordingly, we have not hesitated to stray beyond the solid structure of the disciplines whenever we thought that something useful might be said bearing on the problems of enterprises in the international economy.

Most textbooks come very close to being stolen intellectual goods. Proper acknowledgments for the contributions that go into the making of a textbook, therefore, present a real problem for any author. The situation could hardly be otherwise. The job of a textbook is largely to present the current state of the art. Few scholars individually can do much more than add a few insights, a few clarifications, to a body of ideas already formulated by the culture that spawned them. Inevitably, that is the character of this book.

A word on authorship. This edition, as the names on the cover attest, is the work of two authors, and the general strategy and content of the present edition represents a joint effort of both authors. Wells was principally responsible for Chapters 6, 7, and 11, while Vernon was principally responsible for the rest. Various students at the Harvard Business School and a number of its staff members contributed to the book. The heaviest burden, however, was borne by Marie Castro, whose goodwill and good humor were unfailing.

RAYMOND VERNON
LOUIS T. WELLS, JR.
Boston, Massachusetts

Economic Environment of International Business

PART ONE

THE
FIRM
FROM
WITHIN

Strategies of the

Firm in

International Business

chapter one

This book is for the reader who expects to be involved, one way or the other, in the conduct of international business. If the reader is like most of those that have used this book in the past, he or she will already know something about the concepts and tools of finance, marketing, production, and organization, and something about the interaction between the strategy of the firm and the characteristics of its environment. But the odds are that the reader will feel most at home with these ideas as applied in a single national economy, not in a world made up of many economies.

The object of this book is to add the international dimension: to present the institutions, forces, and problems that are involved when business managers try to operate in many economies at once, and to sort out the threats and promises that develop when they try to link their operations across national boundaries. Because the viewpoint is that of the manager, it begins with the firm itself as it looks outward at the international economy.

FIRMS AND FUNCTIONS

Of course, the transactions that take place across the borders of any country affect every part of its economy, not just the transacting firms. The pervasive impact of changes in the international oil market over the past few years illustrates the point well enough. But some kinds of enterprises are much more caught up than others in the dangers and opportunities that arise from developments that lie outside the home economy.

The "multinational enterprises" of the world (or multinational corporations or transnational enterprises) are especially exposed in this respect. Included in this group are enterprises made up of a cluster of affiliated firms located in a number of countries. Enterprises of this sort commonly operate in such a way that the affiliated firms, although in different countries, nevertheless share the following characteristics:

1. They are linked by ties of common ownership.
2. They draw on a common pool of resources, such as money and credit, information and systems, trade names and patents.
3. They respond to some common strategy.

We shall be exploring the international environment as it relates especially to this sort of enterprise. But a focus of this kind does not narrow the subject very much. Such enterprises, to be sure, confront opportunities and problems of their own. But they also face the problems and opportunities of any importer or exporter, or any lender or borrower, who deals across national boundaries.

Enterprises that are directly involved in the international environment come in all sizes, big and little. But, by and large, international business is the game of big enterprises.

Practically all the 400 or 500 biggest enterprises in the world have substantial business interests in the form of operating units located outside their own country. General Motors, for instance, has one fourth of its employees outside the United States, IBM over one third, and Dow Chemical over one fifth. Siemens, a large German firm, has one fourth of its employees outside Germany and Imperial Chemical Industries one fourth outside Britain. And so on.

Moreover, the tendency of big enterprises to have business interests outside their home base is much greater than the same tendency for small firms. This is true not only of firms that have their home base in the United States but also of firms based in Europe. For Japan, the situation is a bit more complicated; but more on that later.

Firms that have developed a multinational structure not only tend to be large; they also tend to be located in certain kinds of business activities. The manufacturing industries as a group account for more of these enterprises than any other category. Oil and banking each run well behind manufacturing, according to almost any measure. The numerous other activities in which multinational enterprises are prominent include mining, agriculture, and public utilities.

Within the manufacturing category, multinational activity is concentrated in certain sectors of industry; this pattern of concentration, along with the large size of multinational firms, begins to offer some important clues regarding the special strengths and special problems of the multinational enterprise. In the case of U.S.-based companies, the multinational enterprise is especially strong in motor vehicles, chemical products, petroleum refining, drugs, electronic products, and food products; it is notably weak in some very important national industries, including aircraft, iron and steel, textiles, paper, and printing and publishing. Multinational enterprises that are based in other countries, including notably Britain, France, Germany, and Switzerland, exhibit similar profiles by sectors. On the other hand, there are also some important differences between countries in the sector profiles of their multinational enterprises, differences that are especially large for Japanese-based firms.

Why are large firms more heavily committed to multinational activities than small? Why are firms in some kinds of industry more strongly committed than those in other industries? And why do these tendencies appear not only with some similarities but also with some differences for enterprises based in different countries?

In one way or another, most of this book can be thought of as contributing to a response. The first four chapters, concentrating on the firm itself, obviously bear on the questions. But so also do the chapters on international trade, which take the student into the world of international comparative advantage, factor costs, tariffs, and state trading. The chapters on foreign exchange, with their emphasis on exchange rates and capital markets, will shed a little more light. Even the chapter on economic development will provide some of the ingredients for an adequate response.

A key point to be borne in mind is that as a rule firms do not become multinational overnight; ordinarily, no single earth-shattering decision creates a multinational enterprise. These structures generally evolve as the result of a sequence of decisions, each decision representing a response to a pressing issue or a pressing opportunity. However, the patterns of stimulus and response have tended to fall into certain familiar categories, each of which can be thought of as a separate strategy. Firms, especially large firms, have not limited themselves exclusively to any one strategy; different strategies, for instance, can be detected in different product lines within a single firm. Nevertheless, it is useful to distinguish the following strategies and to identify the patterns of multinational behavior they have tended to create:

1. Exploiting a technological lead.
2. Exploiting a strong trade name.
3. Exploiting the advantages of scale.
4. Exploiting a scanning capability.

EXPLOITING A TECHNOLOGICAL LEAD

In any industry heavily engaged in innovation and development, there is a strong likelihood that the leading firms will have numerous contacts with foreign markets outside the home base. In some cases, as in the aeronautical industry, the contact with foreign markets will take the form of exports; for instance, Boeing, Lockheed, Dassault, or McDonnell Douglas depend on exports to a much greater degree than most manufacturing firms. In the chemical, drug, scientific instruments, transportation equipment, and machinery industries, exports also are comparatively heavy. To facilitate their exports abroad, firms commonly appoint agents or develop sales subsidiaries in their foreign markets.

In most cases, however, large firms do not confine their involvement in foreign markets to exports alone. Under one arrangement or another, such firms generally are involved in production abroad. One common arrangement is the ownership and management of producing facilities located outside of the home country. Another common arrangement takes the form of a contract with firms outside the home country, under which the outside firms are linked to the home enterprise in ways that allow the outsiders to tap some of the technological capabilities of the enterprise. These contacts, generally dubbed licensing agreements, may provide a variety of different advantages: a flow of technical information, a license to certain patents, a supply of some exotic line of machinery or industrial supplies, the use of a trade name, or some combination of these.

The linkage between technological leadership and foreign markets can be seen not only for firms based in the United States but also for those based in Europe and Japan. And behind the linkage lies an obvious set of causes.

Since the beginning of modern industry over one-hundred years ago, a good deal of the research and development undertaken by industrial firms has typically resulted in new products. The emphasis on new products has been especially typical of the research and development efforts of firms in the United States, which are responsible for more than half of all the industrial research and development expenditures in the non-Communist world. Some of these products, such as drip-dry shirts, simply perform a familiar job for the consumer better than the existing product. Others, such as computer-controlled machine tools, help the producer perform his tasks more efficiently. But many, such as penicillin and commercial aircraft, are not in serious competition with any existing products at the time of their introduction and can be regarded as satisfying wants that were never previously addressed.

Here already we can begin to see some of the reasons for expecting different patterns of behavior between firms based in the United States and firms based in, say, Germany or France.

The disposition of a country to develop new products is not a matter of pure chance. For substantial industrial innovations to take place in a country, a body of trained engineers and interested businessmen must exist. But that is not quite enough. Businessmen and engineers need an incentive to innovate: the hope of gain or the fear of loss must be strong enough to justify the effort. In some national environments, where the position of individual firms is rendered fairly secure by agreements with potential competitors or by government controls, the motivation to innovate may be quite low; in other environments it will be higher. Even where the capacity and incentive to innovate are strong enough, innovators are likely to react differently in different national environments, developing those products that seem most wanted in the national environment in which they operate.

Some national environments encourage businessmen and engineers to innovate in one direction, some in another. To be sure, all countries welcome new products or processes that will cut costs. But in a country where, say, skilled labor is exceedingly scarce and dear while capital is abundant and cheap, businessmen and engineers are likely to concentrate on labor-saving devices. In countries where labor is the abundant resource and raw materials are scarce, the innovations that capture the interest of businessmen and engineers tend to be material-saving. Various studies show that in past years the innovations emanating from the United States have stressed labor-saving needs while Europe's innovations have been weighted more heavily toward material-saving objectives.

There are also characteristic differences in consumer products. Countries with very high per capita incomes offer opportunities for the sale of new products or services that have not been seen before. Countries with low per capita incomes, on the other hand, offer unique opportunities for the adaptation of existing products to lower-priced versions. European and Japanese innovations commonly fit that pattern.

There are other variables that influence the propensity and direction of industrial innovation in any economy. Countries in which the military buy large quantities of hardware from their producers generate one kind of market, and countries in which the government buys large quantities of medicines quite another. Big countries induce innovations that are associated with economies of scale; small countries may not. And so on.

Once a firm establishes a technological lead in some product, certain characteristic patterns are likely to ensue as the product grows more mature. These patterns, commonly referred to under the rubric of the "product cycle," will be referred to more than once in the chapters that follow.

In any event, the firm's first question is how best to exploit the innovational lead. Sometimes, as in the case of the Boeing 747 or the DC-10, exploitation in foreign markets can be achieved well enough through exports or licensing. A buyer of a Boeing 747 who is located in Delhi does not think of the aircraft as less available or less attractive simply because it is designed and produced in Seattle. In most industries, however, the firm that is exporting a relatively sophisticated product to a foreign market begins to feel the pressure of various forces that push its production facilities in the direction of that market.

Of course, as any market grows, the tendency to move production facilities closer to the market is always present in some degree. In the absence of some offsetting factor, the desire to reduce delivery costs may prompt such a move. But when a product is still new in the marketplace, a manager is not quite as concerned with questions of production cost. For various reasons, his attention at that stage is on other factors:

1. The lines separating the development stage, the pilot-plant stage, and the first commercial production stage for a new product are often not clean-cut. In these early stages, the manager is likely to be most concerned with maintaining effective communication among the key development engineers, production men, controllers, salesmen, and prospective first users of the product. If the product proves successful, the manager is likely to discover suddenly that his first production unit is already in place, at the site where the development of the product was taking place. More than any other factor, this explains the U.S. automobile industry's early location in Detroit and the chemical industry's early location in New Jersey.

2. Even if the manager could take his choice of locations, he would have great difficulty in determining the least-cost points of production and distribution. Products that are in their infancy often come in a variety of experimental shapes, sizes, and materials; witness the radio market of the 1920s. Unsure of the exact inputs that the product eventually will require, unsure of the size of the market or the geographical distribution of demand, the manager is disinclined to give much weight to cost-minimizing calculations that depend on factors such as these.

3. At the early stages, the pressure on the manager to consider cost explicitly and carefully is not likely to be great. In new products such as nylon, video tapes, metal skis, and laser aiming devices, the number of competing producers is small, at least at first. Besides, the earliest customers as a rule are not very sensitive to small variations in price; at that stage, in economic jargon, the product is not very price elastic. The need of the seller to hold down product costs in order to increase sales comes later.

In time, however, the manager is forced to worry about costs again. This is the case for a number of reasons.

1. As the product matures, it begins to assume characteristics that permit easier comparisons from one producer to the next. Automobiles, for instance, took some time before they eventually settled down to a four-wheel vehicle with a steering wheel and a gasoline engine.

2. As the product matures, the original producer's special knowledge and special skills, whatever they may be, are shared with others at home and abroad. The threat of price competition becomes more tangible.

3. As the demand for the product grows, the later users are generally found placing much more weight on questions of price than the first

users. In economic terms, the price elasticity of demand associated with the later users is higher than for the original users. Moreover, differences in price between brands—cross-elasticities—generally matter more with these later users.

4. As total demand grows and as the volume of sales in some foreign markets increases, the possibility of producing from foreign plant locations grows. In these later stages, a formal analysis to determine least-cost production points is more likely to suggest the establishment of foreign production sites by the firm than in the earlier stages. The timing, of course, depends partly on (a) the importance of scale economies in production, and (b) transportation costs for the materials required by the plant and for the plant's output.

5. As the product matures, importing countries may begin to ask if there are ways of encouraging local production to take the place of imports. Import restrictions sometimes develop at this stage. Some are overt restrictions, such as tariffs and import licensing requirements; others are more subtle restrictions, such as "buy-at-home" policies on the part of government agencies and other public buyers.

Accordingly, for many products, multinational enterprises eventually begin to test the attractiveness of various overseas sites as production points. In that connection, the concepts presented in Figure 1–1 come into play.

Figure 1–1 on page 10 indicates the cost situation from the firm's viewpoint prior to establishment of the foreign subsidiary. In this case, the firm is producing $0A$ units for the home market and AB units for the export market. The diagram assumes that marginal costs are falling through most of the production range $0B$. If the price in the export market is given, then the firm's first question is whether the delivered cost per unit in the AB range, reflected in the height of the curve CC', is lower than or higher than the average cost for an equivalent volume of production from a plant set up in the foreign market. This requires an estimate of production costs for such a plant which takes into account the production cost differences that prevail in the foreign market.

To be sure, this method of formulating the issue is only the beginning of the analysis. The possibility has to be explored of separating some aspects of the stages of manufacturing from others, perhaps in order to leave only the later stages to the local market. The possibility that the import duty may be raised, thereby raising the foreign delivered cost, must also be considered. As that contingency is introduced, appropriate account must also be taken of the possibility that the increase in price may lower internal demand or encourage new sources of domestic competition or both. But these aspects of the problem can usually be managed in a systematic way. It is this sort of calculation that has led many U.S. innovators eventually to set up production facilities in Western Europe and

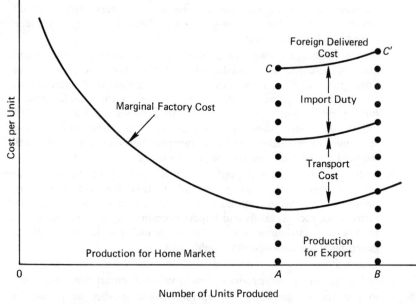

FIG. 1–1   Costs of Exported Product Delivered to Foreign Market

many West European innovators eventually to set up production facilities in the United States.

The maturing of technologically advanced products, therefore, tends to press enterprises toward the establishment of overseas production units, a move necessary to protect or prolong a position that was originally based on a technological lead in those markets. With a decline in the importance of the technological lead, the relatively straightforward calculations of least cost begin to play their familiar role once again.

EXPLOITING A STRONG TRADE NAME

Another strategy that has led enterprises to create producing facilities in foreign countries is to exploit a strong trade name. In the modern world of easy international movement and communication, trade names can sometimes gain strength in a foreign market without much conscious effort on the part of the firm that owns the name. Casual unplanned exports sometimes establish a position for a foreign brand. Military installations on foreign soil sometimes perform that sort of role. International tourists, movies, and television shows can also be the carriers.

In international markets, foreign brands often command a premium because of sheer snob appeal; this appears to be the case in some national markets, for instance, in clothing, automobiles, cigarettes, and wine. (Sometimes, however, foreignness may have exactly the opposite effect.) Apart from snob appeal, however, the strength of the foreign trade name may also be associated with the fact or the illusion of superior performance. Fact or illusion, the expectation of superior performance is often strengthened and fortified by copious promotional expenditures, as is commonly the case for name-branded pharmaceuticals and food preparations.

Sometimes, too, the strength of a brand name is associated not with superior performance but with predictable performance. When that is the case, the existence of a strong trade name may rest on some technological capability. For instance, delivering a packaged food product such as chocolates or biscuits in a reasonably standardized condition on a reasonably reliable basis can be a technically exacting job. As a rule, the processing stage involves a fairly elaborate technique for the standardization of the product. The distribution stage may also entail scheduling and control devices of some complexity to keep the product from aging on shelves and in warehouses.

In any event, whether based on substance or illusion, some trade names command a premium. By selling in foreign markets, many enterprises are in a position to exploit the premium associated with their name. Whether they eventually will also produce in such markets is influenced in part by the technical considerations described in the preceding section.

On these criteria, the decision for some industries has been clear-cut. In packaged foods, soft drinks, and drugs, where trade names play a critical role, enterprises have often discovered that they could not adequately exploit their advantage by way of exports and have commonly established plants in their foreign markets. Once established in such markets, these producers have generally had to confront national competitors who were operating on roughly the same cost basis. Indeed, the foreigners have sometimes been handicapped by added costs, such as the costs of communication and control associated with the maintenance of a multinational organization. In such cases, the special strength of the trade name has usually been indispensable for the foreign firm to maintain a competitive position.

Nevertheless, although foreign trade names have been known to endure for long periods of time in such markets, their ability to command a price premium in a given type of product against the competing offers of national producers often erodes in time. As long as the product itself remains unchanged, the national producers learn either to match the performance of the foreign product or to overcome the illusion of a difference that was never there. When that happens, multinational enterprises find themselves obliged to share their foreign markets with national producers. In most instances, foreign-owned firms continue to sell their product, albeit to a smaller share of the market; in some cases, they find themselves obliged to abandon the market altogether to their national competitors.

EXPLOITING THE ADVANTAGES OF SCALE

In sheer quantity terms, most of the output of multinational enterprises is in products whose sale depends on neither a strong technological lead nor a strong trade name. In oil, copper, aluminum, heavy chemicals, and many other products, differences in technology and differences in trade name strength play a quite secondary role in marketing.

THE STRATEGIC NEED. The strength of the leaders in these industries lies primarily in the fact that large firms are in a position to be more efficient than small. A new challenger, as a rule, has to find some way of assembling the funds, physical assets, and human resources that are capable of producing, distributing, and controlling on a very large scale; otherwise, the firm usually runs the risk of being a high-cost competitor. Besides, assuming the capital, facilities, and human skills could be put together by the newcomer, there would still be the problem of financing a period of learning, a run-in period for the organization. In large, complex organizations, that period generally has to be reckoned in terms of years, not days or months, during which the efficiency of the organization as an operating unit runs at less than its potential.

An enterprise already established on a large scale has an obvious edge over a newcomer. Still, there are latent weaknesses. For one thing, with production facilities in place and determined, the established firm has lost some degree of flexibility in both technology and location. Its strength lies in the fact that its marginal costs are low, so that it has a certain measure of price flexibility for a portion of its output. Its weakness lies in the fact that its fixed costs are high, so that small variations in volume of output have a disproportionate effect on profits. On each of these last two sentences rests a major theme in the strategies of leading firms in this kind of industry. (The reader who finds these concepts heavy going is urged to try to master them by referring to any standard text on pricing. The concepts are basically quite simple, easy to understand, and extremely efficient for communication.) The ability of a firm to exploit the strategies associated with scale is enhanced if that firm is established in a number of countries.

SHUT-OUT PRICING. In oligopolistic markets, a standard reaction on the part of the established leaders to the appearance of a newcomer is the obvious one of drastically, albeit temporarily, reducing the going price. This is a reaction of especial importance in the kind of industry that is dominated by multinational enterprises.

Picture a well-defined market in which the leaders of an industry have settled down into an acceptable equilibrium. Each leader has a stable share of the market and no great uncertainties about the price. Now a newcomer appears in the market. The newcomer may have adequate resources, financial and technical, to make a serious bid for a share of the market. This possibility is based on the fact that the newcomer is already well established in other related lines or in the same line in other markets. Since entry into the market is not easy, profit rates are likely to be fairly high. The newcomer who is able to overcome the entry barriers may therefore be in a position to cut the price in a bid for a share of the market. Confronting the newcomer, the leaders may respond in various ways, but two possibilities are obvious:

1. The leaders may disregard the newcomer's bid and permit him to capture some share of the market, relying on the expectation that the newcomer's goal in share-of-market terms is limited and that equilibrium will reassert itself once the goal has been achieved. In this case, the cost to the leaders of the newcomer's appearance is the quantity of sales lost multiplied by profit per unit.

2. An alternative strategy for the leaders is to reduce the price to a shut-out price, thereby retaining the previous volume of sales but accepting for the necessary period a lower profit margin on all sales. In that case, the cost to the leaders is the quantity of shut-out sales multiplied by decline in profit per unit. Such a strategy, it is apparent, is particularly attractive to one of the leaders if the firm can continue to operate at its old profit margin in other countries while it does battle with a newcomer in a particular market.

For those who feel the need to look at precise quantitative measures, the expected cost of the two alternatives can be calculated by using present value measures. Even on casual inspection, the relative merits of the two strategies begin to sort themselves out. Strategy 1 commends itself more strongly if the newcomer's share-of-market goal is thought to be modest. The relative attractiveness of strategy 1 also increases to the degree that the newcomer's staying power is thought to be long. The agonizing choice occurs when the newcomer in a given product line is both ambitious and strong. That difficult situation commonly occurs as well-established firms move into new products and new markets.

VERTICAL INTEGRATION. The producers of standardized products that are manufactured under conditions of high fixed costs have an especially compelling need to stabilize the demand for their product. One method is to acquire captive customers. The existence of captive customers may not eliminate all the sources of variation in demand; but at least it eliminates the variation that is produced when customers switch between suppliers.

Once the leading producers of such products begin to recognize the need for controlling their downstream users, a difficult strategic choice is offered to the users. Those that do not wish to be absorbed are confronted with a growing need to capture their own source of supply. For as vertical integration proceeds, the users that remain independent find themselves more and more obliged to buy their materials from vertically integrated firms with which they are in direct competition. In periods of shortage, as the experience of independent oil distributors in the early 1970s emphasized, that dependence can be damaging. Under those conditions, the vertically integrated producer may decide to supply its captive downstream users in more generous quantities and on better terms than its independent customers, thereby imperiling the independents' existence. A realization of that risk has led to the pattern of expansion portrayed in Figure 1–2.

The process of vertical integration often leads to the multinationalization of operations. As enterprises move upstream or downstream to complete their vertical structure, they often reach beyond the national economy in which the integrating process began. Either they need new sources of supply not to be had in their part of the world, or they need markets that do not readily exist at home. In either case, national enterprises commonly become multinational enterprises as they pursue the integration strategy.

MULTIPLE MARKETS AND MULTIPLE SOURCES. The dominance of multinational enterprises in the capital-intensive industries that produce standardized products is explained in part by still another factor—a factor that is expressed in the *law of large numbers*.

The managers of a huge capital-intensive aluminum smelter or of a petrochemicals complex may see advantages in serving users located in many different markets. Enterprises that rely on several different markets are less vulnerable to the random variations of demand that affect any national market, and less vulnerable to the interventions of national governments. If the market is shrinking for any reason in one nation, it may possibly be increasing in another. An act of nationalization in one market can be offset by an expansion elsewhere. The strategy in this case is to try to develop facilities around the globe which enjoy the stability that goes with multiple markets.

The same principle applies, of course, with respect to sources of supply.

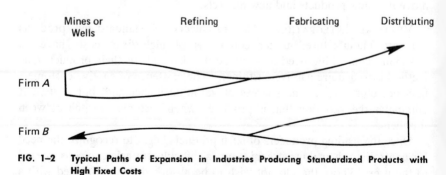

FIG. 1–2   Typical Paths of Expansion in Industries Producing Standardized Products with High Fixed Costs

Enterprises that rely on a number of sources are less vulnerable to stoppages than enterprises that rely upon a single source. Natural calamities, strikes, and the acts of national governments are less likely to affect the total flow. The fact was illustrated pointedly in Libya's negotiations with the international oil companies in 1973; Occidental Oil, being much more dependent on Libya than the others, was also in the weakest position to resist its demands. (Of course, when governments get together to coordinate their demands on the enterprises, as the Organization of Petroleum Exporting Countries has done, the advantages of multiple sources are reduced.)

Managers of multinational enterprises understand these principles well enough; indeed their response to the law of large numbers has often been the cause of their being multinational. In an extension of the same principle, managers have often tried to stretch the geographical spread of their sources of supply by creating joint ventures abroad in partnership with other multinational enterprises in the same industry. In the aluminum industry, for example, a considerable number of the bauxite mines of the world located outside the United States are joint ventures between competing firms, often of different nationality. The same pattern is seen in large oil fields and large copper mines throughout the world. By pursuing the joint venture route, multinational enterprises are able to spread a given amount of investment across a larger number of locations, thereby reducing the risks.

FOLLOW-THE-LEADER.   In an industry made up of a small number of firms that see each other as competitors, another common strategy that often leads to the multinationalization of the dominant enterprises is the follow-the-leader strategy. Although the strategy may appear in any industry in which a few large leaders dominate, it is especially common in industries in which the leaders are selling identical products.

Picture the limiting case, that is, the case in which an industry consists of only two firms, both producing the same standardized product and both located in the same country area. Other firms are barred from entry because of the problem of sheer scale in the industry. Overt agreements between the two firms are illegal and none exists.

Now firm L (the leader) learns of the existence of a new site in another country from which production and distribution would be less costly—a new rich copper ore deposit or a new oil field. Should it set up in the new location?

That, of course, depends in part on its anticipation of the way in which firm F (the follower) is likely to respond.

1. One possibility which firm L may consider is that firm F will not react at all, and that it will passively accept firm L's improvement of its profit

margins. That possibility, although hypothetically possible, would seem unlikely. The existence of major differences in profit margins would place firm F at the mercy of firm L, exposing firm F to the possibility that firm L might try to increase its share of the market at some later date. Moreover, the cash flow of firm L would exceed that of firm F, adding to firm L's aggressive strength. So firm L cannot ordinarily count on inaction from firm F.

2. Firm L must consider another possibility: firm F may follow firm L to the new location; there will be a period of uncertainty, during which each assesses the aggressive intentions of the other in the light of the new cost structures; and the new equilibrium established at the end of the period of uncertainty will generate a price level and profit margin no more favorable than the one that existed before the move. In that case, firm L will hesitate to move. (This situation, by the way, has been said by some analysts to be a reason why the U.S. steel industry delayed for so long in its introduction of oxygen topping in steel production.)

3. A third possibility is that firm F would follow firm L to the new location with favorable results for both. This can occur if both firms retain their old price structure; it would be better still if both—acting as a profit-maximizing monopolist would act—adjust their prices to a new level, a level that would increase their total sales and total profits. (The reader who is not familiar with the concept of optimum pricing in a monopoly situation should pause here to digest the point that it sometimes pays a monopolist to reduce the price of his product because the price reduction may increase both total demand and total profits.) This outcome, seen through the eyes of firm L, would be a happy one.

In the real world of multinational enterprises, of course, industries are rarely made up of just two firms, and barriers to entry are rarely so high as to eliminate the worry on the part of the existing firms that newcomers may enter. Indeed, in oil, aluminum, copper, steel, and basic chemicals, the number of large enterprises in world markets has been increasing, not decreasing, in the quarter-century since World War II.

Managers, therefore, are generally obliged to worry about the possibility of newcomer firms. If such newcomers appear, however, the existing firms may resort to imitative behavior to protect their position. The existing firms, for instance may locate an added productive facility where the newcomer has located. If the new location imparts special strengths to the new firm, imitation by the established firms will have the effect of matching the new firm's strengths. That matching will limit the new firm's ability to upset the existing equilibrium in the market.

To be sure, the facts about production costs or other characteristics relating to some new location are never all that clear. Neither the new investing firm nor the established firms can avoid the possibility that estimates may be prone to major error. That increases risks in all directions: the new firm may have a bonanza or a disaster on its hands. Still, although both possibilities may exist, a consistent practice of follow-the-leader may be the best available response.

For if the new location proves more advantageous than the best prior estimate might have suggested, the desirability of imitation is even stronger. If, on the other hand, the new firm's move proves to be ill-considered and to afford no advantage over existing facilities, the error may still not prove very costly. For if the oligopoly is small enough in number and imitative enough in behavior, the cost of the error may be absorbed by a general increase in the price.

Figure 1–3 illustrates in more detail some typical sequences and indicates more precisely why imitative behavior commends itself as a strategy. In both cases shown, the failure of firms to follow the leader entails high risks, whereas the cost of following the leader is limited. In the end, of course, this kind of strategy may break down. Too many firms may enter the industry. Imitation as a hedge against risk may prove impossible. In that case, a strategy based on the existence of barriers to entry must come to an end.

EXPLOITING A SCANNING CAPABILITY

When the cost of production and distribution takes on major importance in the competitive situation in any industry, the relative efficiency of the multinational enterprise in scanning the world for low-cost sources of production may prove to be an asset of some significance.

Multinational enterprises confront the issue of costs in a particularly acute form when they produce a product whose market is losing its oligopoly characteristics. Picture a product, for instance, in which the firm has lost most of its original technological lead; as far as new entrants are concerned, neither the product nor the related processes present formidable hurdles, whether in terms of money, skills, or organization. Although the product may be sold under a well-known brand name, the power of the name to command a premium is small and appears likely to weaken still further. Sheer scale factors offer no major hurdle for the newcomer and no major element of protection for the leaders. The established leaders in the industry have no intention of remaining forever in a business that is beginning to display the conditions of sharp price competition, but neither are they eager to abandon the business prematurely. The cash flow from the existing business is still large, even though the unit markup may be small and the future dubious.

In cases of this sort, the capacity of the multinational enterprise efficiently to search out new low-cost production sites comes into play. The word "efficiently" needs to be stressed. Any firm presumably can search out a new production site, if it is prepared to pay the price of the search.

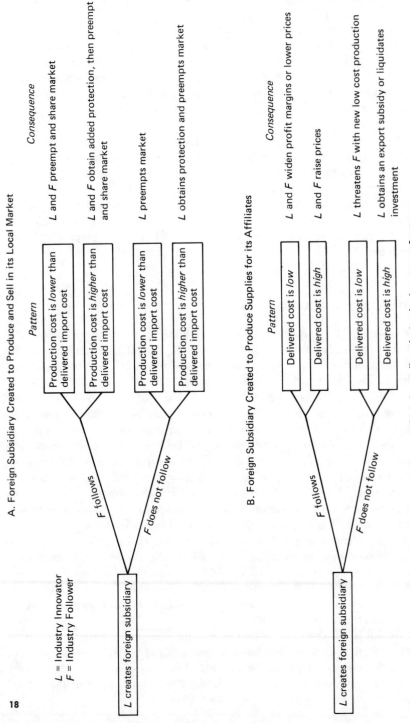

FIG. 1–3 Follow-the-Leader Investment Strategy

18

The problems for most firms starting from scratch in such a search, however, are several:

1. Firms located in an efficient production location may not be aware of the existence of a foreign market for the products that they can efficiently produce; if aware of the market, they feel insecure about their ability to retain it for long.
2. Firms already established in the market as distributors may be unaware of the production possibilities elsewhere; if aware of the possibilities, they may be unsure of the reliability of suppliers.
3. Firms in either situation, to the extent that they require added information, will have to acquire such information at full cost.

The multinational enterprise generally has an advantage on all points. When the enterprise is vertically integrated, it supplies its own market, as in the case of components for automobiles and for consumer electronics; accordingly, hesitations over the availability of a market and the reliability of the suppliers can be held in bounds. Besides, the information that is required for comparing distant places as alternative points of production is more efficiently gathered and assessed by a multinational enterprise in the business than by an entity operating from one end of the prospective chain; at least that is a reasonable starting presumption. For the moment, therefore, the multinational enterprise operates at a distinct advantage.

Of course, if the product is standardized, if trade names are not critical, and if the problem of scale is not important, the information-gathering capabilities of the multinational enterprise may not be a significant asset; the diseconomies and drawbacks of the multinational structure may be more important than the advantages. There are some situations, nonetheless, in which information-gathering capability has been an important element in a successful strategy. Consumer electronics firms, for instance, have managed to survive in highly competitive markets by setting up low-cost producing units for components in Asia. However, perhaps the clearest illustration of the use of information-gathering strength as a basis for multinational activity is provided by a unique kind of Japanese enterprise, the Japanese trading company.

Until the early 1970s, the multinationalizing process in Japanese industry seemed to be taking a form that was somewhat at variance with the process exemplified by U.S.- and European-based firms. For one thing, the products involved were not normally associated with large firms and with concentrated industries. Textiles, biscuits, furniture, and like products were being produced in small overseas plants under the seeming tutelage of relatively small Japanese manufacturing firms. In these arrangements, however, Japanese trading companies almost always held a key position. The preeminence of the trading company in these cases arose from the fact that, in the earliest stages of the multinationalizing process, exports from Japan were heavily emphasized. The trading companies' exporting advantage, as it turned out, lay mainly in three factors: (1) their ability to mobilize credit from associated banks, (2) their ability to scan efficiently the world's markets and to collect the relatively simple and unspecialized information that is needed to sell standardized products on a price basis, and (3) their ability to find the comparatively small-scale producers in Japan who were most efficient in producing the needed products. Compared to any ordinary producer of such standardized products, therefore, the trading companies were in a superior position to sell to markets abroad.

Eventually, however, the position of the trading companies in these markets began to be threatened through the rise of a local group of businessmen—often local distributors of Japanese products—who aspired to get into manufacturing. Neither technology, scale, nor trade names were an overwhelming obstacle to entry. Given that fact and confronted with the latent threat of import barriers, Japanese trading companies responded in the usual way. They helped to set up local production units as joint ventures. In those units, they combined the trading company's strength as financier and integrator, the technical skills (such as they were) of the small Japanese-based manufacturer, and the strengths of the local partner as distributor.

But multinational arrangements of this sort appear to have the same perishable quality as multinational patterns in other competitive industries. Without high entry barriers induced by technology, trade name, or scale, it is to be expected that national firms will rapidly grow in number in many of the simpler industrial sectors. In that case, the drawbacks of the multinational structure are likely to outweigh the advantages, and to lead to a withdrawal of the multinational firms.

The strategies of the multinational enterprise, therefore, are seen as resting on strengths that national enterprises do not readily share. When those strengths are dissipated in any product line or market, the special costs associated with the multinational structure may prove too much of a handicap for the enterprise. At that stage, strategic considerations demand that the multinational enterprise turn its special skills to other lines and other markets.

SUGGESTED READING

BROOKE, MICHAEL Z., and H. LEE REMMERS. *The Strategy of Multinational Enterprises: Organization and Finance* (New York: American Elsevier, 1970).

CAVES, RICHARD E., "International Corporations: The Industrial Economics of Foreign Investment," *Economica,* February 1971.

KNICKERBOCKER, F. T., *Oligopolistic Reaction and Multinational Enterprise* (Boston: Division of Research, Harvard Business School, 1973).

VERNON, RAYMOND, "The Location of Economic Activity," in John H. Dunning (ed.), *Economic Analysis and the Multinational Enterprise* (London: Allen & Unwin, 1974).

VERNON, RAYMOND, *Sovereignty at Bay* (New York: Basic Books, 1971).

Structures of the

Firm in

International Business

chapter two

In Chapter 1, we saw that different firms applied different strategies in the development of their international business. Although the strategies were complex and appeared in various hybrid forms, up to a point they could be systematically identified and analyzed.

The choice of strategies, according to the well-established propositions of organizational theorists, has a profound effect on the way in which an enterprise organizes itself. The exploitation of a technological lead in international business, for instance, makes different demands on an organization than the exploitation of a trademark. These in turn make quite different demands than a strategy based on the barriers of sheer scale or on a special capability for scanning the world's markets and sources of supply. The differences can be seen in the kind of structures that parent firms adopt and in the kind of links they choose when creating their foreign networks.

LINKS WITH FOREIGN AFFILIATES

A CHOICE OF LINKS. Multinational enterprises can implant their presence in foreign locations either by entering into some form of contract with an independent enterprise, by creating or acquiring a local enterprise, or by various hybrid combinations. Although the choices are infinite in variety, the student can think of four "pure" types, always bearing in mind that reality itself is usually a good deal more complex. The four types, arranged in ascending degree of parental control, are as follows:

1. The *licensing agreement* or *technical assistance agreement* is an agreement between the foreign licensor and an entity created under the local law of the host country; the licensor provides a combination of management services, technical information, or patent rights, and receives payment in money.
2. The *foreign–local joint venture* is a corporate entity or partnership created under local law between the parent and local interests.
3. The *foreigners' joint venture* is a corporate entity or partnership involving a number of parents, all foreign to the area in which they operate.
4. The *wholly owned subsidiary* or *branch* is an entity created under the local law of the host country, but wholly owned and wholly managed by the parent.

The labels, of course, can sometimes be misleading. Although licensing agreements generally entail only a limited amount of control by the foreign licensor, there are cases of licensing agreements that tie the local enterprise hand and foot, requiring it to buy its intermediate products from the foreign licensor, adhere to quality standards set by the licensor, and confine its marketing efforts to areas defined in the license; indeed, practically all licenses include some of these limitations. There are also cases of the opposite sort in which wholly owned subsidiaries are scarcely influenced by the foreign parent and operate on so long a leash that the local manager has many of the powers of an unrestrained local owner.

Generally speaking, the strategy that a firm has chosen predisposes it in its choice of links. These preferences develop because the different kinds of links generally have certain predictable costs and benefits, which vary according to the strategy that is pursued.

COST AND BENEFITS. Before trying to tie the firm's strategic choices directly to its preferences in the choice of foreign links, it will be useful to look a little more generally at the costs and benefits associated with each type of link. Table 2–1 on page 25 offers a few statements on comparative costs and benefits ordinarily associated with various local arrangements. The assumption implicit in the table is that a foreign-parent enterprise is linked to a local entity which is engaged mainly in manufacturing for the local market.

A glance at the table indicates the difficulties involved in making one overall generalization about the strengths and drawbacks of any particular arrangement. When measured in costs and benefits, none of the arrangements emerges uniformly as the most desirable. Judgments on the relative merits of the different arrangements depend on two kinds of questions; both involve weighting.

1. Where one arrangement outranks another in some element of cost or benefit, what is the size of the difference?

2. Where an arrangement is ranked high in one element and low in another, is there some common measure that can be applied to the elements so that a single net judgment can be reached by the manager?

The answers to these questions are far from obvious, but a few points may be helpful.

First, one needs to understand perhaps a little more fully the purport of the rankings in Table 2–1. At best, they represent general tendencies rather than ironclad relationships. Some of the factors that lead to the rankings in the table are self-evident nonetheless. Take, for instance, the question of capital commitment and management commitment on the part of the foreign parent. When a license is all that ties the local enterprise to the foreigner, capital and management support from the parent are not ordinarily involved, except on a very restricted scale. Similarly, in terms of capital and management, joint ventures generally draw on the foreign parent to a lesser extent than the wholly owned subsidiary. The order of ranking for capital commitment and management commitment, therefore, is straightforward.

In terms of flexibility, on the other hand, the licensing agreement generally imposes a heavier cost on the foreigner than do most ownership arrangements. Whereas a foreign owner may be able to reshuffle its arrangements with a subsidiary as circumstances require, the rights and obligations of an independent licensor and licensee presumably cannot be changed without an arm's-length renegotiation. In the licensing case, for instance, the foreigner may be irrevocably tied during the life of the license to using the licensee as its instrumentality for serving some given market. In arrangements in which the parent is linked to the local venture by ownership ties, the capacity to redefine the function of the local venture from time to time is likely to be greater.

Table 2–1 gauges not only costs but also benefits. A priori, there is nothing to be said as to relative amounts of payment to parents associated with the various alternatives; a licensing agreement that called for payments of, say, 4 or 5 per cent of gross sales may yield just as much revenue to the licensor as an equity commitment. The return on a joint venture would presumably be less than that on a wholly owned subsidiary, at least in absolute amounts; but it could be more or less than the income from a licensing agreement. The question of stability of payment, however, is more determinate. The stability associated with the anticipated income flows would ordinarily be higher for the licensing arrangement, because such arrangements generally provide for payments that are fixed in amount or are a function of production volume, rather than for payments that are a function of profits.

The other rankings almost speak for themselves, although none is altogether beyond question. The table assumes (despite some occasional

TABLE 2-1   Costs and Benefits from Viewpoint of a Foreign Parent Enterprise,
Ranked According to Form of Local Link
(1 is the lowest and 4 the highest cost or benefit)

	LICENSING ARRANGEMENT	FOREIGN-LOCAL JOINT VENTURE	FOREIGNERS' JOINT VENTURE	WHOLLY OWNED SUBSIDIARY
Costs				
1. Cost of capital commitment	1	2	3	4
2. Cost of management commitment	1	2	3	4
3. Restraint on strategic and operational flexibility of rest of multi-national firm	4	3	2	1
Benefits				
1. Amount of payment to parent	?	?	?	?
2. Stability of payment to parent	4	?	?	?
3. Political security for parent	4	3	2	1
4. Contribution to parent's store of knowledge	1	2	3	4
5. Contribution to value of parent's trademark and trade name	1	2	3	4
6. Future availability of local outlet to parent	1	2	3	4

evidence to the contrary) that licensing arrangements involve less political risk than ownership arrangements. It assumes, too, that the existence of a wholly owned subsidiary allows the foreign firm to capture certain other advantages which are not so surely available through other types of links. The knowledge that foreign firms pick up about the local market, the spread of their trade names in the country, or the access they gain to local distribution systems can more certainly be put to work for other products of foreign firms if the link is a wholly owned subsidiary than if the arrangement entails a lesser degree of control.

JOINT VENTURES AND WHOLLY OWNED SUBSIDIARIES. The cost–benefit calculations suggested by Table 2–1 are difficult to make. But the job is rendered a little easier by the fact that they vary predictably according to certain explicit conditions. These conditions have been carefully studied in connection with the choice between joint ventures and wholly owned subsidiaries. Some of the conditions depend on the host country.

1. Some countries regard local ownership as an important national objective. Western European governments and the United States, although nervous about the possibility of foreign ownership in some industries, are not acutely concerned over the question. Japan, on the other hand, is greatly preoccupied with the issue, strongly preferring licensing to ownership, and preferring joint ventures to wholly owned subsidiaries. Like Japan, the governments of India, Mexico, Nigeria, and Tunisia place heavy weight on this consideration, whereas Israel and Brazil pay less attention to it. Accordingly, in some countries the manager may not have the full range of choices suggested by Table 2–1; or, if he does, he may have to weigh the differences in political risk associated with the various alternatives against the differences in the other costs and benefits listed in the table.

2. Local partners in some countries are in a position to provide local capital and management more readily than in others. A foreign parent that is in a joint venture with a local partner located in Europe, Japan, or the United States may very well be getting a genuine contribution of capital, management, or information; in Haiti or Ecuador, the contribution would be more problematical.

Although some of the factors that determine the manager's choice may be imposed on him by the circumstances in the country he confronts, the manager's choice is likely to be determined even more strongly by the kinds of resources that are already available to his firm and the kind of strategy that the firm is pursuing. A few key propositions have emerged from the studies made so far that offer some guides to an optimum strategy from the manager's point of view:

1. Long overseas experience on the part of a firm tends to go hand in hand with a preference for wholly owned subsidiaries. It may not be the experience itself that causes this tilt, however. Instead, firms with overseas experience may also have readier access to the information, skills, and capital needed to launch a foreign subsidiary. Although local partners in a joint venture may provide information, skills, and capital, the implicit cost to the parent of acquiring these resources from a local

partner may be relatively high. In the terms of Table 2–1, the rankings assigned to capital commitment and management commitment might still be right; but the absolute size of the differences might be smaller for the more experienced firms, thereby tipping the calculation toward the choice of the wholly owned subsidiary.

2. Where an effective strategy demands that the firm should be able to exercise a high degree of control over its foreign affiliate, the presence of others participating in the direction of the affiliate will be counted as a negative factor, especially if the interests of the others threaten at times to be adverse to those of the parent. Although a licensee or a local partner is likely to share many common interests with the foreign parent, there are also issues over which their interests may conflict. Accordingly, where control is important, a wholly owned subsidiary will be preferred. Control is likely to be important if the firm's strategy, for instance, depends critically on its ability to control the quality of output, the production schedule, or the sales area of a foreign affiliate. In that case, the rankings in Table 2–1 will reflect absolute values that give heavy weight to these considerations, thereby tipping the choice toward the wholly owned subsidiary.

Principles such as these suggest that, from the viewpoint of the multinational enterprise, the optimum ownership arrangement may vary from one foreign affiliate to the next. Moreover, from the viewpoint of the multinational enterprise, the optimum ownership arrangement for an affiliate with a given function in a given country may vary over time. When foreign affiliates are set up in protected markets, separated from world competition by high import and high export barriers, a subsidiary's operations often bear very few links to a global strategy. In such cases, joint ventures may not be confining. But as the barriers come down, the utility of the original joint-venture choice is often questioned. If the continuation of the joint venture would interfere with a coordinated global policy relating to the price or quality of a product, or to the choice of location for production, that fact will be counted as a cost to the system.

Of course, a joint venture may break down at some stage not because of its inappropriateness to the foreign parent but because of its inappropriateness to the local partners. Partners that originally thought themselves benefiting from access to a scarce technology or a valued trademark because of their link to a foreign firm may see the value of that link decline as local market conditions change. Developments such as these have commonly led to the end of joint ventures.

LINKS AND STRATEGIES

Certain kinds of strategy have been associated with certain kinds of foreign links. That relationship, already evident from some of the examples in the last few pages, can be sharpened a little by thinking back to the various strategies of the multinational enterprises described in Chapter 1.

THE TECHNOLOGICAL LEAD.　According to various studies, firms that place heavy weight on research and development as a basis for their strategy typically adopt two quite different patterns in the creation of foreign links. Those with very narrow product lines lean in one direction; those with broad product lines in another. Firms with a narrow product line, such as IBM or SKF, lean strongly toward wholly owned subsidiaries; firms with a broad product line, such as Sperry Rand, make greater use of joint ventures or licensees. Although it is always a little reckless to jump to conclusions about the factors that lie behind different approaches of this sort, in this case the reason for the distinction seems fairly clear.

Technologically oriented firms with a narrow product line are generally committed to an effort to maintain their lead in a limited, well-defined market. Confined to that market, they have a high stake in maintaining quality standards, in holding their technological skills close to the chest, and in maintaining a tight control over the market strategy to be applied to their few products. The strategic decisions may be relatively few, but each is highly important and each affects the enterprise as a whole. Hence the emphasis on wholly owned subsidiaries.

Technologically oriented firms with a broad product line are generally playing a different game. They see themselves as comparatively efficient at developing technological leads. Because they know such leads are perishable, their strategy is to make the widest (and presumably the quickest) possible application of any technological lead that they may develop. Since such leads can be exploited over many products and in many markets, these firms rely upon others to provide the specific market information and the specialized distribution machinery needed to exploit such leads. Hence their willingness to enter into licensing arrangements or joint ventures; the expectation is that such arrangements will represent a more efficient way of acquiring information and achieving distribution than the development of the necessary capabilities internally via a system of wholly owned subsidiaries.

THE STRONG TRADE NAME.　The same distinction is seen in the use of trade names. In some cases, such as Ford, the trade name is applied to a very narrow range of products, and in others, such as 3M and FMC, to a much broader range. When the trade name is applied to a broad range of products, it is intended to convey only a general aura of reliability, not a narrow and explicit set of expectations about a particular product. Accordingly, firms with a broad product range have a lesser need for tight control of production and marketing. For such firms, therefore, the risks of weakened control associated with operating through joint ventures are more tolerable.

Yet the case of the trade-named product serves to remind the manager that there are more ways to maintain tight controls than through wholly owned subsidiaries. Coca-Cola, for example, is quite relaxed about taking local interests as partners in its foreign bottling plants, because Coca-Cola still controls the vital marketing functions, such as the trade name, the advertising program, the flavor, and the bottles. Exxon, BP, and Shell also are known to be tolerant of such partnerships at the distribution level. In cases such as these, the local joint venture still exists largely at the pleasure of the foreign parent, relying upon the parent for some critical input. When that is the case, managers of the multinational enterprise are in a position to choose their preferred form of foreign link without concerning themselves greatly over the threat of losing control, and can make their choice on the basis of the other considerations listed in Table 2–1.

THE ADVANTAGES OF SCALE. In industries where firms rely on sheer scale as the barrier to the entry of rivals, as in oil or aluminum, the established firms are likely to give heavy weight to two goals in choosing among different types of foreign links:

1. Achieving stability in the operation of a large capital-intensive facility, including stability in the demand for output.
2. Encouraging an industry structure that will reduce the risk of an outbreak of price competition among the leaders of the industry.

One preference arising out of these considerations already has been noted: multinational enterprises commonly join together as partners to own and operate large capital-intensive facilities such as aluminum smelters, petrochemical complexes, large oil fields, and pipelines. Joint ownership tends to create a common cost structure for the leading firms, a common exposure to risk, and a common vehicle for adjusting supply to demand without upsetting the relative position of the individual firms in the industry.

Downstream from any jointly owned facility, however, each partner is likely to have its own fabricating and distribution network. The preferred patterns of ownership in the downstream facilities depend heavily on how stability of demand can best be assured. If the firm can count on the fact that a joint venture with a local interest will remain tied to the firm's source of supply, such joint ventures may be acceptable and even desired by the firm. If, on the other hand, such joint ventures entail a risk, as is sometimes the case, the firm's need for stability may push it in the direction of favoring wholly owned subsidiaries.

New developments in the early 1970s raised the question of whether new types of links might soon appear between the owners of highly capital-intensive installations on the one hand and foreign fabricators or distributors of the product on the other. New state-owned plants were rapidly coming into being in the Middle East, North Africa, and Venezuela, designed for the fabrication and exportation of petroleum products, aluminum, steel, heavy chemicals, and other such products. Some were joint ventures with the established leaders in the industry, leaders that already owned and managed installations of the same type in other countries. In such cases, active management of the plant often rested in the hands of the established leader despite the existence of a state-owned partner.

In an increasing number of cases, however, the state partners were taking a hand in managing these installations or were grooming themselves for the job. State-owned enterprises in some countries, such as Iran, Algeria, and Venezuela, have every intention of participating actively and independently in the full range of management decisions, including the foreign marketing decisions. The question in these cases is what organizational link can be established with processing and distributing units in foreign countries that would satisfy the usual strategic needs of stability and cooperation in these industries.

One possibility is that the independent state-owned enterprises, lacking organic links to their markets and to the leaders of the industry, will fall into difficulties whenever petroleum and the other products are in easy supply. Another possibility is that some of the Middle East countries themselves will become the home base for multinational enterprises in these standardized products, complete with their own processing and distributing facilities in the countries where the output is marketed. A third possibility, more amorphous and obscure, is that some new type of organic link will be forged between the large-scale, capital-intensive units and their related downstream facilities in foreign markets, a link that will not involve actual common ownership yet will still allow for the application of unitary strategies that cover the whole vertical system.

The expectation that such institutions might be devised and might work has been encouraged a little by the fact that in the years after World War II the Japanese managed to develop a formidable aluminum smelting, copper refining, and steel industry in Japan without having extensive ownership of the foreign mines that provided the raw materials. In those cases, consortia of Japanese buyers were created, often under the guidance of the Japanese government. The institutional link between the Japanese buyers and the overseas mine owners generally consisted of two elements: (1) a long-term development loan from the Japanese to the foreigners, and (2) a long-term purchase and sale contract.

One feature of these Japanese arrangements, however, suggests that the Japanese case may not prove applicable to the Middle East situation. Practically all the final product of the Japanese fabricating firms until the early 1970s was being marketed in Japan proper, and the Japanese market was being effectively protected from the competitive imports of other sources. As long as the leading Japanese firms moved together in the prices they paid for their raw materials, their long-term contracts with foreign sources created no intolerable competitive strains inside Japan; thus, for instance, cheaper sources of the raw material developed elsewhere could not greatly affect Japanese firms selling in the Japanese market. It was only as the Japanese market began to open up to foreign sellers that these long-term purchase arrangements began to show strong signs of strain. By the mid-1970s, the verdict on their durability was not yet in.

ORGANIZATIONS AND STRATEGIES

The challenge for the manager is to find the form of organization that is most consistent with his strategy. Organization in this sense includes both the structure inside the parent enterprise that is intended to guide and control the multinational network and the structure of the network itself which develops through the choice of foreign links. The problem of developing an appropriate organization is rendered all the more difficult by two considerations:

1. The strategy associated with any given product line is likely to change as the product itself changes and as the market evolves. The direction of these changes may be reasonably predictable; but they still leave the manager with the difficult problem not only of adapting the organization to its current strategic needs but also of allowing for future changes in those needs.

2. The organization appropriate to one product line in an enterprise may be quite different from the organization appropriate to another. The firm that produces both nuclear reactors and electric refrigerators may have good reason to produce both; but the organizational requirements for the two lines will be quite different.

Considerations such as these lead at times to the creation of organizations that appear incredibly complex to the outsider. But these complexities should not deter us from trying to find underlying patterns that contribute to an efficient structure for the multinational enterprise.

FIRST PRINCIPLES.   Organizations, it is evident, are created to link the behavior of individuals: to collect and pool information, skills, or capital; to engage in related actions toward the achievement of a set of goals; to monitor performance, initiate corrections, and define new goals.

In the multinational enterprise, three types of building blocks are almost invariably involved in creating an organization to serve these purposes.

1. *Functions,* which are generally defined as production, finance, marketing, control, personnel, research, and government relations.

2. *Products or product groups,* which are generally grouped according to

some key product or market characteristic, so that the items in any such group are more like each other with respect to the key characteristic than like those in any other group.

3. *Countries or areas,* which are generally grouped on the same principle of maximum homogeneity within a class.

In some cases, the strategy of the organization relies so heavily upon one of these three dimensions that the general structure of the organization is almost predetermined.

For instance, the multinational manufacturing organizations that were created by Japanese trading companies depended in their early stages upon two special strengths: a store of information about foreign markets, which the Japanese trading company had developed in the course of its exporting activities, and access to financial resources. As the trading company developed foreign subsidiaries that were engaged in manufacturing, the trading company itself remained intact at the center of a web, reflecting the importance that was attached to maintaining its original functions. Sitting intact at the center, the trading company could continue to perform the financing, search, and control functions. Figure 2–1 portrays the resulting pattern.

Another case of a relatively simple multinational organization is that commonly created by European-based parents, at least until the 1960s,

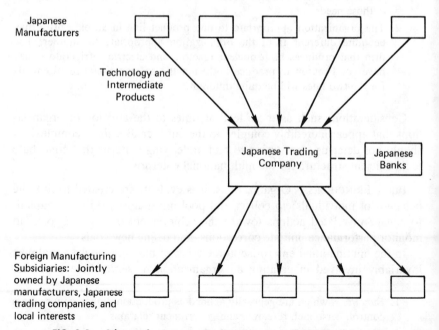

FIG. 2–1   **Schema of a Japanese Trading Company's Multinational Structure**

which is structured on a mother–daughter pattern. In these organizations, the links between parent and subsidiary were mainly forged at the very top of the organization, between the home president and the overseas president. If staff was involved in any respect in these linkages, the finance staff was more likely to be involved than any other. Outside of the area of finance and below the very top of the hierarchy, very little communication occurred.

The simplicity of these European-based organizations was generally a reflection of the simplicity of the multinational strategy that they pursued. Many of their overseas affiliates had been created under the impetus of some historical factor that had temporarily given the parent an edge. In some cases, the foreign subsidiary had come into existence in the colonial era at a time when the parent could be assured of a favored position in the market. The availability of a trusted manager, such as a family member, and of access to credit at especially favorable terms was sufficient to create a basis for a subsidiary. (That kind of pattern, for instance, would nicely fit the case of Siemens, but not of Nestlé or Ciba, whose special strengths rested on other factors.) As long as competition in these distant markets was weak, there were very few stimuli to push the subsidiary and parent toward closer coordination in production, marketing, or research and development. Relations between parent and subsidiary, therefore, were mainly concentrated on two kinds of questions: (1) large strategic choices, involving major questions of expansion or liquidation, and (2) the maintenance of a flow of cash, normally from subsidiary to parent.

But these comparatively simple patterns were transitional forms. In most cases, the strategies of multinational enterprises demanded more complex structures.

A HYPOTHETICAL APPROACH.   Some simple principles of organization are suggested by the Japanese trading organization and the European mother–daughter organization. Picture an enterprise that knows exactly what it wants to do and is only concerned with the appropriate organization for doing it. Assume also that the pattern of needed communication inside the firm can be more or less foreseen. Think of each message in the pattern as stemming from a source inside the firm and going to a destination inside the firm. Each source and each destination is identified according to the function, product, and country to which it relates. The enterprise sees its activities as breaking down into, say, 6 functions, 8 products, and 10 geographical areas. Then the number of points in the communication grid could be thought of as $6 \times 8 \times 10 = 480$.

For simplicity, assume further that every message in the organization originates from one of the 480 points and is directed to another of the 480 points. Some points in the communications grid could be expected to have a heavy flow of communications with another, such as a plastics–market-

ing–France with drugs–marketing–France; some will communicate hardly
at all, such as plastics–production–France with pesticides–finance–India.
The fundamental challenge for the firm is to devise a structure in which
the necessary communications can take place with the highest degree of
efficiency.

Of course, this formulation of the organizational problem, like any
abstract formulation, begs many questions. But it is not a bad starting point
in a search for the appropriate organizational structure.

In addition to establishing the 480 points, the manager is also obliged
to relate the points in some form of organizational grouping. The grouping
will be established on the basis of a number of criteria. But one key
criterion will be to handle the efficiency of communication.

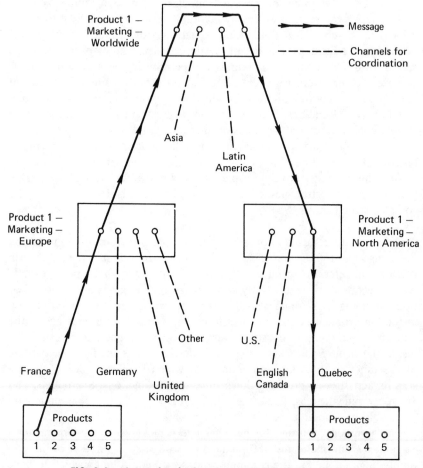

FIG. 2–2   Assumed Path of Message in Multinational Enterprise,
Product 1–Marketing–France to Product 1–Marketing–Quebec

Now look at Figure 2–2. Here we see the case of the firm that has decided to create a series of worldwide product divisions and to organize each product division on a geographical breakdown. Such an organization will mean that when product 1–marketing–France communicates with product 1–marketing–Europe, the message remains inside the product 1 division. If it moves in formal channels, it ascends first to Europe, then to worldwide, whereupon it descends to North America and finally to Quebec. Is this an efficient way for the message to be communicated? To help the firm find the answer to this question, the student has to bear in mind a number of other considerations, which are familiar to specialists in organizational theory:

1. Junctures or nodes will have to be set up where control and coordination take place in the organization. Yet each such node entails a cost; so the efficiency with which communications flow between two points in the organization depends in part on the number of nodes through which the communication must pass from sender to receiver.
2. The cost of passing through a node is a function of the number of channels that the node controls; the larger the number of channels being controlled, the higher the cost of passage. In other words, where the span of control is very wide, the cost of passing through the node is very high.
3. When messages originate and terminate within the same group, they avoid the need to pass through a coordinating node. The length of the journey is thereby shortened. One way of reducing the number of coordinating nodes, therefore, is to enlarge the number of originating points that fall within a single group. This possibility has its disadvantages, however, which derive from the fact that the efficiency of communication within a single group is a function of the size of the group; the larger the group, the lower the efficiency.

These concepts allow one to formulate the organizational problem in the following way: How does one best organize the $6 \times 8 \times 10 = 480$ communications points in groups and in coordinating nodes such that the formal channels for communication promise the highest degree of efficiency? Intuitively, one can frame a number of propositions. One of these is that the shape of the optimum organization is greatly influenced by the anticipated pattern of messages. If the common element of identity shared by senders and receivers in an organization is usually the product, then "product" will be used as the principal coordinating category. If the common element of identity is usually the area, "area" will be the principal coordinator.

Responsive to these general propositions, different segments of the organization may be set up in different ways. If the main divisional breakdown of the organization is by product, for instance, some product divisions may be organized quite differently from others. The main breakdown within the "plastics" division could conceivably be functional in nature, whereas the main breakdown in the "drugs" division might be geographical in nature. Everything will depend on the pattern of communications envisaged within each product division.

In fact, on the basis of the criteria suggested earlier, one can even picture a solution that raises some given function above all the products and area levels for global coordination. The finance function, for instance, is often a candidate for such treatment. Since money is a fungible resource that flows across product divisions and areas, financial officers often demand much more communication with one another than with officers identified with a specific area or a specific product.

TYPICAL PATTERNS. So much for introductory principles. In practice, functioning organizations evolve over time by adjusting to visible strain. As strain develops, informal, out-of-channel contacts are generally used at first to deal with the new problem. When the formal adjustment is finally made, it is greatly influenced by the structure that preceded it and by the personalities that have to be accommodated within it.

Despite all the qualifications, however, there have been some visible regularities in the organizational change of multinational enterprises. To understand the nature of these regularities and the forces underlying them, one can begin with Figure 2–3. The figure describes some of the features of two typical organizations before they have embarked on a program of overseas investment. At this stage, the organizations can be thought of as relatively "small" by the standards of multinational enterprises, confined to a few product lines or a few markets, and wrestling with a comparatively limited number of strategic decisions. In organizations of this sort, strategic decisions are typically made by the president, based on the contributions of the vice-presidents. Contact with foreign markets is achieved mainly through exports. An export manager, if he exists, is thought of as an adjunct to marketing, whose principal communication needs are with the marketing vice-president and others in the marketing group.

As the enterprise grows, the diversity of its problems increases. This is especially the case if growth occurs by adding to the number of product lines. As the strategies described in Chapter 1 suggest, each product may well require a different kind of integration between marketing and production, as well as different ties with research. At the same time, if the products are increasing, the chances are that the exports of the enterprise will be growing too, perhaps even faster than domestic sales. Out of the growing choice of products, several, in product-cycle terms, will have reached their time for rapid growth in overseas demand. At first, the increased traffic may be handled by an export manager on the pattern sug-

A. Organization with Narrow Product Line

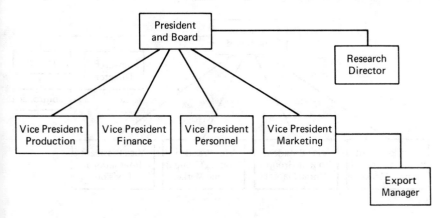

B. Organization with Wide Product Line

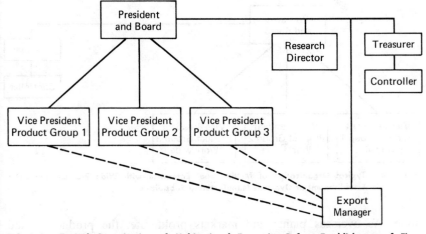

FIG. 2–3 Typical Organization of Multinational Enterprise Before Establishment of First Overseas Manufacturing Subsidiary

gested by Figure 2–3. Eventually, however, an organization along the lines of Figure 2–4A is likely to emerge.

One key assumption about the communication patterns that lie behind the organization shown in Figure 2–4A is fairly evident. Those concerned with production and marketing for areas outside the home market, it is assumed, will have more to communicate with one another than with their counterparts in the product groups. This key assumption has been widely made in the first stages of overseas expansion, especially by U.S.-based firms and other firms with large home markets. Typically, however, the assumption begins to be discredited within a relatively short period of

A. Organization at Early Stage of Overseas Expansion

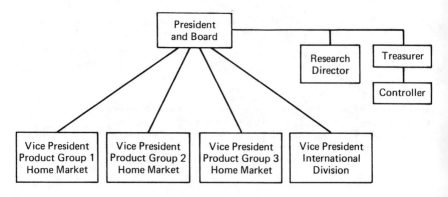

B. Organization at Advanced Stage of Overseas Expansion

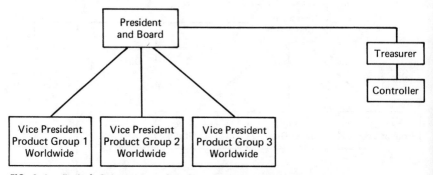

FIG. 2–4   Typical Organization of Multinational Enterprise with Wide Product Line After Establishment of Overseas Manufacturing Subsidiaries

time. As overseas plants and markets proliferate, the production and marketing specialists in the international division find themselves obliged more and more to consult with their counterparts in the various home product divisions. Information must be exchanged; plans must be coordinated. Accordingly, two sources of strain begin to break the international division apart: (1) the strain of sheer size, creating a problem of declining efficiency in communications within the division, and (2) the strain of a heavy flow of communication with other divisions involving attenuated lines of communication between sender and receiver.

The outcome is to be seen in the short life and high rate of mortality for international divisions in large, U.S.-based multinational enterprises, and by the similar strains that are beginning to appear in European-based enterprises and Japanese trading companies. Once the international division is gone, Figure 2–4A is no longer representative and is superseded by

Figure 2–4B. As the international division disappears, the product group divisions are concurrently assigned worldwide responsibility for production and marketing. At this stage, too, they may be delegated responsibilities for some or all of their related research activities, which reflects the fact that the communications of the researchers need no longer be directed to two constituents, the international division and the appropriate home product division.

A special point has to be made, however, with regard to enterprises that expand overseas on the basis of comparatively narrow product lines. Enterprises with narrow product lines, such as IBM or Volkswagen, have tended to organize their operations on a highly integrated basis in any region of the world and to link the separate production and marketing facilities of the region into fairly tight interdependent patterns. Within their regional markets, the pricing practices, trademark practices, quality-control standards, and production patterns of the enterprises are closely related. A plant in one country may be assigned to a specialized task, such as the manufacture of a limited range of components for assembly and sale in a number of contiguous countries.

Enterprises of this sort have been relatively slow to adopt a product division organization. Among firms of this sort, for instance, there has been a preference for an organization based on functional divisions. Besides, once such firms have established an international division to handle their overseas business, they have tended to find such a division adequate for a relatively long period of time. Because the patterns of communication inside such organizations are heavily influenced by affinities of geography rather than by affinities of product, the organizational breakdown between the home market and elsewhere has not been wholly inefficient. Eventually, however, enterprises of this sort based in the United States have been found to break up their non-U.S. interests into regional divisions, to produce the sort of structure depicted in Figure 2–5.

Whatever the choice of organizational structure, whether in the directions suggested by Figure 2–4 or those suggested by Figure 2–5, the process of coordination and communication seems repeatedly to flush up apparent shortcomings in the structure. Organizations structured on product lines find their product groups operating at cross purposes in a given country or region, simply because of the inefficient lines of communication among product groups within each region. Those organized on a regional basis find that the interregional coordination of product strategy leaves something to be desired. The result of that discovery has often been to try to create three-dimensional organizations.

Three-dimensional structures are extraordinarily difficult to picture in conceptual terms. Can an originating point such as product 1–France–plastics be coordinated simultaneously and coequally on all three dimensions? The answer to that question is usually no. The lines of authority

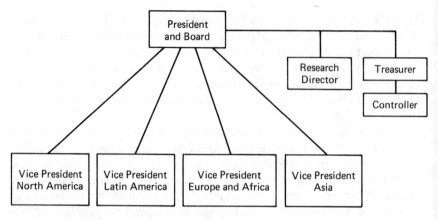

FIG. 2–5   Typical Organization of Multinational Enterprise with Narrow Product Line at Advanced Stage of Overseas Expansion

generated by any such effort are too ambiguous. The result is generally a compromise: one element in a decision is coordinated by the line, another element by the staff.

For instance, although the main divisional breakdown in any organization may be set up by areas, as in Figure 2–5, a staff of product managers may be appointed to create coordination among the areas. Their job can be viewed as that of increasing the efficiency of communications relating to a common product when the messages originate in one geographical area and terminate in another. By the same token, when the main divisional breakdown is by products, as in Figure 2–5, an "umbrella company" may be created in each country or in each regional area so that the various product specialists who happen to be located in that country or area will have some way of coordinating their local activity. The function of these "umbrella companies" can be thought of as a way of short-circuiting some of the messages that otherwise would have to be passed up the organizational hierarchy and down again.

For all the experiment and experience, however, the problem of organizational structure has proved a constant headache for multinational enterprises. The desire simultaneously to coordinate in at least three dimensions —by function, product, and geographical area—has created tension. Trade offs between one approach and the other have been constantly reassessed and adaptations constantly made. As long as the strategies of multinational enterprises do not stand still, changes in structure will be one of the unavoidable features of the continued existence of the enterprise.

SUGGESTED READING

CHANDLER, ALFRED D., JR., *Strategy and Structure* (Cambridge, Mass.: MIT Press, 1962).

DAVIS, STANLEY M., "Two Models of Organization: Unity of Command Versus Balance of Power," *Sloan Management Review,* Fall, 1974.

FRANKO, LAWRENCE G., *Joint Venture Survival in Multinational Corporations* (New York: Praeger, 1971).

FRANKO, LAWRENCE G., *The Other Multinationals: The International Activity of Continental European Enterprise* (New York: Harper & Row, 1976).

STOPFORD, JOHN M., and LOUIS T. WELLS, JR., *Managing the Multinational Enterprise: Organization of the Firm and Ownership of Subsidiaries* (New York: Basic Books, 1972).

Multinational Enterprises as a System of National Units

chapter three

A multinational enterprise may be composed of separate units in different national economies; but the separate units are generally responsive to an integrating strategy. As Chapter 1 indicated, there is bound to be a common thread linking the seemingly independent units: a common use of credit, information, manpower, trade names, or patents among the affiliates; a commitment to specialization and cross-hauling among the affiliates; or other manifestations of common resources and common purpose. If such common elements are absent, a multinational enterprise has no reason for existence.

At the same time, however, the managers of multinational enterprises constantly find themselves obliged to treat their business as if it were made up of national units, however artificial the breakup may be. This stems especially from the need to satisfy the requirements of taxation, public disclosure, legal accountability, and internal control. Thus, the multinational enterprise is engaged in constant efforts to reconcile its identity as an integral enterprise with its identity as a series of national units.

NATIONAL BOUNDARIES AND MULTINATIONAL OPERATIONS

In response to the requirements of a common strategy, the units of a multinational enterprise are engaged in a variety of transfers among themselves. Figure 3–1 portrays in a schematic way some typical transfers among such units, which characteristically come about as follows:

1. A given unit of the enterprise may be specialized in the production of some intermediate material, component, or final product on behalf of the enterprise as a whole. Transfers are dubbed "sales" and ordinarily bear a transfer price, even when both sides of the transaction fall under the general direction and control of a single global product manager and lie within the ambit of the same profit center in the enterprise.

2. A given unit may be specialized in research and development for the benefit of the multinational enterprise as a whole. At some point, transfers of patent rights and know-how must take place between affiliates. These transfers are often regarded as sales and the payments generally appear as "royalties" or administrative charges.

3. The cash generated in some units of the enterprise can sometimes be used more efficiently in other units. Accordingly, cash transfers are arranged. If the desired cash flows do not take place in the form of interest, dividends, royalties, charges, or payment for goods, they are generally arranged as loans and advances or as purchases of equity among the affiliates.

For a multinational enterprise that is composed of a parent and wholly owned subsidiaries, it may not be immediately apparent why any of these internal transfers should be explicitly identified and labeled; the transfers, after all, are all taking place entirely within the bounds of one integral business unit and under the direction of one general intelligence. But there

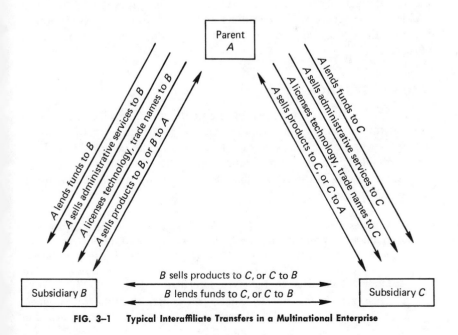

FIG. 3–1   Typical Interaffiliate Transfers in a Multinational Enterprise

are at least four reasons why such explicit identification and labeling are required.

1. There is a need to develop a separate taxable income figure for each affiliate to serve as the basis for tax payments in each national jurisdiction.

2. There is a need to measure the performance of various parts of the enterprise for internal control purposes, such as measuring the performance of managers and generating yardsticks to guide added investment.

3. There may be a need to establish a profit figure in a foreign subsidiary because a portion of the ownership of the subsidiary is held by some outside interest, such as a local partner.

4. There may be a need to report the operations of the enterprise or its parts to various national authorities for purposes other than taxation, including those concerned with credit, import licensing, or price control.

Because several objectives exist, a familiar and inescapable problem arises: from the viewpoint of the firm, no one set of figures is optimal for all these purposes. The figures that bring taxes down to the minimum level permitted by law are not necessarily those that best measure the performance of each affiliate; the figures that are useful for measuring performance for internal control purposes are not usually appropriate for reporting the firm's operations to stockholders or to public authorities. The problem is not usually one of deception or avoidance, as is so often supposed; although deception or avoidance may sometimes occur, the main problem is that there is no such thing as a wholly objective description of the operations of a firm and no such thing as a description optimal for all purposes.

ISSUES IN TAXATION

MINIMIZING TAXES. Managers of multinational enterprises share with most of the human race a common reaction to the problem of taxation: where choices exist in the law, they tend to elect the course that reduces their tax obligations to the minimum. Multinational enterprises, however, have some choices in this regard that are not normally available to national enterprises:

1. Affiliates that perform certain specialized functions, such as the distribution of products and licensing of patents, may be just as readily placed in one country as another without greatly affecting their efficiency. In such cases, countries with low or nonexistent tax levies, such as Bermuda and Luxembourg, have a special attraction.

2. When one affiliate provides capital to another, the multinational enterprise is often free to choose whether the capital should be advanced in

the form of debt or of equity. Debt entails subsequent payments in the form of interest; equity, in the form of dividends. The choice generally affects the paying affiliate's taxable income, and sometimes the receiving affiliate's taxable income as well.

3. In the transfer of some products and services between affiliates, no arm's-length measure of value exists that can objectively be attached to the transfer. Unless arm's-length bargaining has actually taken place, the price appropriate to a patent license, a credit guarantee, a set of procedure manuals, or access to the information of other affiliates is usually indeterminate. The same can be said of a wide range of specialized intermediate products. In such cases, the manager is not greatly inhibited in choosing a transfer price, and the choice can be influenced by its effects on the firm's tax bill.

4. Even where an arm's-length price appears to be available, there is often room for genuine dispute as to whether that is the price which the multinational enterprise should apply. One field in which disputes have been particularly bitter is pharmaceuticals. Leading manufacturers will claim that they are entitled to a higher price for some intermediate ingredient because materials that bear their name carry a higher probability of consistency and purity. To make matters more complex, they are likely to assert that prices charged by independent producers operating in jurisdictions where pharmaceutical patents do not exist (such as Italy) cannot be used as an appropriate yardstick for sales by an enterprise in a market in which a valid patent exists.

5. Finally, even where a price exists that is unequivocally arm's length in nature, local tax law and regulation may not require that the standard should apply. In some tax jurisdictions, the law may simply be silent on the question. The silence may represent a simple oversight; but it may also be due to the fact that tax authorities are interested in preserving the option to impose a price that is different from the arm's-length price. (In the case of an oil refinery that buys its petroleum from a foreign affiliate, for instance, national tax authorities have been known to require that the local refinery should figure its purchases at lower-than-market prices, thus increasing the amount of local income that is taxable.)

The upshot of all this is that the managers of multinational enterprises often have considerable discretion in reporting the income of each affiliate for tax purposes. That discretion will sometimes be exercised in ways that reduce the tax burden to a minimum; but it will sometimes be used with other objectives in mind. Other criteria will prevail, for instance, when the actions that would be needed to minimize taxes have undesired side effects on sales or other costs. Efforts to minimize taxes, for instance, may generate cash flows to the wrong affiliates; they may set the price of imports in some national markets too high or too low for maximum profit; they may create an historical record that in future years would be used by regulatory authorities to the detriment of the firm. So any policy on tax payments has to be considered fully before a judgment can be made as to the net impact of the policy.

DOUBLE TAXATION POLICIES. Numerous considerations affect the firm's policies in taxation. One key factor is the effects of double taxation: How will the profit of a subsidiary be treated by tax authorities in the parent's country when it is passed from the subsidiary to the parent; how will the parent's tax authorities take account, if they do, of the fact that the income has already been taxed in the subsidiary's country?

The answer depends, among other things, upon the identity of the parent's country. In most jurisdictions, tax-paying corporations with subsidiaries in other countries are entitled, according to one principle or another, to some recognition of the fact that the subsidiary has paid taxes in the country where it was domiciled. It is unnecessary to reproduce the various national systems in all their extraordinary complexity. However, certain basic approaches, such as the following, appear repeatedly.

1. Many countries rely on bilateral tax treaties to establish the basis for calculating the tax liability that is due on income originating in some other country; in such cases, the taxpayer's obligation to his home government with regard to income earned abroad may vary according to the source of that income.

2. Some countries, including Germany and the United States, do not ordinarily assess their home corporations for any tax liability arising from the profits of their foreign subsidiaries, until the home corporation becomes entitled to that profit through the declaration of dividends.

3. Another approach, found in French law, requires the parent to base its domestic tax liability on its consolidated worldwide income, whether or not that parent actually received such income from its foreign subsidiaries. Where that approach is followed, the parent generally may take a credit for the foreign income taxes paid by its subsidiaries.

4. A variant of the preceding approach, found in Dutch law, relies on a proportionality principle. The parent's tax liability at home is based on its worldwide consolidated income. But that income is divided into two parts: income originating abroad and entitled to exemption, and other income. The parent's tax liability is then reduced in proportion to the share of worldwide income that is entitled to exemption. In other words, if one third of its total worldwide income is entitled to exemption, the domestic tax liability of the parent corporation is reduced by one third.

U.S. TAX LAW. United States tax law, as it applies to multinational enterprises, has its own distinctive features. Although it starts with the proposition that a U.S. taxpayer is subject to taxation on all of his income whether that income has been earned at home or abroad, the concept of income is carefully limited. As the law stood in 1975, a U.S. parent that maintained a branch abroad—that is, an entity that under U.S. corporate law has no separate juridical personality from the U.S. parent—was regarded as having received income from the moment that the branch earned it. But if the parent maintained a subsidiary abroad—an entity that possesses a separate personality from the viewpoint of U.S. authorities—the parent was not construed to receive income until the subsidiary had declared a dividend.

For the manager, this distinction presents both problems and opportunities. For instance, a parent company may anticipate that there will be losses in a new overseas operation for the first few years. If the overseas operation is a separate subsidiary, there is usually no way of using the loss as an offset against the income of the parent in the United States. On the other hand, if the overseas operation is nothing more than a branch of the parent establishment and therefore a part of the parent, the loss will offset income earned elsewhere inside the parent company and will reduce the aggregate tax liability of the parent to the U.S. government.

Contrariwise, when profits are anticipated, the U.S. parent usually finds it advantageous to incorporate overseas establishments as separate entities under the laws of the countries in which they operate. These subsidiaries, of course, are obliged to pay taxes to their host governments (for that matter, so are the branches of U.S. parents, as a rule). In the treatment of these foreign taxes, another fundamental principle of U.S. tax law, alluded to several pages back, comes into play:

When the profits of the foreign branch or subsidiary become income to the U.S. parent, any income taxes that the subsidiary may have paid to the foreign government represent a basis for reducing the parent's tax liability to the U.S. government. The foreign government is expected to take a first cut at the income generated in its jurisdiction; the U.S. government then imposes only such additional taxes on the income as will bring the total up to U.S. rates. In general, therefore, the principle is one of the avoidance of double taxation.

This approach has interesting consequences. One arises when a foreign government grants a "tax holiday" to a selected enterprise. When such an exemption is granted to the subsidiary of a U.S. parent, the exemption simply has the effect of reducing the size of the foreign tax credit that its U.S. parent will eventually be entitled to take in the United States. The attraction of such exemptions for U.S. investors, therefore, is reduced.

Many complexities and technicalities surround the calculation of the foreign tax credit. For instance, some U.S. taxpayers have an option in the way in which they can calculate the foreign tax credit. In the ordinary course, the U.S. taxpayer would make the calculation for income from its subsidiaries country by country—the "per country" approach. But in 1975, a U.S. taxpayer that had subsidiaries in more than one foreign country also had the option of pooling income from its branches and subsidiaries, as well as the credits applicable to such income, as if they all came from a single foreign source. In that case, any surplus tax credits arising in one foreign country could be used to reduce the taxable income from another foreign country.

Another feature of U.S. tax law deserves special mention: this is the difference between the calculation of tax credits for subsidiaries located in less-developed countries and those located in advanced economies. An accidental quirk in the U.S. tax law has been retained so that the U.S. tax credit is applied more generously to income from less-developed countries than to income from the richer countries. In the case of the less-developed countries, wherever the U.S. income tax rate exceeds the foreign rate, the U.S. parent's liability on income received from such a foreign subsidiary is computed by multiplying (1) the difference between the rates by (2) the net income received by the parent. This strange formula has some curious properties. If the foreign tax rate is zero, or if the foreign tax rate is exactly equal to the U.S. tax rate, there is no special tax advantage to the U.S. parent; that is, the total tax liability is the same as it would be for income from the richer countries. In between those extremes, however, the U.S. parent receives a tax break. For instance, if the tax rate of the less-developed foreign country is 24 per cent and the U.S. rate is 48 per cent, the formula produces a total tax liability of 42.25 per cent for income that has been transmitted as dividends to the parent.

United States tax law is tilted in other directions as well. One such tilt is intended to limit the use of foreign tax credits on the part of U.S. companies that are engaged in overseas oil operations. As the effective tax rates imposed by foreign governments on oil and gas extraction activities rose to astronomical heights in the 1970s, some U.S. companies acquired huge amounts of foreign tax credits, enough to wipe out their tax liabilities on all their foreign-earned income. Amendments to the U.S. tax law cut back the use of such credits, so that unusually high rates imposed by foreign countries would not provide a basis for building up further foreign tax credits. The ability of U.S. firms in the oil and gas business to reduce their U.S. taxable income when they incurred losses in their foreign branches was also placed under limits.

The U.S. government has taken other steps as well to ensure that U.S. taxpayers become liable for U.S. taxes on the basis of their profitable foreign operations. One important step, taken as far back as 1962, has to do with the use of tax havens in foreign countries.

As was pointed out earlier, a U.S. parent company normally incurs a

U.S. tax liability on income from a foreign subsidiary only after dividends have been declared by the subsidiary. One way of avoiding dividend receipts in the United States is to create and interpose a foreign holding company, preferably situated in a country whose income tax rates are very low. These holding companies can be assigned many functions, some of them of a management nature. But, for the most part, their purpose is to serve as intermediaries to which foreign subsidiaries channel their payments of commissions, royalties, interest, and dividends for eventual distribution as working capital to other members of the system. Since these funds are kept out of the hands of the U.S. parent, they would ordinarily be expected to escape U.S. taxes.

In 1962, however, the U.S. government devised a complex formula that greatly reduced the attractiveness of the tax-haven subsidiary. Some of the dividends and other intermediary income that a foreign holding company receives from subsidiaries were made subject to U.S. taxation even if the U.S. parent never received the income. The amount subject to U.S. taxation varies according to the relative importance that these intermediary transactions have in the foreign holding company's total operations. To the extent that local income taxes have been paid, these are credited in the usual way. But, all told, the uninhibited use of the tax-haven device has received a major setback.

Still another direction taken by U.S. tax law is systematically to encourage exports from the U.S. home base by lowering the tax rates that apply to profits from such activities. (This is a tax feature widely shared with other countries.) The U.S. technique for using the tax structure to favor exports is to authorize taxpayers to create a Domestic International Sales Corporation (DISC). Such a corporation is not subject to federal income taxes.

To qualify as a DISC, a corporation must have generated 95 per cent or more of its receipts through export of goods and services from the United States. And 95 per cent or more of its assets must be of the sort that are related to the export business. A corporation of this kind has a right to buy "export property" from its parent, sell the goods abroad, and take a profit, limited by a complex set of formulas. Although the DISC is not subject to federal income taxes, the U.S. parent that owns the DISC must pay taxes when it receives dividends from the DISC. Even if the parent receives no dividends, it is still deemed to have received half the DISC's profits annually. Accordingly, the manufacturer or exporter that has created the DISC can arrange to cut his U.S. tax liabilities roughly in half on the business that the DISC handles.

There have been fairly widespread misgivings regarding the DISC's operations based on the view that the device added little or nothing to U.S. exports. But the existence of similar preferential devices in other national tax systems suggests, in accordance with a well-known variant of Gresham's law, that the preference favoring exports will be retained in U.S. law as well.

MEASURING PERFORMANCE

THE PROBLEM.   It would be a staggering coincidence if the figures that had been generated for tax purposes inside the multinational enterprise served equally well to measure performance for other purposes, such as the measurement of management performance and the measurement of returns. The points of incompatibility are large in number and substantial in impact.

Some problems of measuring managerial performance are quite familiar and are encountered in any organization, whether multinational or not. One such problem, for instance, is whether the manager whose performance is being measured has an area of management responsibility that corresponds to the subsidiary or branch for which records are compiled. In the case of multinational enterprises, that problem can be a little more acute than usual. For instance, the manager of France–paint may have responsibilities and authority that do not correspond to any accounting unit. There may be an accounting record for the French subsidiary as a whole, covering all its manifold products; there may be an accounting unit for a world paint division covering all paint activities throughout the world. But France–paint may not exist as an accounting unit.

Even if France–paint does exist as an accounting unit, its records may not reflect either the performance of the France–paint manager or the return to the multinational enterprise from France–paint activities. The performance of France–paint will be profoundly affected by a variety of constraints that are dictated by the strategic needs of the multinational enterprise as a whole; these will express themselves in many ways, notably in transfer prices, royalties, and administrative charges, and in other prices "charged" between units in the multinational system. Where these problems exist, the resulting record for any unit does not provide an appropriate base for measuring either managerial performance or financial return.

TRANSACTIONS IN FOREIGN EXCHANGE.   Similar kinds of measurement problems arise in accounting for the effects of foreign exchange fluctuations. Like any other businessman, the manager of any unit of a multinational enterprise is likely to find himself from time to time paying or receiving funds in a "foreign" currency, that is, a currency different from the one in which his unit ordinarily conducts its business. Of course, any enterprise, whether part of a multinational enterprise or not, may make a commitment to pay in a foreign currency or may accept a commitment to receive payment in a foreign currency. In that case, the commitment is likely to generate special problems.

A firm in Leeds, England, for instance, may borrow U.S. dollars, use these dollars to buy sterling, and pay its local bills with the sterling proceeds. Problems arise because the value of the pound sterling may vary from month to month or even day to day in relation to the U.S. dollar. Accordingly, the borrower in Leeds may find sixty days later that the repayment of its dollar debt requires more sterling than it had received sixty days earlier. If no prior provision had been made for the contingency, the firm in Leeds would find that it had suffered a loss in sterling. By the same token, an exporter of machinery from Pittsburgh who accepted a 60-day note from a Paris buyer denominated in francs might find that the dollar value of the note had changed when the time for payment arrived. (For an indication of what firms may do to forestall such losses, see Chapter 4.)

Losses or gains of this sort affect the units of a multinational enterprise just as they do any national enterprise. At times, however, in measuring the performance of a manager of a unit of a multinational enterprise, it may be necessary to consider whether the policies that generate gains or losses of this sort are part of the manager's responsibilities. In multinational enterprises, such decisions, for obvious reasons, are often kept out of the hands of the local manager. The interests of the manager and those of the enterprise as a whole are likely to be perceived differently. The interests of the enterprise may, for instance, suggest that a subsidiary in a weak currency area that has borrowed from the parent should denominate its debt obligation in the parent's currency; yet this might be quite contrary to the interests of the local manager. At times, too, the interests of the managers of two affiliates of the same multinational enterprise may be flatly at loggerheads—one wanting a prospective payment to be denominated in one currency, the other in another currency. Decisions of this sort, therefore, are commonly handled by delegation to some higher center; when they are, the problem of measuring the performance of individual managers takes on an added difficulty.

Another issue arises that is of special importance to the multinational enterprise: How should the enterprise as a whole and its constituent parts evaluate and record assets and liabilities that are in different currencies, as the currencies themselves change in value? There are two aspects to this issue—the conversion problem and the translation problem.

The *conversion problem* is simply an extension of the issue already discussed. Any firm at all, whether in Leeds, Pittsburgh, or Paris, will find itself adjusting the value of assets or liabilities on its books that are not denominated in its own currency. Accordingly, if our Pittsburgh exporter were obliged to produce a balance sheet at a time when it was carrying accounts receivable denominated in francs, the dollar value of the franc account would have to be calculated on an up-to-date basis. That sort of adjustment is required of all business units, whether they are independent entities or units of a multinational enterprise.

The *translation problem,* however, is quite another story; this presents issues that are uniquely associated with the multinational enterprise. Although there are occasional exceptions, each unit of the multinational enterprise ordinarily does its business in the currency of the country in which it is located. Local currency is received from local sales, and local currency is used to pay local taxes, meet local payrolls, and buy local supplies. Accordingly, the assets and liabilities, income and outgo, of the subsidiaries are commonly denominated in a currency which differs from that of the parent. When the parent is faced with the need to consolidate the statements of the various units into a single statement for the multinational system as a whole, the existence of many different currencies can create considerable difficulties.

The faint glimmerings of this problem can sometimes be detected in the consolidated financial statements of parent companies. Here, obviously, some convention has been applied to convert cruzeiros, pounds, quetzals, francs, and dollars all into one currency. If the parent is in the United States, that one currency will presumably be dollars; if British, pounds sterling; if German, deutschemarks; and so on. An occasional note may appear in such statements, perhaps indicating that the enterprise has reduced its consolidated profits or its earned surplus by some explicit amount in order to reflect the "losses" that accompanied the devaluation of the currency of one of the subsidiaries. The accounting conventions that determine the nature of these entries represent a major pitfall for the manager in the international economy. As a rule, they do not accurately reflect the changes in either the business value of the units of the multinational enterprise or the performance of the managers of those units. Let us see why.

The foreign subsidiaries of any multinational enterprise are exposed to an endless series of interrelated events, all bearing on the outcome of the investment. Picture a specific situation. The country is Italy in the year 1975. The value of the lira in relation to the dollar has been falling steadily, while internal prices in terms of the lira have been going up continuously. There is every expectation that more of the same is in the offing. A parent company located in the United States is assessing the implications of the change in the value of the lira upon its investment, and is wondering what adjustments ought to be made upon its books to reflect the changes.

Suppose, then, that the manager of the parent company, being innocent of accounting translation practices, simply requests his staff to undertake two groups of projections for the years ahead: (1) a projection of the balance sheet and profit-and-loss statement for the Italian subsidiary, denominated in the lira, and (2) a projection of the net flow of earnings to the parent across the lira–dollar exchange, taking fully into account the probability of a continued decline in the value of the lira.

The staff, of course, could make all sorts of assumptions about price trends, projecting item by item the prices of goods and services that the company would have to buy, and item by item the prices of goods it would have for sale. By estimating cash needs and cash flows, it could come to some kind of estimate of cash throw-off. And on given assumptions about the change in the exchange rate and the parent's policies toward the subsidiary, it could estimate the schedule of dollar yield to the parent.

Since the price relationships among different goods and services do not remain forever fixed, and since the depreciating price of foreign exchange cannot be a perfect negative image of every domestic price within an inflating economy, there is nothing foreordained about the outcome of such a calculation. It may show that the prospective inflation-with-devaluation spells trouble for the subsidiary because of a squeeze between raw material prices and sales prices and because of the need for increases in working capital; it may show that the inflation-with-devaluation would leave the subsidiary's future largely undisturbed; or it may show that the inflation-with-devaluation will provide a bonanza for the subsidiary, even after due allowance for increased working capital needs.

The staff, let us assume, has done its projections and has concluded that, by and large, inflation-with-devaluation will leave largely unimpaired the subsidiary's capacity to generate a net flow of dollars to the parent. Lira prices may change inside Italy and the dollar–lira relation may change as well. But, all told, the effect of the two different kinds of price changes will simply be to leave the dollar cash flow roughly where it is.

TABLE 3-1   Typical Effects of Inflation and
Devaluation upon Italian Subsidiary

ITEM	CAUSE	EFFECT IN LIRE
Sources of funds		
Gross revenues from local sales	Inflation	Increase
Gross revenues from export sales	Devaluation	Increase
Windfall profit from nonlira assets	Devaluation	Increase
Uses of funds		
Expenditures on local materials and labor	Inflation	Increase
Expenditures on imported materials and labor	Devaluation	Increase
Taxes	Inflation or devaluation	Indeterminate
Additions to working capital	Inflation	Increase
Additions to fixed capital	Inflation or devaluation	Increase
Windfall loss from nonlira liabilities	Devaluation	Increase

That outcome is no less plausible than any other. Table 3–1 lists the changes that occur inside the Italian subsidiary as inflation, punctuated by devaluations, takes its course. As one runs down the list of effects, he begins to realize that the net effect of inflation-with-devaluation upon the subsidiary's generation of local currency depends on the circumstances of the subsidiary; on balance, the effect may increase cash flows or diminish them. Accordingly, it is unclear whether the net flow of funds to the parent across the exchanges, that is, the flow of funds converted to the currency desired by the parent, will rise or fall; even with periodic devaluations, the flow may well increase.

But logic is one thing and accounting conventions another. Under these conventions, the enterprise is obliged to record the effect of a devaluation in such a way that it almost invariably represents a bookkeeping loss to the parent. These conventions, it should be emphasized, have nothing to do with the question of taxable income, which is determined under different rules; they relate simply to the question of accounting practice. There are some minor disagreements among accounting authorities over the adjustments that are appropriate for this purpose; a variety of practices are encountered. It will suffice to describe in skeleton form some typical patterns of adjustments.

Assume that an Italian devaluation occurred on December 31, just a split second before the close of business. Suddenly, the value of the lira was changed from L.100 = $1 to L.200 = $1. The parent in the United States has received the financial returns of the subsidiary, measured in lire for the year ending December 31. The parent wants to include the subsidiary's returns in a consolidated system-wide report, reflecting in U.S. dollars the situation of the system at the opening of business on the next day, January 1. What does it do?

As far as the operating results on the profit-and-loss statement are concerned, no "adjusting" is necessary in the translation from lire to dollars. They represent transactions entered into prior to the devaluation; according to convention, they may be translated at the lira–dollar rate prevailing when they occurred, that is, at L.100 = $1. The balance sheet, however, is another story. This is supposed to reflect the condition of the business at the year's close. By that time, the lira had changed in value relative to the dollar. This change, according to accounting convention, must be appropriately reflected.

First, there are the conversion gains and conversion losses, that is, the adjustments of assets and liabilities that ultimately will be paid in a currency other than the lira. These adjustments are straightforward enough, according to the principles discussed earlier. Once the subsidiary's balance sheet has been restated in the new lira totals, however, there is still a need for "translation," that is, the translation of the subsidiary's adjusted balance sheet into appropriate dollar equivalents. At what exchange rates should

TABLE 3-2   Translation Rates Applied to Subsidiary Balance Sheet After Devaluation

	LIRE PER DOLLAR	
ITEM	FINANCIAL ASSETS METHOD	CURRENT ACCOUNTS METHOD
Assets		
Cash in lire	200	200
Cash in dollars	200	200
Accounts receivable in lire	200	200
Inventories of foreign origin	100	200
Inventories of local origin	100	200
Fixed assets	Historical rates (i.e., 100 or less)	
Liabilities		
Accounts payable in lire	200	200
Accounts payable in dollars	200	200
Unremitted declared dividends	200	200
Long-term debt in lire	200	100
Net worth	Historical rates (i.e., 100 or less)	

the translation take place? Table 3–2 lists the main items of the balance sheet, together with a set of translations that reflects rules typically applied by U.S. enterprises.

Insofar as translation practices differ, the differences tend to center on two items: how to treat inventories of local origin, and how to treat long-term debt denominated in lire. One approach, dubbed the "current accounts" approach, limits adjustments to current items only, bypassing the long-term items. Another, labeled the "financial assets" approach, limits adjustments to financial assets, bypassing the inventory item.

Quite obviously, the effect of all these manipulations is to produce an inconsistency in the accounts of the subsidiary that are to be recorded in the consolidation. This requires a balancing adjustment somewhere in the consolidated balance sheet. The general effect of the adjustments is to put a lower dollar valuation on the subsidiary's current assets and current liabilities. Since assets are usually greater than liabilities, a net write-down is necessary. A "conservative" way of handling the write-down is to charge it against the consolidated profits of the current year, in this instance, the year ending December 31. If this is done, the subsidiary's profits for that year and its net worth at year end are accordingly reduced in the consolidation. In some cases, other balance sheet accounts are debited, such as the earned income account or a capital reserve account previously set up for the devaluation contingency.

Enterprises that follow the policies just described and that take their own records seriously as a basis for management control sometimes gain the impression that subsidiaries located in inflating–devaluing countries are experiencing erratic year-to-year earnings. In some years, for instance, prices inside the country will rise considerably while the country's exchange rate remains relatively unchanged. During these years, even though local prices and local profit margins may be rising in terms of the local currency, the translation of the results into the home currency of the parent takes place at unchanging rates. These are the bonanza years, if there are any bonanza years at all; in these years, the subsidiary's paper performance, translated into the home currency, is at its best.

Then comes the devaluation. Suddenly, a less favorable rate is applied to sales and profits. On top of that, a write-down is required that bears no direct relationship to either sales or profits, but rather to certain items on the balance sheet. The erstwhile bonanza is suddenly seen as a disaster.

Yet throughout the cycle, the local subsidiary's performance, if measured in terms that would have been applied to a production unit at home, may be quite unchanged and exemplary. Small wonder that managers of foreign subsidiaries are sometimes bewildered by the roller-coaster quality of home-office appraisals.

What answers could be provided to the complex bundle of problems that are posed when continuous inflation occurs, punctuated by sporadic devaluations? If the problems are sorted out by their constituent parts, they become a bit more manageable.

How, for instance, should the subsidiary's lira profits be recorded in their dollar equivalents when inflation is continuing and a devaluation has not yet occurred? For the internal purpose of evaluating performance, some enterprises deal with this issue (1) by using arbitrary rates of translation for sales and profits for subsidiaries, and (2) by reserving from profits, both in local-currency accounts and in dollar accounts, such sums as they anticipate will have to be added to working capital requirements as a result of the inflation. These measures are intended to distribute the impact of the inflation–devaluation process over the full period of overvaluation and undervaluation of the local currency.

Calculating a credible measure for performance is not the only problem that is brought on by fluctuating exchange rates, however. A problem of a very different sort still remains. If the devaluation occurs, the parent may be obliged in its published financial statements to write down its equity in the subsidiary; this may be required, for instance, to secure independent certification of its consolidated statement. The possibility that the certifiers may require a write-down is clearly a "risk"—if not in the usual economic terms, then surely in business management terms. Accordingly, managers may be tempted to try to avoid such a risk.

Measures can certainly be taken. When the risk arises, a subsidiary can be directed to take steps that force the level of its current assets in lire to equal its current liabilities in lire. The subsidiary can do this in various ways: by declaring a dividend to the parent, by paying off long-term debts, or by assuming short-term lira liabilities in order to acquire fixed assets. (The reader will find it useful to reconstruct the effect of each of these policies upon the balance sheet; then, by referring back to Table 3–2, note how these maneuvers affect the translation adjustment.) As current assets in lire approach current liabilities in lire, the adverse effects of translating these items by the new depreciated lira rate tend to shrink.

But these cautionary measures have a cost. Draining a subsidiary of cash could hurt its ability to do business, and loading it with local debt could add to interest charges. Whether the "cost" is worth the benefits is for the manager to determine according to the circumstances of the firm. The assumption that the answer is "yes," so common in many enterprises, is far from self-evident.

CALCULATING THE SUBSIDIARY'S PROFITABILITY.   The reader by now will be aware of some of the pitfalls that are present in trying to calculate the profitability of any separate entity in a multinational enterprise system. In most cases, there is a strong element of artificiality in any such calculation because the entity cannot be thought of as an independent profit-making unit. Each entity operates under the restraints of a unifying strategy; each has access to a common set of guarantees or credit, a common organizational memory, a common set of well-tested procedures, a common trade name, and a set of mutual assurances regarding the availability of markets, materials, skills, or money. Each entity in the end justifies its continued existence by its contribution to the system as a whole, not by its own performance.

The problems of calculating an individual subsidiary's profit in these circumstances are formidable.

Take the case of an automobile enterprise that sets up an assembly plant abroad. The main purpose of such a plant is to secure a local market for the firm's product. Most of the product, however, is fabricated by other subsidiaries of the enterprise, not by the assembly plant. Some of the return may show up on the books of the other subsidiaries. The assembly plant's return on investment, therefore, may be grossly misleading from the manager's point of view.

Or take the case of a chemical company that maintains its research laboratories and pilot plants in the home country and manufactures the products generated by these facilities all over the world. The human resources that determine the productivity of the overseas facilities of the company lie partly in the home country; the investment in those resources appears mainly on the parent's balance sheet, if it appears anywhere. Once again, there is a risk of grossly misleading calculations.

The "ideal" solution for estimating the yield on any added investment anywhere in the multinational enterprise involves the multinational enterprise as a whole; it requires a calculation of the incremental return to the whole multinational enterprise system, irrespective of where the investment may take place. In practice, this approach is sometimes formally used. Oil companies calculating the yield on investment in new producing wells, for instance, sometimes include a provision for the capital that will have to be invested in seemingly unprofitable downstream refining and distributing facilities.

As a general rule, however, the local managers of multinational enterprises that are charged with the operation of the separate facilities of the enterprise are likely to be judged on the basis of the performance of only a part of the enterprise. From their viewpoint, an investment that benefited the enterprise as a whole without benefiting their particular part would not be attractive, whereas an investment that seemed to benefit their area of responsibility at the expense of the rest of the enterprise might well be supported.

Both in the internal calculations of multinational enterprises and in the external evaluations of their performance, a common tendency is to overlook the system-wide costs and benefits of an investment proposal and to concentrate narrowly on the costs and benefits that fall inside a single subsidiary or a single profit center. When staff work inside the multinational enterprise is based on an incomplete approach of this sort, it often leads to staff recommendations that seem intuitively wrong when viewed from the vantage point of the higher strategic levels of the multinational enterprise. In these cases, the intuition of the board of directors may be superior to the seemingly refined calculations offered by the staff.

In addition to the problem of devising measurements that reflect the impact of a proposal upon the enterprise as a whole, there is also the problem of placing a value on benefits or costs inside the system that have elusive price tags. Sometimes, satisfactory price tags can be devised for such purposes. A subsidiary that uses an intermediate product fabricated by the parent, for instance, can be charged the market price for the product, provided a market price exists; the caustic soda manufactured by an entity in a chemical enterprise can be priced to its downstream affiliates at the price it would bring in the open market. On the same principle, a producing subsidiary that uses the distribution services of an affiliate to sell its exports can be charged the price that such services would command if offered to other exporters. Cases of this sort cover a considerable proportion of the transactions of the subsidiary with its affiliates.

Difficulties begin to arise when the resources used and the benefits provided by the subsidiary are not so easily priced. Tracking back over the past few pages, one can easily identify the items difficult to price. Table 3–3 provides such a list.

The items listed in Table 3–3 do not, of course, wholly defy quantification. For instance, the parent's management commitment in the establish-

TABLE 3-3   Resources Used and Benefits Generated by a Subsidiary
That Are Difficult to Price

Resources used

1. Parent's management commitment in the establishment of the subsidiary and in its subsequent operation.
2. Subsidiary's use of parent's guarantee in raising funds.
3. Subsidiary's use of accumulated information and procedures of the enterprise.
4. Subsidiary's use of trademark and trade name of the enterprise.

Benefits generated

1. Subsidiary's availability to parent and affiliates as a source of supply or an outlet.
2. Subsidiary's availability to parent and affiliates as an alternative source of supply in emergency.
3. Subsidiary's contribution to information regarding local economy or similar economies for benefit of parent and affiliates.
4. Subsidiary's contribution to parent and affiliates in extending use of trademark and trade name.

ment of a foreign subsidiary could be capitalized, presumably on the basis of the opportunity cost to the parent that was involved in the diversion of its energies. In theory, at least, if the top management of Dow Chemical were diverted from planning the expansion of a plant in Peoria because it was completely absorbed in planning the expansion of a plant in Brussels, the cost of expanding the plant in Brussels should include the profits that were foregone in Peoria. On the same principle, a parent's guarantee of funds could be carried as a running cost to the subsidiary equivalent to the increased burden, if any, that the rest of the system would have to bear by virtue of the guarantee.

Some valuable resources might not entail any cost to the firm; this would depend on whether their utilization by the subsidiary involved an opportunity cost or out-of-pocket cost for the rest of the system. The subsidiary's use of the accumulated information and procedures of affiliates might fall in the category of a costless resource, for instance. Nor would there necessarily be any cost involved in the subsidiary's use of the parent's trade name and trademark. If the trade name and trademark could be licensed for the use to which they are put by the subsidiary, then of course there is an opportunity cost involved in the subsidiary's use; but if no such licensing is possible, the subsidiary's use is costless.

A pricing of the benefits, however, presents rather more formidable difficulties. If the existence of the subsidiary provides assurances to affiliates that a predictable source of supply or a predictable market exists, then the affiliates are capable of planning for production on a basis that involves lower risks. The caustic soda plant operated by the chemical enterprise can plan its output against a more predictable demand. The oil enterprise can plan its refining activities on a basis that worries less over a cutting off of supplies. Accordingly, the subsidiary's presence may either reduce the risk to affiliates or reduce their costs or both. But none of the factors involved is easily expressed in money terms.

As for the contribution of the subsidiary to the aggregate knowledge of the multinational enterprise system, this, of course, can be thought of as a contribution to intangible capital. The experience that an enterprise develops in selling office machines in the Argentine market will presumably increase its knowledge of how to sell office machines in Chile. On similar lines, the subsidiary's introduction of a trade name or trademark may contribute value to the enterprise as a whole if it increases the power of the trade name or trademark for other purposes.

The challenge for the manager in the international economy is to find the quantitative equivalents that can reflect measures of this sort in a return-on-investment calculation. The temptation will be to disregard these factors simply because they are so difficult to quantify. But that is a temptation to be resisted. Otherwise, the investment decision may well be made on false premises.

SUGGESTED READING

AHARONI, YAIR, *The Foreign Investment Decision Process* (Boston: Division of Research, Harvard Business School, 1966).

BROOKE, MICHAEL Z., and H. LEE REMMERS, *The Strategy of Multinational Enterprise; Organization and Finance* (New York: American Elsevier, 1970).

BROOKE, MICHAEL Z., and H. LEE REMMERS (eds.), *The Multinational Company in Europe: Some Key Problems* (Ann Arbor, Mich.: University of Michigan Press, 1974).

STOPFORD, JOHN M., and LOUIS T. WELLS, JR., *Managing the Multinational Enterprise: Organization of the Firm and Ownership of Subsidiaries* (New York: Basic Books, 1972), Chapters 7 and 8.

Moving Money
Across
National Borders

chapter four

Doing business in the international economy differs in various ways from doing business inside a single national market. As earlier chapters have repeatedly indicated, one important source of these differences is the fact that the manager must deal in a number of national currencies and in a number of national money markets, all at the same time. But currencies are constantly changing in value, and money markets are constantly changing in condition. To exploit the opportunities and reduce the risks of these changes, managers make use of various institutions and facilities outside of their own firm.

Anyone who has been close to the institutions that help to move money across international borders is aware of how mercurial they can be. New money instruments are constantly being created; old ones are constantly disappearing. But there are certain basic institutions and concepts relating to the movement of money across borders that endure.

MULTINATIONAL BANKING

One key set of institutions on which the manager relies is, of course, the banks that specialize in international business. These institutions serve the multinational enterprise by extending credit, moving money across borders, and reducing the risks associated with doing business in more than one currency.

Many of these banks are multinational enterprises in their own right. Such banks maintain separate facilities in several countries, the facilities

are operated pursuant to some common strategy, and the facilities draw
on a common pool of financial resources, managerial skills, and operational
capabilities. It is not our objective here to explore all the problems associated with the operation of these banks; that subject would require specialized coverage over the whole range of topics presented in Chapters 1 to 3.
Nevertheless, it may help those who intend to pursue the subject further
to recognize that most of the observations of Chapters 1 to 3 do have a
strong bearing on any such study. Let us see why.

Recall, for example, the four categories of oligopolistic strength listed
in Chapter 1, which have accounted for the multinationalization of
industry. These were the strength of a technological lead, the strength of
a trade name, the strength associated with size and spread, and the
strength associated with a scanning capability. All have figured in the vast
growth of multinational banking institutions since the 1950s.

Take the case of the technological lead. Throughout the evolution and
expansion of banking institutions, innovations of various sorts have played
a role in the competitive seesawing of rival institutions. These innovations
have generally taken the form of new credit instruments and new services.
As a rule, the innovations have responded to a new kind of demand, such
as the demand of consumers for the financing of automobiles and housing;
they have often reflected a new technological capability, such as the
capacity for near-instantaneous retrieval of information from computer-
operated discs.

The widespread penetration by U.S. banks into foreign markets—an
expansion from about 100 foreign branches in 1950 to about 700 branches
in 1974—is to be explained partly in these terms. But technological leads
of this sort are easily copied and easily diffused; in time, local banks could
learn how to manage a consumer loan activity and how to use a computer
on the premises. Accordingly, innovations of this sort could only be relied
on to offer a brief competitive advantage to the U.S. banks operating
abroad.

More important and enduring in multinational banking has been the
power of the trade name. The importance of the trade name in banking
does not need much elaboration. Customers are ordinarily in no position to
gauge the risks associated with doing business through different banks.
Accordingly, there is a strong tendency for customers to be attracted to
the "most reputable" name in the business. The staying power of the leading British banks in international commercial banking is to be attributed
partly to that factor; in its absence, the relative decline in the British
economy and in the status of the pound sterling after World War II might
have been expected to reduce the role of British-based banks somewhat
more rapidly than in fact occurred. On the same lines, the weakening role
of the U.S. dollar in the 1970s did not immediately affect the position of
the U.S. banks abroad. The capacity of leading U.S. banks, such as the

Bank of America, the First National City Bank, and the Chase Manhattan Bank, to maintain their position in Europe and elsewhere can also be attributed in part to their general reputation for capability and strength.

However, the largest single factor in the multinationalization of banking has been the advantages associated with geographical spread, that is, with the creation of branches or subsidiaries in many countries rather than just one or two. Those banks that could readily achieve such spread enjoyed a major advantage over their competitors; conversely, those banks that wished to enter the race for multinational business had to find some way of developing the network if it did not already exist.

The importance of developing a widespread network stems from different factors:

1. As noted in Chapter 2, industrial enterprises that are multinational in scope tend to conduct their large financial strategies from headquarters. As a rule, the headquarters staff plays a large role in determining the form and the extent of the money movements generated by the system, especially the movements that cross international borders. As a result of the centralized pattern of financial control in multinational enterprises, banks that are capable of effectively serving the headquarters staff tend to be favored over others. The global scanning capabilities of such banks are seen as an advantage; so is their capacity to lend efficiently and to receive deposits in many currencies. In the United States, these considerations generate a major advantage for banks located in New York and other headquarters cities, provided they also command the services of a multinational network of their own.

2. Relying upon the law of large numbers, banks try to reduce their risks by locating in many markets, by drawing on many sources of money supply, and by lending to many customers. Indeed, the principle is much more important in the case of banking than in industrial undertakings. As far as international banks are concerned, both regulation and practice push the banker toward limiting the size of his commitments to any customer, country, or currency. As for the bank's sources of funds, access to many countries means that tight money conditions in one market may conceivably be offset by the existence of easy money conditions in another so that surplus funds can be shuttled between countries. (But more on that when the Eurocurrency markets are discussed below.) Growth, therefore, is achieved partly by spread; conversely, the absence of spread is an impediment to growth.

3. Banks that have facilities in many countries have another major advantage. Dealing with separate units of a single multinational enterprise located in different countries, multinational banks are in a position to provide funds to one unit of a multinational enterprise in its local currency and to receive compensating funds from another unit in a different country denominated in its local currency. In that way, the

parent of an enterprise may be relieved of the exchange risks that are associated with increasing its assets or liabilities held in another currency, and its subsidiary is similarly relieved. The multinational bank's ability to serve both parent and subsidiary in this way adds to its competitive advantages.

The power of factors such as these has been so great that the leading banks in every industrialized country have found themselves obliged to extend their scope from national to multinational operations. Apart from the longtime British leaders such as Barclays and National Westminster and the well-known U.S. leaders already mentioned, banking institutions in France, Germany, and Japan have also developed huge overseas networks, comparable in size to those of the U.S. and U.K. multinational banks.

The importance of size and spread in the conduct of multinational banking has been responsible for the appearance of another kind of institution, the international banking *consortium*. Groups of banks have pooled their facilities, both at home and abroad, for the conduct of international business. The exact legal form of these consortia has varied according to the requirements of the particular jurisdiction and the preferences of the participants. In many cases, the member banks in a consortium have taken equity interests in a new banking institution that specializes in international banking. For instance, Allied Bank International, whose participants in 1974 consisted of eighteen regional U.S. banks, has taken this form. Other well-known consortia have drawn their members from more than one nationality. Such groups include Western American, with members from Japan, Britain, and the United States, and the Orion Group, with members from Britain, the United States, Italy, Germany, Japan, and Canada.

Banks of different nationalities have participated in international consortia not only to acquire the servicing capabilities that go with geographical spread, but also to reduce the risks of international operations. Other means have also been used to hold down the risk associated with going abroad. Some U.S. banks, for instance, have confined their foreign commitments to loose correspondent ties with other banks located abroad. Others have established Edge Act corporations, operating under the general regulatory mantle of the Federal Reserve Board; units of this type, which numbered about 100 in the mid-1970s, were entitled in their own right to do foreign banking business.

In addition to the multinational networks created for commercial banking, similar networks have been created for investment banking. These, too, are enormously varied in structure. Whatever the structure adopted, the motivations have been the same: to follow the multinational customer to overseas locations, to exploit some special skill developed inside the organization, to diversify risk, and to achieve scale economies.

INTERNATIONAL MONEY MOVEMENTS

The manager cannot operate for very long in the international economy without encountering some problem entailing the international movement of money. In the handling of such problems, he is exposed to a set of institutions and a group of risks that his domestic counterpart ordinarily does not encounter.

THE FOREIGN EXCHANGE MARKET. Money, of course, is traded like any commodity. On any given day, a dollar will buy so many francs or deutschemarks; a deutschemark will buy so many pesos or guilders; and so on. A holder of one currency can ordinarily go into the foreign exchange market and can sell his currency for another currency that he needs. It is a normal function of large banks, linked together by various means of instantaneous communication, to maintain a market in foreign currencies for their customers and for one another.

When managers turn to the foreign exchange market, however, they are often engaged in something more than a simple conversion of one currency into another. Commonly, their concern is to hedge against a future fluctuation in exchange rates.

Consider the enterprise that sees itself coming into possession of a foreign currency at a future date, or sees itself needing a foreign currency at a future date. Its managers are acutely aware of the message in Figure 4-1; the prices of currencies can vary considerably over any period of several months. Conscious of that fact, managers often want to fix their exchange rate now to avoid the risks associated with future changes. Sometimes insurance is available in one form or another, sometimes not. When it is available in more than one form, the manager may have to choose.

To understand the choices available, assume that the date is March 15, 1975. Begin with a manager located in the United States who expects to receive 90 days hence a check for 10,000 guilders drawn on the Amsterdam–Rotterdam Bank in the Netherlands. At that very moment, if the manager had the check in hand, he could "sell it" at the rate of f.1 = 42.23 U.S. cents. That is, the manager would deposit the check with his own bank in New York; the bank would sell the guilders for "spot" dollars, that is, dollars for immediate delivery; and the bank would credit the manager with $4,223 (less some small handling charges). Our manager, being a risk avoider, does not relish the fact that 90 days hence, when he finally gets the check, the rate might well be different. To be sure, as Figure 4-1 shows, the guilder has tended to increase in value relative to the dollar in the months preceding. But speculating on the continuation of that trend is not a risk the manager wants to assume. What is he to do?

At least two courses are available to him. One involves the use of the

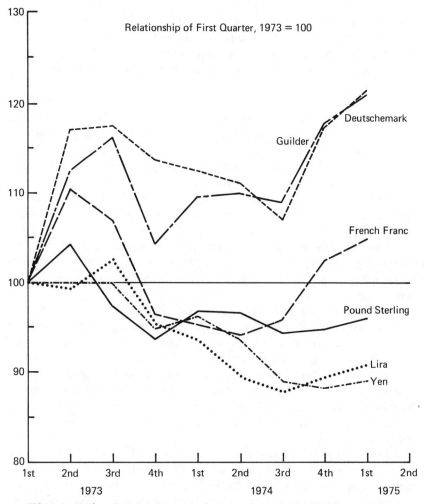

FIG. 4–1   Value of Six Foreign Currencies in Relation to the U.S. Dollar, by Quarters

Dutch banking facilities; the other the use of a *forward contract* in the foreign exchange market. Pushing aside a few technical details that would otherwise complicate the illustrations, the choices come to the following:

1. As his first alternative, he can forthwith borrow f.10,000 from a Dutch bank for a period of 90 days and immediately convert the f.10,000 into $4,223 in a spot transaction on the foreign exchange market. If he takes that course, he simply repays the loan 90 days later, using the f.10,000 check he is to receive at that time. Of course, he has to pay interest to the Dutch banks on the 90-day loan; but he also may earn

interest in the United States on the dollars that he has managed to acquire 90 days ahead of schedule. So his yield is made up of the following elements: proceeds from spot sale *minus* Dutch interest paid *plus* U.S. interest received.

2. As his second alternative, our manager can forthwith make a contract to sell the guilders for a stated sum in dollars even though he does not yet have the guilders, with the undertaking to deliver the guilders and receive the dollars in 90 days. This is what is meant by a forward exchange contract. Although the spot rate on the day of the decision was f.1 = 42.23 U.S. cents, the 90-day forward rate might be something else again, a figure higher or lower than the spot rate. In this case, let us assume that the forward rate is 42.10 cents. For expository convenience, we can call the difference of .13 cents the *forward discount*. In this case, the net yield from the use of the forward rate can be restated as follows: proceeds from spot sale *minus* forward discount (or *plus* forward premium, if it had been a premium).

Which of the two hedging strategies should the manager select? Clearly, the choice depends on whether the forward discount is greater than or less than the difference between Dutch and U.S. interest rates. Suppose that the Dutch rate for a 90-day loan were 8 per cent per annum and the U.S. interest rate on 90-day deposits was 6½ per cent. In this case, the first alternative strategy would produce a net interest cost of 1½ per cent. If this cost were less than the forward discount, the latter having been suitably converted for comparative purposes to an annual-interest-rate basis, the first alternative would be preferred. On the other hand, if the forward discount were less than the interest cost, the strategy involving the use of the forward exchange market would be indicated. (It is good practice for the reader to work out the appropriate choice for the example given.)

Note all the permutations of circumstances that the manager may encounter. He may be a buyer or a seller of foreign exchange; he may encounter a premium or a discount in the relevant forward market; he may find interest-rate differentials running one way or the other between the two money markets. These are the main variables.

As one plays with these variables and tries them out for their effect in different situations, a powerful generalization emerges: where the foreign exchange and capital markets between two currency areas are open and free, there is a strong link between the short-term interest rates prevailing in the two areas and the forward exchange discount rates. Because money can be shuttled between the two areas in search of higher yields, and because the forward exchange market can guarantee against any unforeseen changes in exchange rates, money should be expected to flow to the higher-yield market until the point at which the forward exchange discount is equivalent to the net interest gain.

In a perfectly frictionless world, therefore, one might perhaps anticipate a continuous equilibrium in which the forward discount or forward premium hovered just at the very point that made the manager indifferent in choosing between hedging through short-term borrowing or hedging through forward exchange. But, of course, the relationship in practice proves to be less than perfect. Speculators who are interested in the movement of the foreign exchange rate itself, without regard to its use as a hedging device, are quite prepared to buy or sell forward exchange at rates that are inconsistent with interest-rate differentials. Central banks interested in creating the appearance of stability in their currencies are prepared to intervene in the foreign exchange markets at levels that temporarily may be inconsistent with interest-rate differentials.

One important implication of this fact should be quite clear. The manager cannot be certain in advance about which of the various hedging routes is likely to be cheaper. It often proves worthwhile—provided, of course, that the amount at stake is reasonably large—to cost out both routes to determine the cheaper.

Despite the emphasis on the alternative means of hedging foreign exchange risks, one ought not to draw the inference that managers always have some way of arranging such a hedge. When managers want to use the borrowing route as their method of risk avoidance, the first of our two alternatives, they are sometimes inhibited by limitations on the use of local borrowing facilities or by restrictions on the use of the foreign exchange market. Local bank credit is often scarce, especially in an economy in which foreign exchange risks exist. Even if such credit is not scarce in general, local regulations may prohibit its use for the purpose of buying and remitting foreign currencies.

As for the second hedging alternative, the foreign exchange hedge, this may also be difficult to use in troubled times. Managers may learn to their sorrow that no forward contracts are available in the market, or that such contracts are not available precisely for the period of time that they would like to cover.

Some hedging transactions depend for their total success upon the existence of a market that can speedily produce contracts of odd durations. Take the case of the manager who is an exporter, entitled to payment of an agreed amount of foreign exchange upon the arrival of a shipment in the buyer's home port or upon completion of some other event of uncertain date. If the manager wants to cover his foreign exchange risk until that date, it is a matter of guesswork to decide on the length of the forward exchange contract. In all likelihood, any period chosen in advance will prove either too short or too long. For instance, the manager who has covered his risk with a 90-day contract to deliver foreign exchange may find that he is actually paid on the 75th day and has the foreign exchange available

15 days too early. Having received these foreign funds, his first desire may be to convert them into his own currency and put them back to work in the business. To take this step, however, would mean to carry a 15-day foreign exchange risk; for the manager still is committed, pursuant to his 90-day forward contract, to deliver foreign exchange at the end of that period.

In that event, if the manager is still in a risk-avoiding mood, he may want to enter into another forward contract to bridge the remaining 15 days of foreign exchange risk exposure. The full sequence of his transactions, therefore, would consist of the elements in Table 4–1. Only a well-developed foreign exchange market, however, could be expected to provide the necessary buyers or sellers willing to enter into contracts for the odd number of days involved in transactions of this sort. Forward exchange markets, therefore, cannot always be counted on to provide facilities for the total elimination of foreign exchange risk.

SWAPPING DIFFERENT CURRENCIES. When the manager has access to local credit and a spot market, his problem of hedging against foreign exchange risk is eased; when he can find a forward market as well, his hedging options increase further. But when neither of these conditions is satisfied, the possibility of some sort of hedge is not wholly excluded; there may be other ways of hedging in certain cases.

Take the case of a multinational enterprise whose foreign subsidiary is in need of working capital. The parent, located in Zurich, could conceivably provide the capital by lending some of its own currency, Swiss francs, to the subsidiary. The subsidiary could buy local currency, say pesos, with the Swiss francs and accept the obligation to repay those francs later. But the managers of the multinational enterprise are not eager to

TABLE 4-1   Sequence of Transactions in a Forward Contract

TRANSACTION	CUMULATIVE FOREIGN EXCHANGE POSITION
1. On first day, agrees to export product, and to receive £1,000 upon arrival in buyer's port, date unspecified	Zero
2. On first day, sells £1,000 forward, for delivery in 90 days	Short £1,000
3. On 75th day, deliver to buyer's port, receives £1,000	Zero
4. On 7th day, sells £1,000 in spot market for $, to replenish working capital	Short £1,000
5. On 75th day, buys £1,000 forward, for receipt in 15 days	Zero
6. On 90th day, (a) Receives £1,000 per para. 5 (b) Delivers £1,000 per para. 2	Zero

finance the subsidiary in this way. There is a danger that the value of the pesos may decline in relation to the Swiss franc, thereby saddling the firm with problems:

1. The subsidiary will be obliged to record a translation loss on its books, as described in Chapter 3.
2. To pay back the Swiss franc loan, the subsidiary will be obliged to find more pesos than it originally received.

Accordingly, a local loan in pesos is preferred. But local funds may be scarce. Can the multinational enterprise exploit its multinational character to ease the subsidiary's problem? The answer is yes, especially if the multinational enterprise is doing business with a multinational bank.

When that is the case, the kind of transaction sketched in Figure 4–2 is easy to envisage. In currency area 2, the peso area, a unit of the multinational enterprise (the subsidiary in Figure 4–2) borrows pesos from a local unit of a multinational bank. At about the same time, another unit of the multinational enterprise located in the Swiss franc area (the parent in Figure 4–2) makes a compensating deposit in francs to another unit of the multinational bank.

The idea that the deposit in Swiss francs and the loan in pesos are compensating and offsetting may be explicitly understood by the parties, or it may not. In many cases, the compensating quality of such transactions will be only vaguely acknowledged; the parties involved will simply see their complex interconnections in the various markets as likely to throw the exchange risk in different directions at different times, and will be content to assume that the risk is more or less evenly distributed.

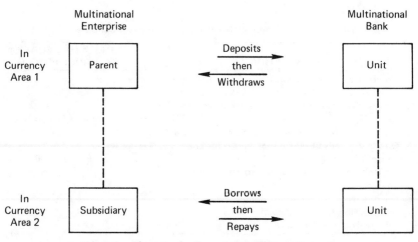

FIG. 4–2   Elements of a Swap Loan in Different Currencies

When the offsetting nature of the loan in one currency and the deposit in another is explicitly recognized, it raises an interesting question: Why should a banking institution ever be able and willing to make loans in the weak currency and to borrow in the strong currency? Picture a bank in Switzerland with a number of major corporate clients. When the corporate clients establish subsidiaries abroad, they offer the bank an opportunity to serve the subsidiaries by setting up branch facilities or subsidiary facilities abroad. The bank's response is conditioned in part by its calculation of the full implications, including the bearing on its relations with the parent. If the bank fails to follow its clients' subsidiaries into foreign areas, will it also lose the business of the enterprise throughout the world? That consideration thereafter governs its calculations in dealing with the foreign subsidiaries of the enterprise; on that basis, the bank's risks of lending in a weak currency and borrowing in a strong may be justified.

There are, of course, many other reasons why a multinational bank may be found engaged in such a transaction:

1. The bank's estimates of the relative strengths of the two currencies involved may differ from those of the hedging enterprise.
2. The bank's opportunities for offsetting its loan in the weak currency may be greater than those of the enterprise.
3. The bank's net earnings from the deposits it receives in the hard currency and from the loans it makes in the weak currency may be deemed sufficient to offset the risk of lending in the weak currency.

Although an arrangement between a multinational enterprise and a multinational bank of the sort just described may be broad and general, there are also situations in which the offsetting transactions in the two areas may be quite explicit and consciously paired. On the more explicit side, large banks headquartered in weak-currency areas have sometimes offered "swaps" along the following lines. The local subsidiary of a foreign parent has been extended a loan, denominated in local currency, chargeable at the going interest rate, say 15 per cent. Simultaneously, the foreign parent has been obliged to make a deposit in a foreign unit of the same multinational bank—that is, create a compensating balance—denominated in a hard currency such as the dollar or the deutschemark, free of interest. The size of the hard-currency loan has usually borne some relation to the size of the local loan, suitably converted by some prevailing rate of exchange; but the exact size relationship has been a matter for negotiation. The two transactions have usually had identical timing, being entered into and liquidated simultaneously. Accordingly, the costs of the arrangement have included (1) the hard-currency cost to the parent in having its funds tied up in an interest-free dollar loan, and (2) the subsidiary's soft-currency interest payments, payable in connection with the loan. Despite the costs and difficulties in setting up such a hedge, it does have value in some situations for the manager who is attempting to reduce his exposure to the vagaries of the foreign exchange rate.

KEY CURRENCIES AND EUROCURRENCIES

For all the difficulties in dealing with foreign exchange risk, there is still another way in which that risk can be avoided. A manager may insist that his purchases and sales and his loans and borrowings, even those undertaken with foreigners, should be denominated in the currency of his own country. If he is British, he may insist that his transactions be denominated in pounds sterling; if American, in dollars. In that way, he can avoid the risk of a change in the nominal value of the receipts or the payments that he anticipates from his transactions, at least to the extent that the change might be the result of a devaluation.

To be sure, this strategy does not wholly ensure against losses of a certain kind. If the value of sterling declines in relation to deutschemarks, for instance, a British seller or lender may wish that the transaction had been denominated in deutschemarks. But the pain to the British manager of missing a windfall profit in deutschemarks would not be great. More important to him is the fact that, by conducting his international transactions in his home currency, the main money inflows and outflows of his business are denominated in the same medium.

One difficulty with a "solution" of this kind is that it cannot apply to both parties in an international transaction; either one or the other, but not both, can trade in his home currency. A further difficulty is that the businessman who insists on doing his buying and selling and borrowing and lending in only one currency ordinarily handicaps his negotiating position to some extent. If the businessman is selling goods or services, his insistence on designating the currency may have the effect of discouraging the prospective buyer, because it would force the buyer to borrow a currency that he may have trouble in getting. The same problem exists in international borrowing; if a businessman is a borrower of funds, his designation of the currency may cut off various prospective lenders.

This is one of many reasons why certain currencies have been accepted from time to time as near-universal media of international payment—as *key* currencies in the parlance of international finance. The pound sterling played that role practically until World War II; the U.S. dollar performed that role until the early 1970s. The U.S. decision in 1971 to allow the dollar's value to vary in relation to gold and other currencies somewhat reduced its attractiveness as a key currency. Today, it shares that function with other currencies, including the deutschemark and the yen.

As long as the U.S. dollar was the dominant unit by which international transactions were conducted, the supply of dollars owned by persons outside the United States was very high; and so was the demand. The heightened flow of dollars in the hands of non-Americans helped to create one of the more novel financial institutions of the postwar period, the Eurodollar.

The unique aspect of the Eurodollar is that its users can gain access to dollars and make deposits in dollars without having any direct contact with a bank in the United States. In the 1960s, this was more important than it may appear. A number of difficulties inhibited foreigners from maintaining dollar deposits in the United States, and some stood in the way of U.S. banks lending to foreigners.

On the deposit side, one difficulty at times has been the comparatively low interest rates in the United States. Regulations of the Federal Reserve System, embodied in Regulation Q, limited the payment of interest on deposits of less than 30-day duration. Moreover, it placed a ceiling on the rate at which banks could pay interest on time deposits, a ceiling that made such deposits exceedingly unattractive at times. On top of that, some deposits of foreigners in interest-earning accounts in the United States were subject to tax deductions from their interest earnings levied by the U.S. tax authorities at the U.S. source. Some foreigners also had to concern themselves with the possibility that, under agreements between the United States and their home governments, their identity might eventually be known to their home governments.

On the dollar-borrowing side, there were also problems for foreigners. Until quite recently, the commercial intelligence networks of U.S. banks were not as widely developed as, say, the networks of some of the British and Dutch banks, especially for prospective dollar borrowers located in remote corners of the earth in Africa and Asia. Accordingly, prospective borrowers from remote points often found themselves unable to establish a ready line of dollar credit with U.S. institutions.

As long as prospective foreign depositors and borrowers were being frustrated in their desire to do business in dollars with U.S. banks, an opportunity existed for bridge building by institutions located outside the dollar area itself. These overseas institutions, which consisted mainly of the London branches of U.S. banks and of European banking institutions, set about their bridge building by denominating loans and deposits in dollars, thus creating the Eurodollar. Claims in this form on banks outside the United States grew so rapidly that by the middle of the 1970s they had reached a level of nearly $140 billion. At the same time, claims in deutschemarks on banks outside Germany were being created by a similar process, as were claims in pounds sterling on banks outside Britain. Indeed, by the mid-1970s, nondollar Eurocurrencies had come to represent claims equal to about one third of the claims in Eurodollars.

Where does the supply of currencies of this sort come from? Take the case of Eurodollars. Middle East governments, Greek shipowners, and others with spare dollars approach banking institutions located outside the United States with offers to turn their dollars over to such banks; all that the banks are required to do is to agree that the deposits may be redeemed in dollars as requested, and to pay interest for the dollars on terms that are sufficiently attractive to top the depositor's alternatives in the United States. In addition, there are also U.S. residents who see some advantages in placing their dollar funds in the hands of banks outside the United States if higher interest rates can be earned.

In one sense, these Eurodollars are inevitably linked to the U.S. economy. When the European bank that receives a deposit is actually receiving a claim on a bank in the United States, that link is self-evident. When the European bank receives a promise from another bank in Europe to pay U.S. dollars, that pledge is normally backed up by an offsetting claim on dollars to which the pledging bank is entitled. There may be some fairly long chains of lenders and borrowers involved; but, eventually, all roads lead back to bank deposits in the United States.

From the viewpoint of U.S. banks located at home, a dollar acquired through the Eurodollar market is just like any other dollar. If the amount of earnings that the dollar can generate when in the possession of the U.S. bank exceeds the cost of acquiring it, the acquisition makes sense. Accordingly, U.S. banks that have branches in London have at times instructed their branches to acquire Eurodollars, which then were made available to their parents in the United States. In transactions of this sort, the London branch may actually be getting its dollars from one part of the U.S. economy and returning them to another part of the U.S. economy. In that case, the London branch becomes a link in a complex international chain that begins and ends in the United States and that has the effect of reshuffling deposits among U.S. banks. The extent of the reshuffle is suggested by the fact that, toward the close of the 1960s, borrowings of Eurodollars by U.S. banks were about $10 billion at times, a result of the big banks with London branches or other overseas facilities having borrowed the dollars that these facilities were drawing away from other dollar sources.

Although it may be evident why Japanese traders, Middle East governments, and New York banks see some advantage in doing business in Eurodollars, the question still remains as to what European financial institutions get out of that medium.

As for European banks, one advantage they derive is simply that of increasing their regular commercial banking business in their home market. To illustrate:

A borrower in the United Kingdom, being well established with Barclays, requests an ordinary 90-day loan in sterling. Because of the stringent monetary situation in Britain, Barclays is fully loaned up. But under the relevant regulations in effect at the time, Barclays is not prevented from acting as an intermediary in the loan. Having acquired U.S. dollars from a holder on payment of an 8 per cent interest charge, Barclays lends these dollars to the British borrower at 10 per cent. The British borrower, to be sure, wants sterling, not dollars. So a conversion of dollars to sterling through the spot sterling market is necessary. But there is also an uncovered risk to be dealt with, the risk that sterling may be devalued between the inception and the liquidation of the 90-day loan. At a suitable cost, the forward discount, this risk is hedged; that is, the borrower can simultaneously (1) buy spot sterling with his dollars and (2) buy dollars forward, for delivery 90 days later. If the forward exchange discount is the equivalent of, say, 2 per cent per annum, the full cost of money to the borrower comes to 12 per cent.

Another advantage for European financial institutions in the existence of the Eurodollar market is that it has generally received their idle funds, when idle funds existed, in quantities and in maturities that could not be provided by national money markets at home. In a typical illustration of the virtuous circle, the widespread expectation that the market could perform in this way was sufficient to increase the probability that it would so perform.

Indeed, the central banks of Europe have commonly used the Eurodollar market as a repository into which they could dump excess funds that may have piled up in the home market and come to represent an inflationary threat. In typical transactions of this sort, the central banks of some countries have persuaded or coerced their own national commercial banks to invest some of their accumulated dollars in the Eurodollar market. The dumping of these dollars into the Eurodollar market by national commercial banks has had the effect of reducing the capacity of those banks to make more loans at home, thereby reducing inflationary forces in the home economy.

Uses such as these make the Eurocurrency markets a convenient international facility that banking authorities in most countries have been reluctant to restrain.

LONG-TERM MONEY MOVEMENTS

Most of the money that crosses international boundaries is intended for a short-run transitory purpose: to pay for goods or services, to hedge against an early change in the value of a currency, to gamble on an imminent change in the currency, or to make or receive a short-term loan.

But money is also sent across borders with much longer commitments in mind. Lenders in one country may commit their funds on a long-term basis to borrowers in another, or enterprises in one country may use their funds to acquire subsidiaries in another.

In the mid-1970s, two things could be said of the international flow of long-term money: (1) money movements of this sort were going on at a rate that was unmatched in history, and (2) such movements were being achieved in spite of a labyrinth of restrictions laid down by the various sovereign states.

Some large long-term movements have occurred in connection with the growth of multinational enterprises. Since "multinational enterprises" is not a very precise concept, the official balance-of-payment statistics of most countries generally do not segregate these flows. Instead, they record the capital transactions of such entities under the general rubric of "foreign direct investment," that is, transactions associated with the acquisition or expansion of any parent company's interest in a foreign subsidiary. Another major flow of international long-term capital is "foreign indirect investment," sometimes dubbed "foreign portfolio investment." This is the sale of securities across international boundaries to buyers who are acquiring them for investment purposes, not for management control. Bond issues generally make up a considerable part of that total. Accordingly, Table 4–2 records for 1973 the volume of public bond issues offered across international borders. The table indicates that most of that activity fell into a few well-known channels.

As Table 4–2 shows, there was a substantial dependence of U.S. corporate issuers upon the Eurobond market, that is, upon the sale of dollar-denominated bonds offered on behalf of U.S. parent enterprises in Europe. For the most part, the proceeds of these issues were intended as capital for the foreign subsidiaries of the U.S. enterprises in Europe. In addition, foreign governments made heavy use of the Eurobond market, offering their long-term obligations on commercial terms to public buyers outside their own country.

The relatively heavy volume of transactions in the Eurobond market in the mid-1970s was made possible by an elaborate multinational infrastructure that had been put in place in the years preceding. Eurodollars were in plentiful supply. The intelligence networks of the investment bankers were highly developed. Securities-distributing syndicates were well oiled and operating. All the attributes of a well-developed capital market seemed in place.

On the other hand, some of the data in Table 4–2 reflect the fact that numerous obstacles still exist to the easy and efficient flow of international capital. For instance, why should various countries have been borrowing dollars in the United States during 1973 while U.S. issuers were busy borrowing dollars in Europe? Part of the answer to questions such as this lies in the fact that, despite the pervasive networks of commercial and investment banking institutions, the capital markets of different countries are

TABLE 4-2 Foreigners' Offerings of Bond Issues, 1973 (in millions of U.S. dollar equivalents)

| COUNTRY OR AREA OF FOREIGN ISSUER | TOTAL | OFFERINGS BY FOREIGNERS IN NONLOCAL CURRENCIES (EUROBONDS) IN EUROCURRENCIES | | | | OFFERINGS BY FOREIGNERS IN LOCAL CURRENCIES | TOTAL FOREIGN OFFERINGS |
		DEUTSCHE-MARK	GUILDER	U.S. DOLLAR	OTHER		
United States	$ 820	$ 50	$ 10	$ 710	$ 50	$ 480	$1,300
Canada	200	170	0	30	0	960	1,160
Western Europe	2,060	540	160	1,110	250	850	2,910
Rest of world	600	210	20	370	0	450	1,050
International institutions	410	20	0	170	220	1,720	2,130
Total	4,090	990	190	2,390	520	4,460	8,550

Source: Adapted from Bank for International Settlements, *Forty-fourth Annual Report*, 1973-1974, pp. 175-179.

far from perfectly linked. The bonds of some issuers are more favorably received in one market than in another; for instance, the investment banking community of the United States and the bond buyers they serve would provide a better reception to well-known Latin American issuers, on the whole, than would the bankers and buyers in Europe. And even where information is adequate, the pervasive governmental regulations described in Chapter 5 provide numerous roadblocks to the movement of long-term capital. Accordingly, the manager who sets out to raise long-term funds outside of the capital market of his home country may have a good chance of succeeding. But he will ordinarily have to steer his undertaking through a labyrinth of obstacles.

SUGGESTED READING

BAKER, JAMES C., and M. GERALD BRADFORD, *American Banks Abroad: Edge Act Companies and Multinational Banking* (New York: Praeger, 1974).

LEES, FRANCIS A., *International Banking and Finance* (New York: Wiley, 1974).

ROBBINS, SIDNEY M., and ROBERT B. STOBAUGH, *Money in the Multinational Enterprise: A Study of Financial Policy* (New York: Basic Books, 1973).

STONEHILL, ARTHUR I., and DAVID K. EITEMAN, *Multinational Business Finance* (Reading, Mass.: Addison-Wesley, 1973).

PART TWO

THE
FIRM
AND
THE
NATION

Multinational Enterprises
and
National Institutions

chapter five

TWO POINTS OF VIEW

As earlier chapters have emphasized, the multinational enterprise builds its strategy and structure around two disparate sets of forces. On the one hand, the advantages of being multinational can only be realized if the firm adopts a strategy and structure that build on and exploit these advantages; accordingly, the strategy and structure of such an enterprise contain certain unifying elements that transcend national boundaries. On the other hand, each multinational enterprise is actually a network of many national entities, not just one entity alone; and the distinctiveness of such entities will not be disregarded by various institutions that deal with the multinational enterprise. Accordingly, as Figure 5–1 suggests, the managers of the multinational enterprise view the enterprise from one angle of vision while the leaders of national institutions, such as governments or labor unions, see it from a very different perspective. The fable of the blind men and the elephant is constantly being reenacted.

In theory, any country whose jurisdiction contains one of the units of a multinational enterprise can direct the unit to do its bidding, just as it would any other entity in its jurisdiction. Accordingly, the government that holds the parent company inside its jurisdiction can command the parent, while the government that holds a subsidiary inside its jurisdiction can command the subsidiary.

That inescapable situation creates a series of dilemmas for managers of the multinational enterprise. For instance, when a unit of a multinational

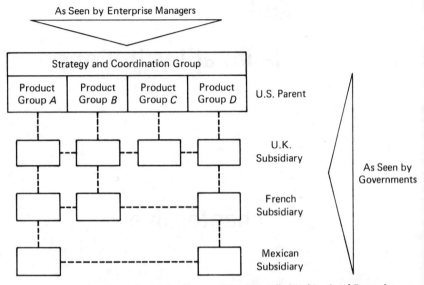

FIG. 5–1   Two Views of a Product-Centered, U.S.-Controlled Multinational Enterprise

enterprise responds to the command of its government, that action generally affects the rest of the multinational system, often in the most profound ways. The U.S. government directs a parent unit, IBM US, not to send some of its advanced nuclear reactor controls to IBM France; as a result, the objectives of the French government are threatened. The monarch of Saudi Arabia directs ARAMCO, a partnership of four U.S. firms, not to ship oil to the U.S. Seventh Fleet; as a result, U.S. military operations are affected. The Mexican government commands Ford Mexico —once again, a subsidiary—to increase its exports of automobile components to the United States; as a result, the economic activity of Detroit is affected. The Japanese government refuses Mitsubishi Japan, a parent, the right to make further investments in its subsidiary in Taiwan; so Taiwan's growth is affected. The Colombian government puts a ceiling on the profit remissions of the Colombian subsidiaries of foreign-owned companies; as a result, the stockholders of the parent company are hurt, not to mention the balance of payments of the country where they live.

On the other hand, multinational enterprises may operate not as a conduit for governmental influences but as the originator of such influence. The parent unit of a multinational enterprise can try to invoke the protection of the country where it is headquartered on behalf of an affiliate in another country. The petition of the initiating parent may not always generate a response from its home government; governments often insist that the foreign units of a parent are not unambiguously entitled to their protection. But sometimes the parent may succeed in spreading its government's protective mantle fairly wide. Pechiney invokes General de Gaulle's persuasive powers to secure special rights from the Greek government for Pechiney Greece; the U.S. ambassador to Liberia invites the Liberian government to deal gently with the U.S.-owned firms in that country; ITT in the United States tries to invoke the U.S. government's covert powers to promote the interests of ITT Chile; the Japanese government offers Saudi Arabia special incentives to be nice to the Arabian Oil Co., in which its nationals have an interest.

Here and there, of course, governments have recognized the anomalous fact that the independent commands of any two of them can converge on a single enterprise, often in ways that are unintentionally contradictory or unintentionally destructive. As Chapter 3 points out, numerous bilateral treaties exist that deal with the status of the nationals of each signatory when operating inside the jurisdiction of the other. The usual principle of these bilateral treaties is that each government extends to the nationals of the other and to the enterprises those nationals control the same treatment that the government accords to its own nationals. Some familiar exceptions exist. For instance, countries tend to limit the right of foreign-controlled enterprises to enter the defense industries, shipping, utilities, banking, radio, television, and newspapers. The less-developed countries tend to push their right to control the entry of foreign-owned enterprises even further, essentially preserving total freedom of action for themselves regarding entry conditions.

Although treaties of this sort are a first step, they barely touch the edges of the problems of multiple jurisdiction. Besides, any rights that are conferred on foreigners and foreign-owned enterprises are hard to enforce; a manager that places much weight on such a treaty as a basis for defining the obligations or establishing the rights of an affiliate in a foreign country often finds himself leaning on a hollow reed.

In practice, experienced managers are aware that they are largely on their own when they confront conflicting commands from different states and when their rights are challenged outside the home jurisdiction. Accordingly, the tendency is to try to bridge or fudge or compromise the issue, not to highlight it. And when a foreign-owned unit operating in some distant land is discriminated against by the national government—when, for instance, it is denied the research subsidies its local competitors are receiving or denied the right to sell its local output to government agencies— the usual reaction is to avoid dealing with the issue on the level of principle.

In practice, therefore, problems of national discrimination and of double jurisdiction continue. Indeed, of late, they seem to have been increasing in frequency and intensity. It would be an endless chore to identify all the issues that multiple jurisdiction is capable of generating for multinational enterprises and for the national institutions with which they interact. A foretaste of these problems appeared in Chapter 3, where some of the issues of taxation were discussed. To orient the reader a little more fully to the kind of problem the manager is likely to confront, however, it may help to look at some of the issues that arise in two selected fields: issues of labor relations and issues of capital movement.

LABOR RELATIONS

As Chapter 1 suggested, one potential strength of the multinational enterprise is its capacity, at relatively small cost, to scan the world for locations where production costs promise to be low. Such a location having been pinpointed, a multinational enterprise has the seeming option of buying from a local source or setting up its own productive facility in the area. That choice rests on certain strategic considerations, such as the importance to the enterprise of maintaining control over production quality or production scheduling. When such a need exists, the enterprise may prefer to create a local subsidiary rather than to buy from an independent local supplier.

In practice, the choice between buying from a local source and establishing a local subsidiary does not always exist. The regulations of the parent country or the prospective host country may prevent the option; tariff barriers or transportation costs may impede. Still, the multinational enterprises commonly do create local subsidiaries to serve a global network of affiliates. In relations with labor unions in one country or another, the fact that such a network exists is often critical. Witness the well-advertised statement of Henry Ford II to Prime Minister Heath in 1971, asserting that Ford's operations in the United Kingdom might have to be curtailed if U.K. labor continued its disconcerting practice of staging sporadic wildcat strikes.

One concern of the managers of multinational enterprises has been whether national labor movements might begin to organize themselves in such a way as to pool their bargaining power across international borders. Signs of this sort of initiative have appeared from several different quarters. During the 1950s and 1960s, an important stimulus came from the U.S. labor movement, especially from the national headquarters of the AFL–CIO and from the United Automobile Workers. The motivations of U.S. labor in these cases have been fairly clear-cut. As one of the highest paid labor forces of the world, U.S. labor has had a major incentive to increase the bargaining power of labor unions in other areas. If successful, that strategy could not only increase labor's share of world product; it could also reduce the temptation of multinational enterprises to shift their facilities out of the United States to countries with lower wages. The UAW has had a special stake in the strategy because the U.S. automobile companies were linked with special intimacy to their Canadian affiliates by the existence of a free-trade regime in automobiles between the two countries, a regime that practically eliminated any restraints on the movement of automobiles and parts across the U.S.–Canadian border. With Canadian labor slightly cheaper than U.S. labor, the temptation on the part of General Motors, Ford, or Chrysler to move facilities and jobs northward across the border was strong. As a result, the UAW placed a high priority on integrating the bargaining strategy of its U.S. and Canadian labor union affiliates.

Building on the UAW initiative, the International Metalworkers' Federation in Geneva has sought to coordinate the negotiating strategies of the various national labor movements whenever they confronted the same multinational automobile enterprise. In the same vein, the International Federation of Chemical and General Workers has sought to coordinate the negotiations of national labor organizations with such multinational enterprises as AKZO, Michelin, Solvay, and Monsanto. (The tendency, of course, has been accentuated by the development of the European Economic Community, on which more will be found in Chapter 12.) The result has been that multinational enterprises have found themselves a little less free, especially in times of labor strife, to shift their production from one country to another. Occasionally, labor unions in one country have refused to work overtime when the result would be to fill the needs of a multinational enterprise created by a strike in another country.

Nevertheless, in general, the efforts of national labor movements to coordinate their negotiating efforts have not been outstandingly successful. Two kinds of problems have been apparent.

One problem has been the differences in history, philosophy, structure, and tactics of the various national labor movements. In many continental European countries, separate labor organizations have been created by communist, socialist, and Catholic political movements; each such organization sees its objectives partly in terms of the goals of the movement with which it identifies. By contrast, practically all the organized labor movement of the United Kingdom identifies with the Labor Party, while that of the United States identifies with the Democratic Party.

In any situation involving a multinational enterprise, therefore, the priorities of the different national groups concerned tend to be somewhat different. A U.S. group is likely to concentrate narrowly on bread-and-butter issues. A German group, while not neglecting such issues, is likely to place a very high priority on the perennial objective of securing *Mitbestimmungsrecht,* or participation for workers in the supervisory board of the enterprise. A British group, although also concerned with pay scales and benefits, will likely stand on its right to refuse any form of cooperation with the managers. Finally, some elements of the French and Italian labor structure will never lose sight of the fact that one of their prime long-run objectives is to gain control of the government and to alter the economic and political system by way of such control.

Apart from ideologies and priorities, the labor union organizations that multinational enterprises confront in different countries are based on entirely different types of membership. In the United States, many unions are organized on industrial lines; unions such as the United Rubber Workers and the United Mine Workers cover any worker in their industry and are the largest single labor organization in that industry. In the United Kingdom, on the other hand, a single plant is likely to be organized in hundreds of little craft-related units, each under the authority of an autonomous shop steward and each committed to follow the lead of any other unit that precipitates a strike. In Germany, the employer confronts a few monolithic industrial unions, such as IG Metall, whose national positions may determine the outcome of any local dispute. In the Netherlands and Sweden, local disputes tend to be settled by comprehensive national organizations of employers and labor.

Apart from national differences based on history, philosophy, structure, and tactics, the different national labor groups that confront a multinational enterprise are also bound to recognize that their respective interests are not always in harmony and are sometimes in direct conflict. To be sure, there are cases in which labor units in different countries can all gain if they manage to maintain a common front against a multinational enterprise; a coordinated demand by such groups for increased fringe benefits, for instance, can come out of the firm's profits or from the customers of the enterprise. On the other hand, when the multinational enterprise is in a position to shift the location of its production, the different national labor groups are themselves in competition; a labor group in one country can win at the expense of a labor group in another. In these cases, it is sometimes difficult for labor to maintain a solid front across international boundaries.

The problem of diverse interests has been evident in a number of situations involving national labor groups. United States labor's sponsorship of the highly restrictive Burke–Hartke bill in the early 1970s drew sharp dissent from labor groups in Canada and Europe. United States labor movements have looked with undiluted hostility at the production operations of U.S.-based multinational enterprises in the border zones of Mexico and in southeast Asia. More generally, labor's commitment to a given national area has limited its ability to pool its negotiating power when facing enterprises that have greater territorial flexibility.

One final point. Although labor is often thought of as the adversary of multinational enterprise, there are also situations in which labor is regarded as its close ally. For instance, politicians, reformers, and revolutionaries in many developing countries often take the view expressed by Lenin many decades ago—workers employed in the modern industrial sector of such countries come to identify their interests with their employers and come to see their interests differently from national labor as a whole. Linked to the relatively productive modern sector of their countries, where foreign firms tend to be heavily represented, these local workers can sometimes aspire to far higher incomes than the prevailing level in their countries. Numerous surveys suggest that in fact such workers do manage to secure higher wages. Sometimes, the higher wages are due to labor's bargaining power, sometimes to national legislation, and sometimes to the policies of the enterprises themselves. Whatever the reason, the outcome is not counted as an unmixed blessing by others in the developing countries, since it is thought to drive a wedge into the solidarity of the national groups confronting foreign interests.

All told, therefore, multinational enterprises confront a diffuse and uncoordinated array of labor groups in various countries, whose disposition and capacity for joint action across international boundaries or even with other national groups inside their own country are quite circumscribed.

CAPITAL MOVEMENTS

In the ordinary course, multinational enterprises find themselves moving very considerable amounts of money across the borders of nation states as their affiliated units go about the business of making and selling goods and services. These transactions are of various sorts. Affiliates buy and sell in transactions between them and with third parties. Parents' investments in the long-term assets and the working capital of subsidiaries and branches are increased or reduced. Hedges by the enterprise against currency fluctuations are established, liquidated, and reestablished. Estimates of the amounts of these flows vary greatly. However, the international money flows of all sorts in which multinational enterprises participate have to be reckoned in the hundreds of billions of U.S. dollars annually. And a considerable part of the total has to be thought of as arising out of inter-affiliate transactions inside a single multinational system, rather than as transactions at arms' length among independent buyers and sellers, lenders, and borrowers.

RESTRICTIONS BY GOVERNMENT. The huge flows of capital across international boundaries each year represent a triumph for man's ingenuity in overcoming bureaucratic regulation. Practically every country regulates the flow of capital across its borders. One result of this network of regulations is that the prevailing interest rates for comparable types of investment can differ substantially and persistently from one country to the next. In 1974, for instance, Swiss government bonds yielded about 7 per cent while U.K. government bonds yielded about 14 per cent. At about the same time, 3-month bank deposits in France paid interest at the annual rate of about

11 per cent, although the equivalent German rate was 7 per cent. These differences did not mean that national money markets were being totally segregated from one another. But the differences were larger than the costs of any hedge, and they reflected the fact that some channels for the flow of money were being restricted or blocked.

As a general rule, in any country the shape of the regulations relating to capital movements has depended on their purpose. If a country is concerned about the adverse effect upon its balance-of-payment position of a capital outflow, onerous regulations will apply on the outflow side; this is exactly where the weight of U.K. regulations was to be found in the 1970s. On the other hand, if the national concern is over foreigners' domination of local enterprise, as it is in the case of France and Japan, the regulations will apply to the inflow of capital, especially to capital inflows associated with the creation or expansion of subsidiaries. If nations worry that the movements of foreign capital in and out of the country may prove to be a destabilizing nuisance, they are likely to regulate its flow both ways. If, however, a nation looks on the easy flow of capital as a positive feature for the country—because, for instance, such freedom is indispensable for the country's role as an international money center—the capital regulations will be carefully tailored not to pinch these activities too much. Finally, whatever else nations may do to restrict the flow of money across their borders, they are likely to show some sensitivity to political relationships, as the United States has typically done in tailoring its capital controls to the needs of Canada.

It would be difficult to attempt to describe the extraordinarily complex network of national regulations affecting capital movements. Besides, any such description would be out of date before the ink had dried. In the 1960s and early 1970s, for instance, U.S. regulations over capital flows had mainly been intended for one prime purpose: to safeguard the U.S. balance-of-payment position against an outflow of capital. For about ten years beginning in 1963, the U.S. administration applied an *interest-equalization tax* applicable to offerings of bonds and stocks by foreigners in the U.S. market; Canadian issuers were exempted from the measure, as were issuers in poor, developing countries and even some Japanese issuers. On the basis of a complex formula, the interest-equalization tax in effect reduced the net proceeds to foreign issuers, the equivalent of elevating annual interest charges or dividend costs. As the U.S. government periodically sought to tighten or relax restrictions on capital movements, the taxation rate was altered to suit the need. By 1974, the interest-equalization tax had disappeared; but there is no reason to assume that it or something like it will not reappear whenever U.S. interests seemed to require.

The U.S. government has also been known to control the flows of foreign private direct investment, that is, the movement of funds between U.S. parent enterprises and their foreign branches and subsidiaries. Beginning in 1965, the U.S. government took the first of a series of steps that culminated in a system of mandatory controls over the flow of foreign private direct investment. After many revisions, the "voluntary" program was superseded in January 1968 by mandatory regulations. The regulations distinguished among different groups of countries and imposed different restraints on U.S. parents with regard to their investments in each group: in poor, less-developed countries; in Canada, Japan, Australia, United Kingdom, and the oil-producing areas; and in most other countries, notably those in continental Europe. By 1975, these regulations too had disappeared, along with a companion program covering commercial loans by U.S. banks to foreigners.

The regulatory style of the United States, as this sketch suggests, has been explicit, voluble, and, by and large, nonselective among different enterprises—in short, a style typical of U.S. regulations in general. But national regulatory styles differ greatly; the U.K. regulatory approach has a flavor all its own, that of France is something else again, and that of Japan different still.

To give the reader a taste of the variation in regulatory styles that he is likely to encounter, it is worth contrasting the U.S. pattern in the field of capital controls to that of the Japanese. It would be only a slight exaggeration to say that the Japanese style in applying its regulations, at least as that style is seen and interpreted by the foreigner, was the reverse image of that in the United States. In general, the regulations were inexplicit in their published versions, reserved in their official elaborations, and highly selective in their application.

The basic rule of Japanese regulations is that all capital transactions, whether inflows or outflows, are subject in Japan to validation by the government. That basic point having been established, the government from time to time has indicated the treatment that applicants could expect. In mid-1971, for instance, the Japanese ground rules specified that, as far as Japanese firms already in existence were concerned, foreigners would ordinarily be limited to small minority holdings. By the fall of 1971, the collective pressures of U.S. and European interests were pushing the Japanese toward further liberalization, and by the mid-1970s the Japanese had gone a very long way in that direction.

The main regulatory device of Japan, in practice, has proved to be a screening delay. During the period in which the screening process occurred, an alert and diligent applicant was able to pick up some hints of the steps by which the process could be accelerated and a favorable outcome ensured. Sometimes the hints were generated from government sources and sometimes from Japanese private interests with which the foreigner was negotiating. Eventually, if the foreigner responded appropriately to the signals, the needed validation was forthcoming. The required response sometimes consisted of accepting a designated Japanese partner, reducing a patent royalty rate, undertaking to provide more capital to the enterprise, agreeing to achieve certain export goals, or similar measures.

The Japanese style of control on the direct investments of foreigners represents a model to which many less-developed countries aspire. As discussed in Chapter 6, most developing countries impose fairly tight controls over the establishment of foreign-owned enterprises, hoping to exclude the investments that they consider harmful for their economy and to secure the rest on better terms. Like the Japanese provisions, these requirements generally place limits on the foreigner's right to take over going businesses, and they generally specify the extent to which equity in the proposed enterprise must be placed with local owners. In some cases, they also include requirements for the training of local employees, the use of local sources of materials, the export of some proportion of the output, and so on. Sometimes the foreigner is obliged to agree not to borrow funds in local capital markets. As a rule, however, none of these requirements is an ironbound rule. After a pattern that may appear arbitrary to businessmen accustomed to other traditions of regulation, each project generally can be negotiated on its own terms.

INCENTIVES BY GOVERNMENT. From the viewpoint of the multinational enterprise, however, national incentives for the attraction of foreign capital have been just as important as restrictive measures. What is more, the incentives have appeared at both ends of the international flow of capital. Some have been maintained by rich countries, such as the United States and Germany, to encourage timid or reluctant investors in their respective economies to venture abroad; and some have been maintained by countries that are eager to attract foreign investors for selected projects.

To develop an impression of the type of incentive that the manager is likely to encounter, consider the oldest, largest, and most ambitious program of them all, the U.S. foreign investment guarantee program. Investment guarantees were inaugurated by the U.S. government in 1948 as part of the European Recovery Program. Originally designed to stimulate the flow of investments to Europe, the program was eventually extended and modified so that it applied to investments in less-developed countries. Despite the extensive controls that the U.S. government felt obliged to place on the export of capital in the 1960s, it continued to provide guarantees under the program to certain types of investment in the less-developed countries. By the early 1970s, the program had been taken out of the direct control of government agencies and placed in an autonomous public corporation, the Overseas Private Investment Corporation (OPIC). By that time, there were over ninety such countries in which U.S. investors could secure guarantees of various sorts under the program.

For a small fee, OPIC is prepared to extend three kinds of guarantees to its overseas investors: (1) guarantees against inconvertibility of either the profits or the principal involved in an approved investment; (2) guarantees against losses arising out of expropriation or confiscation by a foreign government; and (3) guarantees against losses due to war or revolution. In addition, in very special cases where the U.S. government is unusually eager to promote some investment, OPIC may even guarantee against ordinary commercial losses.

The devices that prospective countries use to lure foreign investors into their economies have a certain similarity from one country to the next. In advanced countries, they are generally part of a program that is available to all prospective investors, foreign or domestic, and intended to encourage the settlement of industry in backward areas of the country. Ambitious programs of this sort are found, for instance, in southern Italy, in lagging areas of the United Kingdom, and in many states of the United States. In cases of this sort, the lures for the investor usually consist of cheap loans from public lending institutions, subsidies for factory construction, subsidies for training labor, and generous depreciation allowances or other devices for reducing income tax liability. Although the programs are available to any investor, whether foreign or domestic, foreigners have often responded more enthusiastically than their domestic competitors. The domestic firms, after all, are already well fixed in some familiar or traditional center, whereas the foreign firms are often rootless, searching for a new site in which to locate a subsidiary. Accordingly, it has been much easier for an FMC or a Dow Chemical to contemplate the establishment of a subsidiary in some remote corner of Italy or of the United Kingdom than for one of their well-established local counterparts.

In less-developed countries, incentive programs intended for prospective investors have often had the foreign investor much more explicitly in mind. Apart from offering generous tax holidays, these programs have generally promised such inducements as the duty-free entry of materials and equipment, the guaranteed right to remit profits and even to repatriate capital, and similar rights. Since incentives of this sort have generally been available to enterprises at the discretion of the government concerned rather than as a matter of right, their availability has depended on how attractive the proposals of the enterprise appeared to the receiving government and how effectively they were pressed.

COOPERATION AND CONFLICT. Despite the preoccupation of the managers of multinational enterprises with the restrictions and incentives that relate to capital flows, there are numerous indications that these factors have comparatively little effect upon the basic strategies of such enterprises. The strategies outlined in Chapter 1 continue to represent the compelling forces that motivate multinational enterprises in deciding whether and where to implant their subsidiaries and affiliates.

There are exceptions to that generalization, of course. Until the early 1970s, for instance, Japanese-based enterprises had quite restricted access to external sources of funds, and accordingly could be effectively restrained by Japanese government authorities from implanting their subsidiaries abroad. (By the middle 1970s, as Japanese-based firms spread over the world, the power of Japanese authorities had grown much weaker.) Similarly, French tutelary ministries managed to steer some French-based firms in their overseas ventures. And even more commonly, governments that wished to exclude foreign-owned subsidiaries or to modify their form of entry into the economy could wield some measure of influence.

All told, however, governmental restrictions have not greatly inhibited multinational enterprises from the pursuit of their basic strategies. When governments sought to prevent their home-based enterprises from exporting capital abroad, the enterprises often found it possible to mobilize the needed funds from sources outside the country. Sometimes, of course, the government itself had no objection to that solution, particularly if the main concern of the government was based on the balance of payments. But sometimes, the solution frustrated the government's purposes, especially when the official concern was with blocking a transfer of jobs abroad. Moreover, when governments sought to prevent foreign-owned sub- sidiaries from establishing themselves in the national economy, the multi- national enterprise often satisfied its strategic needs through other arrangements, such as tight licensing agreements and even, although less commonly, through management contracts of various sorts with local enterprises.

Nevertheless, the official obstacles and blandishments associated with capital flows have had a large impact on the second-order strategies and the day-to-day tactics of multinational enterprises. When confronted with the need to establish a producing facility in a low-wage country, enterprises have tended to weigh the rival regulatory structures of different countries in making their choice. Once established in a country, enterprises have taken governmental provisions into account in choosing a financing struc- ture and in deciding on the form in which profits were to be remitted. Thus far, therefore, the basic operations and structure of the multinational enter- prise have still retained a certain unity despite the maze of govern- mental capital regulations in which they operate.

The managers of multinational enterprises in the decades ahead can be expected to confront an increasing realization on the part of national governmental agencies that national regulations have their limitations. In some cases, that realization will lead to inaction; in other cases, to stiffer national regulations; and in still other cases, to international cooperation among governments.

SUGGESTED READING

GRIFFEN, J. P., "The Power of the Host Countries over the Multinational: Lifting the Veil in the European Communities and the United States," *Law and Policy in International Business,* Spring 1974.

HELLMANN, RAINER, *The Challenge to U.S. Dominance of the International Corporation* (New York: Dunellen Publishing Co., 1970).

KUJAWA, DUANE, *International Labor Relations Management in the Automotive Industry: A Comparative Study of Chrysler, Ford and General Motors* (New York: Praeger, 1971).

LITVAK, ISAIAH A., et al., *Duàl Loyalty: Canadian–U.S. Business Arrangements* (New York: McGraw-Hill, 1971).

NORTHRUP, HERBERT, and RICHARD L. ROWAN, "Multinational Collective Bargaining Activity: The Factual Record in Chemicals, Glass, and Rubber Tires," Part I in *Columbia Journal of World Business,* Spring 1974; Part II in *Columbia Journal of World Business,* Summer 1974.

STEIN, ERIC, "Conflict-of-Laws Rule by Treaty: Recognition of Companies in a Regional Market," *Michigan Law Review,* June 1970.

ROBBINS, SIDNEY M., and ROBERT B. STOBAUGH, *Money in the Multinational Enterprise: A Study of Financial Policy* (New York: Basic Books, 1973).

The National Evaluation

of a

Foreign Investment

chapter six

When a multinational enterprise considers whether to set up a subsidiary in a foreign country, it is interested in the contribution that the project may make to the well-being of the enterprise. A government, on the other hand, is likely to be concerned with the net impact that the proposed project has upon its country. Although the investment may be attractive to the enterprise, it may be unattractive to the countries affected by it.

In situations of this sort, at least two governments are generally involved: the *host* government in whose territory the multinational enterprise proposes to invest, and the *home* government in whose territory the headquarters of the enterprises is based. Let us turn first to the analysis of the project as seen through the eyes of the host government.

THE HOST GOVERNMENT'S ANALYSIS

There are many reasons why the analysis of the benefits of a project as seen through the eyes of a multinational enterprise may differ from the evaluation of a host government. The benefits from the viewpoint of the multinational enterprise are likely to be calculated in economic terms, whereas the government is likely to do its calculations in political and social terms as well. Moreover, as indicated in Chapter 3, the benefits from the viewpoint of the multinational enterprise may arise outside the host country in the form of added profits or reduced risks to other parts of the multinational system. The benefits to the government, on the other hand, are likely to be confined to the consequences that arise on its own turf.

For the present, however, let us concentrate on the narrowest and simplest case. A multinational enterprise intends to invest in an autonomous facility in a foreign country—autonomous in the sense that costs and benefits all will be visible in the facility itself. The host government proposes to evaluate the project in economic terms alone. What are the divergences between the private calculation and the governmental calculation?

WHY PRIVATE AND SOCIAL BENEFITS DIFFER.   To begin, we can put aside the fact that it is a foreign-owned enterprise making the investment. Once a domestic investor is involved, there is a case for asserting that no difference should exist between the private benefits and the social benefits that derive from a particular project. In the assumptions underlying a laissez-faire economy, market prices serve as the key to an efficient use of resources: capital, labor, materials, and land. If a business can produce at costs that allow it a profit, it is efficient. The prices it pays for inputs, such as labor, reflect the productivity of those inputs wherever they may be used in the economy. Competition with other manufacturers assures that the prices of the output, as determined in the market, will pay a return to capital that is in accord with its contribution.

If market prices are to work in this way, however, the prices of the inputs must reflect the value that they would have if the inputs were used elsewhere in the economy, and competition must determine the prices of the producer's output. In many countries, especially in developing countries, neither of these conditions holds.

Distorted prices may arise because competition is weak or because the government itself intervenes in the marketplace. Whatever the cause of the disturbed price signals may be, they are likely to lead investors and governments to have different views of an investment.

Competition may be weak for various reasons. Small countries offer such tiny markets that only a few firms can share the market and still produce at low costs. Moreover, where firms are few in number, they may collude to keep prices up. Labor unions may also be the source of misleading price signals in some countries; the unions may exercise such an influence over wage rates that wages do not reflect labor's contribution to output.

The investor's response to the prices that result from weak competition often leads to business decisions that are wrong from the government's point of view. If the price of a consumer product is kept high by collusion, inefficient producers are drawn into local production of that product. High wages may dissuade investors from taking up labor-intensive projects.

Prices that lead to decisions that are undesirable in terms of their social yield frequently arise as a result of policies originally instituted by the government itself, policies instituted with other objectives in mind. Take, for example, the practice in some countries of requiring a license for any new industrial installation. When licenses are withheld for any reason, prices rise to a level that is higher than a competitive market would generate. Another common source of misleading price signals is the tariffs or import restrictions that are levied on imported goods. Government levies such as sales and excise taxes also affect investment decisions. Moreover, prices are often affected by the decision of the government to subsidize the sale of certain commodities. Subsidies on an input in a processing operation, such as fuel oil, can affect the quantity of the input used by a factory. Social project evaluation is intended to help the analyst determine the profitability of a project as if the prices of the inputs and the output were free of such distortions.

THE FIRST STEP.   The first step in a government's evaluation of a project is to estimate the value of the project's output to the economy, that is, what it would cost the country to acquire the output if the project were turned down. In this step, the output of the project is valued as if the product or service were obtained from the best feasible alternative source. In many cases, this alternative source is the world market.

Consider a project, a tire plant proposed by a local businessman, with a pro forma income statement, calculated by normal business conventions, that would look as follows for a typical year:

		(PESOS)	
Sales of tires		1,000	
Cost of goods sold		700	
Labor			200
Raw materials			
Imported			400
Local			100
Overhead		50	
Interest		50	
Profit		200	

If the plant is to be the only tire factory in the country and is to have tariff protection, its prices will not be controlled by strongly competitive forces. In fact, local prices are likely to reflect the costs of imported tires plus a large portion of the import duties that an imported tire would bear. Instead of using such local prices in the calculation of sales value, the government analyst will try to determine a better figure. The world market price provides such a measure. If import duties were not imposed, the world market price would presumably set the prevailing price in the country.

For the hypothetical example, assume that the world market price is 30 per cent below the projected price of the tires produced locally. The 1,000 pesos of output becomes 700 pesos measured in social value terms. The firm's profit of 200 pesos disappears from the social point of view:

	GOVERNMENT'S CALCULATION (PESOS)	
Value of tires	700	
Cost of goods sold	700	
Labor		200
Raw materials		
Imported		400
Local		100
Overhead	50	
Interest	50	
Profit	− 100	

THE SECOND STEP. The prices of inputs may also be distorted. They may not reflect the value of the labor, capital, and materials used by the plant, at least as measured by alternative uses. For the hypothetical tire factory, we shall deal only with labor and capital as possibly mispriced inputs.

Assume that the country where the project is to be placed has a high level of unemployment. If the project failed to materialize, the labor that the project proposes to use might be idle and produce little or nothing of value for the economy. To be sure, if labor were being offered on a competitive labor market, the wages would presumably fall to the point at which unemployment disappeared. But in most countries a dramatic fall in wages is contrary to public policy and unlikely to occur. The labor, therefore, has no "opportunity cost" to the economy regardless of the actual wages. In that case, the government analyst would say that the "shadow" wage rate is close to zero. The government official might therefore replace the 200-peso wage bill with a zero. Once that adjustment is made, the tire plant again shows a profit from the point of view of the government:

	GOVERNMENT'S CALCULATION (PESOS)	
Value of tires	700	
Cost of goods sold	500	
Labor		0
Raw materials		
Imported		400
Local		100
Overhead	50	
Interest	50	
Profit	100	

Adjustments for the cost of capital are slightly more complicated. According to one commonly used method, the government will use a measure very much like conventional return on capital. But, even then, some changes are required.

Assume that the tire plant requires a total of 900 pesos of capital, made up of 500 pesos of debt and 400 pesos of equity. The enterprise thinks of its return as the return on its equity of 400 pesos. In this case, the calculation would yield 200/400, or 50 per cent. If this return is as high as the business could earn on the funds elsewhere, the enterprise finds it acceptable.

The approach of the government is similar, but it is likely to yield a rather different answer. The government is not concerned with the equity capital alone; it is concerned with that amount of capital used in the proposed project, whatever the source or ownership of the capital, which would be put to work somewhere in the economy. If a local investor is involved, as here, the appropriate sum is probably both the local debt and the equity, a total of 900 pesos. When calculating the return on the 900 pesos, the interest payment is no longer an item of cost to the project; it is instead a part of the social return. The social return, therefore, becomes 150 pesos, made up of profit and interest. From the social point of view, the rate of return in the tire plant is 150/900, or 17 per cent. Like the business manager, the government official must decide whether this return is as large as the capital would generate in an alternative project in the country. If "yes," the project has survived the return test.

Another common measure of return is conceptually identical to the preceding. In this approach, the project is charged with an *opportunity cost* or "shadow cost" for the capital. That charge reflects what the capital would yield in an alternative use. If the opportunity cost is 15 per cent, the income statement will simply bear a capital charge of 15 per cent, or 135 pesos. If the bottom line remains positive, the project is socially profitable. The hypothetical tire plant still looks good:

	GOVERNMENT'S CALCULATION (PESOS)	
Value of tires	700	
Cost of goods sold	500	
Labor		0
Raw materials		
Imported		400
Local		100
Overhead	50	
Cost of capital	135	
Social return	15	

In more complex cases, additional price adjustments are required. In many projects, inputs must be revalued to adjust for the effects of indirect taxes, such as tariffs, sales, or excise taxes. Levies of this sort, from the social viewpoint, simply transfer the benefit from one part of the economy to another without changing the total benefit. So they are subtracted from the price of the inputs. These changes reflect a basic principle in most project evaluation techniques: payments that represent mere transfers within an economy rather than the actual use of resources in the economy are not counted as costs or benefits.

Another common modification involves the exchange rate. Often, the official rate of exchange for the local currency does not reflect the real value of foreign exchange to the country. An additional dollar available from earnings on exports or from savings on imports enables the country to import more goods or services. Imports are being deliberately inhibited, either by tariffs or by import licensing. Accordingly, the additional import of, say, a machine can have more value in terms of the local currency than the official exchange rate indicates. In such a case, the value of the output and the cost of imported inputs will have to be recalculated, using the "shadow" price of foreign exchange. In practice, the government analyst usually guesses at such a rate, using vague and imprecise criteria. If adjustments were made to the calculations for the tire plant to reflect an overvalued exchange rate, the alternative costs of tires, in pesos, would be higher; that is, the value of the tires manufactured would be greater than 700 pesos. The costs of imported inputs, measured in pesos, would be raised by the same percentage. The net result would be to make the tire plant look more profitable to the government than it did before the adjustment.

Thus far, the calculations for the tire project have been made for a typical year. In an effort to improve the calculations, some government analysts attempt to calculate costs and benefits for each year of the project. Then they discount those figures to yield a present value of the net costs and benefits. Just as in similar calculations undertaken from the point of view of the enterprise, adjustments to reflect the flow of costs and benefits over time can yield results rather different from those done on the basis of a typical or average year. But the more sophisticated calculations involve no new principles.

THE THIRD STEP. Besides adjusting prices, the analyst may try to place some value on the *externalities* that are associated with the project. One way of viewing externalities is to consider them as costs and benefits to the economy that result from the project, but that are not captured in the company's income statement.

Take some familiar examples. If the proposed plant causes litter or pollution, the government analyst may add a charge to cover the resources that the government will have to provide for clean up. Even if the litter or pollution is not cleaned up, a charge can be imputed to reflect the damage to the environment as perceived by others who must view the litter or breathe the polluted air. Not all externalities are costs; some are benefits. If the existence of the tire factory gives promise of attracting other facilities to the country, the tire factory may be credited with an additional benefit. If the tire factory is just what is needed to speed up the establishment of a chemical plant in the country so that it will appear two years earlier, then for purposes of evaluation the tire plant project should be allocated some portion of the benefits of the speedup. Even if the tire plant alone did not meet the social return test, the benefits of attracting the chemical plant two years earlier may tilt the balance.

FOREIGN-OWNED PROJECTS.   Thus far, we have assumed that the tire plant is locally owned. If it is foreign owned, a few adjustments are required; but there are no new principles to be mastered.

The critical difference between the foreign-owned project and the domestic one usually lies in the handling of the costs of capital. In the case of the locally owned plant, the government charged the project with the opportunity cost of all the capital as long as the capital was of a kind that would be used elsewhere in the country if the project were not undertaken. However, for a foreign-owned project, it is very likely that some of the capital would not be available to the country if that project were not undertaken. The foreign investor would probably take his funds and invest them elsewhere; for such capital, therefore, there is no opportunity cost to the host country. Nevertheless, it would be a mistake not to charge the project for that capital. The host country incurs costs for the capital, in the form of dividends, interest, and similar payments that leave the country. These payments are counted as costs in the government's calculation of the social profitability of the foreign investment.

Of course, even when foreign capital is involved, there are cases in which the approval of a given project means that less capital will be available to the country for other projects. For example, funds from an international lending institution may be available for a wide range of uses, but only up to a ceiling amount. In considering capital that could be used in alternative projects, opportunity cost is again relevant. The government analyst charges the project with the opportunity cost of the capital if that cost is higher than the actual payments to foreigners for the use of the capital. On the other hand, if the actual payments are higher, they represent the appropriate charge.

Now consider all the changes that are required in the government's calculations to reflect the fact that the tire plant is foreign owned. For this purpose, assume that all the capital comes from abroad and would not be available to the host country if the tire plant were not built. If all the profits and interest are remitted abroad, these payments become costs from the government's point of view.

	GOVERNMENT'S CALCULATION (PESOS)	
Value of tires	700	
Cost of goods sold	500	
Labor		0
Raw materials		
Imported		400
Local		100
Overhead	50	
Cost of foreign capital		
Interest	50	
Foreign profit	200	
Profit	− 100	

The project is no longer profitable from a social viewpoint. Observe, however, that imposition of a local income tax could make the project attractive to the host government. A 50 per cent tax would reduce the foreign payments by 100; in that case, the project would just break even from the government's point of view.

ALTERNATIVE FORMS OF PRESENTATION. The manager who has dealt with governments in the evaluation of projects will have recognized that governments do not always present their figures in the ways shown here. In fact, it is improbable that any government makes its social calculations simply by adjusting the figures in the firm's income statements. Nonetheless, when governments calculate a social benefit–cost ratio, social return, or a domestic resource cost the principles are identical with the preceding illustrations. For most purposes, the outcome is the same no matter which method is chosen. Yet, the manager needs to understand the variants so that he can deal with governments on their own terms.

Two methods of presenting the government's analysis have been demonstrated thus far. In the first, the *social return* for the tire plant was calculated by figuring the social profit as a percentage of the capital that the government could allocate elsewhere in the economy if it were to reject this project. The hypothetical domestic tire plant yielded a 17 per cent return on capital according to this approach. This figure is adequate to pass the project if it is greater than what the capital would yield in an alternative project.

The second format involved a calculation of the difference between the social benefits and the social costs, including as a cost the yield that the capital would provide in another project. In the domestic example, the social benefits were 700 pesos and the social costs, 685 pesos. The project

is attractive if the benefits are greater than the costs. The distinction between the two formats is of no practical importance because the two
methods lead to identical decisions.

The *social benefit–cost ratio* is another approach that is conceptually
similar. To calculate the ratio, the government analyst simply divides the
benefit of 700 pesos by the total costs (including capital costs) of 685 to
yield a social benefit–cost ratio of 1.02. As long as this ratio is greater than
1, the benefits exceed the costs.

The manager will see his project evaluated by governments in still another format. The *domestic resource cost* approach has much appeal to
officials and is spreading rapidly. Although a little more difficult to understand at first, the method is the same in principle as those already presented.
The approach of the analyst is to compare the value of the domestic resources—labor, capital, and so on—that would be used in the project with
the value of the output if it were secured abroad. For the calculation,
the domestic resources are valued in local currency, say pesos, while the
product purchased abroad is valued in foreign currency, say dollars. The
two figures produce an implicit exchange rate of so many pesos per dollar.
The more pesos it takes to produce a dollar's worth of value, the less
attractive is the project.

To illustrate, we shall restate the income statement of the hypothetical
tire plant in the appropriate currencies. Return to the case in which the
plant is locally owned and let 2 pesos equal $1.

	GOVERNMENT'S CALCULATION
Value of tires	$350
Cost of goods sold	
Labor	P 0
Raw materials	
Imported	$200
Local	P100
Overhead	P 50
Cost of capital	P135

The total domestic resources used (all the peso costs) add up to P285.
The net value added in the economy is the difference between what it would
cost to import the tires, $350, and the purchases from outside the economy,
$200, a net figure of $150. The "implicit exchange rate" is $\frac{P285}{\$150}$, or 1.9
pesos per dollar. As long as this rate is better than the rate that the analyst
thinks would "clear the market" (the "shadow exchange rate" mentioned
earlier), the project passes the test.

Table 6–1 summarizes the four methods of presentation in algebraic

TABLE 6-1   Principal Forms of Social Profitability Calculations

METHOD	FORMULA	TEST
Social return =	social benefits *minus* social costs for inputs other than capital, *divided by* relevant amount of capital	Should exceed the yield that the capital would bring in alternative uses
Net benefits =	social benefits *minus* social costs for all inputs	Should exceed zero
Benefit/cost =	social benefits *divided by* social costs for all inputs	Should exceed one
Implicit exchange rate =	social costs for all local inputs denominated in local currency *divided by* the difference between social benefits of the project and the social costs of all foreign inputs, both denominated in foreign currency	Should be equal to or better than a "shadow exchange rate"

form. A project that passes or fails any of these tests will pass or fail all of them. But if the government analyst wishes to rank projects from best to worst, the measures can yield different orderings. As long as the government analyst is concerned only with a "go" or "no go" decision, the methods differ only in convenience of calculation or presentation.

EVALUATING THE CALCULATIONS.   Although analytically useful, social calculations have their limitations.

For one thing, none of these methods can be applied in evaluating projects whose output cannot be purchased on world markets. Consider a hospital, for example. How does one measure its social value? Luckily, most projects undertaken by the manager in the international economy do not fall into this kind of wonderland. Most are for the manufacture of products that do enter world trade and which can be subjected to fairly rational analysis. Even for such products, however, the various measures suffer from important limitations. The most important derives from the fact that the calculations usually measure the project in terms of only one goal. As presented here, the methods evaluate a project only on how efficiently it uses domestic resources to increase national income. Some analysts will try to overcome this limitation by supplementing the basic calculations with others designed to measure the project against other criteria. Typical analyses are aimed at measuring the effect of the project on income distribution, on government revenue, on the country's balance of payments, and on the generation of skills in the country. Some analysts attempt to embody in one single measure the effects of a project on a number of goals.

In practice, efforts to capture all goals in one measure prove altogether arbitrary, since they oblige government officials to specify the weights to be attached to possibly conflicting goals, such as the goal of increasing national income and the goal of increasing government revenue. Apart from the difficulty of handling multiple goals, measures of the sort presented here are also inadequate because they fail to capture adequately the dynamic economic effects of a project, as well as the political implications of a project in terms of control over the economy. Beyond a certain point, therefore—a point that is quickly reached—the analyst will find himself in unknown territory, working more by taste and instinct than by rational calculation.

UNBUNDLING THE COMPONENTS OF FOREIGN INVESTMENTS

As a rule, governments are likely to view foreign ownership and control as real costs sitting on top of the more obvious economic costs. Ownership is ceded to foreigners only reluctantly. Control is equally sensitive. The ramifications of foreign control touch political and economic issues that are important to most governments. In an effort to decrease foreign ownership and control as well as to improve the net economic benefits of foreign investment, some governments have tried to develop alternatives beyond those of simply importing a product or allowing the subsidiary of a multinational firm to manufacture the product locally.

The efforts are most easily understood if one thinks of the possible benefits of foreign investment as consisting of capital, technical and managerial capabilities, and access to export markets. The government's approach is to "unbundle" the project—to acquire some or all of these elements separately and thereby to reduce or eliminate the problem of foreign ownership and control.

Consider a project that involves manufacture for the local market. The inputs needed from abroad may be technical know-how and capital. Local management skills may be adequate and access to markets assured. In that case, the government may try to secure the capital by borrowing abroad rather than by accepting the foreigner's investment in a local subsidiary. The technical capabilities might also come from abroad under a licensing arrangement with a foreign firm that holds no equity in the local project.

More generally, from the host country's point of view, the options break down roughly as shown in Table 6–2, which shows that the arrangements with the least costs to the host government appear also to offer the least benefits. The policy issue that must be faced by the host is whether the reduction in costs associated with a particular investment arrangement more than offsets the loss in benefits. If, for example, a licensing arrangement could be generated as a feasible alternative to a wholly owned subsidiary, the question is whether the reduced capital, management, and

TABLE 6-2   Benefits and Costs from Viewpoint of Host Government of
             Alternative Investment Options

OPTION	BENEFITS	COSTS
Wholly owned subsidiary	Capital, technical and managerial capability, access to export markets	Foreign ownership and control; dividends, fees, claim on retained earnings
Foreign-local joint venture	Probably less capital, technical and managerial capability, and access to export markets than for wholly owned subsidiary	Foreign ownership and control; dividends and fees, but perhaps different in volume, mix, and timing from wholly owned subsidiary
Licensing	Technical capability only	Fees
Management contract	Primarily managerial capability	Fees

access to export markets that might be associated with the licensing arrangement are worth the advantages of retaining local control and the difference in payments abroad from the local economy.

The view of a country toward its options changes as the country develops. At the early stages, a developing country sees its alternatives as few. As long as the home market is still poor and small, potential investors may find the country insufficiently attractive to be willing to consider any departure from their preferred form of investment. With development, the country may find it can squeeze some of the resources, such as management capability and capital, out of the local economy.

Moreover, a country's needs for technology and access to export markets shift as the country's development proceeds. At the outset, the requirements for technology are of a very simple kind. However, as industry develops, the requirements are likely to be more complex. Special access to export markets may become important, for example. Initially, the country is likely to be exporting products that are sold on a price basis on an open market, without the need for direct ties to foreign buyers. Gray cloth or jute bags illustrate that stage. As development progresses, the manufactured goods that make up the country's exports may be more complex. To sell sophisticated products successfully abroad, greater knowledge about foreign markets is essential. Indeed, for some types of export sales, such as some automobile components and electronic components, the foreign buyer may have to be involved directly in the local production process. To export these products successfully, the country may have to accept some measure of foreign ownership and control.

Accordingly, the perceptions on the part of the host country of what is needed from the foreign investor change with time. Some of the early foreign investors may eventually be seen as offering nothing very critical to the host country. From the government's viewpoint, the costs of servicing those investments appear to be incommensurate with current benefits. In many developing countries and in some of the more industrialized nations, governments take a direct role in readjusting arrangements with past investors to reflect the new perceptions. The history of a hypothetical U.S. automobile firm in Mexico illustrates the pattern.

> Let us say that the firm went to Mexico in the 1920s with the offer of a little capital, some technology, and some management skills much desired by the Mexicans. In exchange, the Mexicans allowed a wholly owned subsidiary to be established to assemble imported automobile parts for the local Mexican market. Soon the simple technology of assembly was mastered by the Mexicans. In effect, the Mexicans began to ask whether the arrangement was not too costly for the few benefits continuing to accrue to the nation. In such a case, the American automobile firm might try to reinforce its shaky position by adding a new and more difficult function. It could manufacture in Mexico many of the components that it had been importing for local assembly. As a result, the investor may be able to resist pressures to sell a portion of its equity to Mexicans or to "Mexicanize" his operations in some other way.
>
> Eventually, however, the Mexican government may see its economy as quite capable of manufacturing an automobile. Skilled management is available locally. Capital can be raised by issuing bonds in the New York capital market. Our hypothetical automobile firm would have found itself once more under great pressure to "Mexicanize."

However, many foreign firms in countries such as Mexico manage to survive with wholly owned subsidiaries. Some control technologies and skills not otherwise available to the country. The technology may relate to the production of well-established products or to a stream of products. When a stream of products is involved, the usual pattern is for foreigners gradually to lose their share of the local market to national firms in older products, while holding or enlarging their overall position with the introduction of new products.

Other foreign investors have found that their position of strength in confronting the Mexican government rests on their special access to export markets. The hypothetical American automobile firm, for example, may manage to retain its control over its Mexican operations simply because of its capacity to sell Mexican-made parts to its assembly plants in the United States.

Generally, as industries grow older and as the barriers to entry decline, the options for host countries increase. More firms enter the industry and their bargaining power with host countries declines. Faced with competitors that are willing to yield to host countries' desires, some multinational firms change their policies with regard to overseas arrangements. General Motors, for example, long opposed joint ventures and licensing arrangements, explaining that unambiguous control was essential to its worldwide strategy. By the mid-1970s, however, GM had begun to form joint ventures outside the United States and had stated its willingness to license technology without equity interest. No doubt, the growth of competitors such as Fiat, with a more flexible approach to foreign ties, played an important role in changing GM's policy.

The extent to which governments will concern themselves with issues of foreign control in their economy varies from country to country, according to complex factors. History plays a part; so does the stage of a country's development; so, too, does the size of total foreign involvement in the country. In Europe, for instance, the issue of the foreign-owned investment does not ordinarily generate as much tension as in the developing countries. In Europe, governments depend in fact on the growth of local firms to contain the foreigner. In many industries, lower overheads and better familiarity with the market assure the European enterprise a growing market share as the initial advantages of the foreign-owned subsidiary decline.

In some cases, nevertheless, European governments have played an active role in accelerating the process. Unwilling to wait for local firms to grow on their own, European governments have also stepped in, but in their own styles. The usual vehicles for intervention have been local "national champions" supported by the government to do battle with the foreign-based, often U.S.-based, multinational. The champions may be state-owned or private firms. In automobiles, France has its state-owned firm of Renault, Italy has state-owned Alfa Romeo and privately owned Fiat, and Germany has Volkswagen, with mixed private and state ownership. Whatever the form of ownership, governments have used subsidies, preferences in government purchasing, and other forms of support to assure that national firms would survive against the foreign-owned intruder.

There are other alternatives besides the approaches common in Latin America and Europe. Canada, for example, has chosen another route. The Canadian Development Corporation was created partly to buy up foreign investments in Canada. Its charter is not very specific as to criteria, but its first major purchase was an American firm, Texas Gulf Incorporated, whose principal assets consisted of mining ventures located in Canada. In this case, Canadian ownership would not significantly reduce the technology or other benefits flowing to Canada, but it would make a contribution toward reducing foreign control of industries in Canada. The savings in payments of dividends outside Canada might be worth the purchase price to the Canadians.

In some cases, the policies of host countries are embodied in national legislation; in other cases, not. In some instances the rules are universally applied; in others, on an ad hoc basis. Commonly, governments maintain a list of industries that are closed to foreign investment. Indonesia, for example, has published such a list. These include bicycle tires, simple rubber goods, selected cement operations and cement products, and so on. In most of the industries on the list, local investors have already demonstrated their capability to provide the capital and technology. Exports appear either to be unlikely in those industries or to be feasible without the development of ties to foreign investors. Many countries also restrict investments in industries that are oriented to national defense or to other vital national interests. For example, the United States restricts foreign investment in domestic aviation, coastal shipping, communications, hydroelectric installations, and nuclear power.

In addition to covering prohibited sectors, host government legislation dealing with foreign investment may also list investments that are particularly desired by the country. As was discussed in Chapter 5, many nations offer incentives to attract such projects. In some cases, the government has estimated that the private benefits are inadequate to attract an investor. Many countries offer incentives for projects located in remote areas, for projects in regions with large unemployment, and for industries that will earn foreign exchange by exporting. Note that these are projects for which the firm's calculation of cost and benefits is particularly likely to differ from the social calculation.

Foreign investment legislation sometimes spells out the form of investment that is desired or which might be allowed. The country may leave some sectors open to wholly owned foreign subsidiaries; others may be open only to joint ventures that include local interests. Where such distinctions exist, there is usually some implicit weighting of the need for foreign contributions and the economic and political cost associated with the particular investment form.

RESOLVING THE TWO VIEWS

If a project looks profitable to a firm, but unattractive to the host government, changes in the project may overcome the problem. If the project is unattractive to the firm but attractive to the government, incentives, subsidies, or protection may resolve the difference in views. However, some of the most difficult problems revolve around the structure that foreign participation is to take. To deal with that complex and sensitive issue, new kinds of ties between multinational enterprises and host countries are being developed.

Issues of ownership and control create the impasse in many negotiations. Governments have one set of objectives in the handling of these issues; managers, another set. As the discussion in Chapter 2 indicated, managers are often desirous of unambiguous control over decisions critical to the firm's global strategy; ownership sometimes appears to be an essential ingredient to obtain the required control.

When ownership and control have caused difficulties in negotiations between governments and potential foreign investors, novel solutions have sometimes been arranged. Co-production agreements in the socialist countries of Eastern Europe illustrate the kind of accommodation that is possible. In the typical case, the foreign firm has no ownership in the facility. However, it may have wide ranging control over the operations. And its financial benefits, perhaps paid in the form of goods produced by the project, bear no direct relationship to ownership or control.

More conventional are joint ventures that allocate control and financial benefits to the partners in proportions that are different from the shares in ownership. In such an arrangement, a partner with minority ownership may have the right to appoint certain officers of the venture. Such a partner may also be entitled to financial benefits from royalties, management fees, or other payments apart from dividends. And these payments need not bear a direct relationship to the actual costs of services rendered.

In many situations, the type of decision that is critical to the multinational firm can be identified. When international trade names are being used, for instance, quality control may be critical. In that case it may be possible to make arrangements by which the firm retains control over the critical areas of decision, even though it does not have complete ownership.

To solve an impasse, special rights can sometimes be given to either the foreign investor or the local partner. In Colombia, negotiations with Hanna Mining Company were stalled over the issue of control in 1970. The deadlock was finally broken when the government, a minority partner, was able to spell out the kinds of decisions that it thought it must control. The company granted government members of the board of directors veto rights in those areas of great concern to the government, but retained for itself control over the decisions it regarded as strategic.

In some cases, the task in negotiations is to build provisions into the arrangement that allow for likely shifts in the future position of the parties. The investment rules of the Andean Group, described in more detail in Chapter 12, take into account in a rather rough way the changes that might occur in the relationship between investor and host country by calling for a scheduled decline in foreign ownership over a specified number of years. In other nations, agreements have been struck that have attempted to build in an orderly procedure for change.

A number of investments in refining facilities for petroleum illustrate this particular genre. In the mid-1960s, for example, AGIP (an Italian, state-owned oil firm) reached an agreement with the Ghanaian government that provided for an eventual change of ownership. For the first eleven years, AGIP would own and manage the facilities. After that time, the government could purchase them, receiving a credit toward the purchase price equal in amount to the tax exemptions granted to AGIP in the early years. AGIP would have a guaranteed market for its crude oil, which in those days was considered to be in surplus. Ghana would receive the technology it required and would be able to exercise eventual control.

An arrangement for the reconstitution of powdered milk in an Asian country was, in some ways, similar to AGIP's deal in Ghana, although the agreement was between two private entities. In this case, the foreign partner was an exporter of milk powder. The joint venture was with a local partner, who contributed local political power and management skills. The agreement between the two partners called for a starting arrangement under which the foreign firm had most of the stock. Over a certain time period, however, the local partner was entitled to buy added shares of the enterprise. Nevertheless, the joint venture was to continue to buy its milk powder from the original foreign partner, with an appropriate guarantee of a competitive price. The foreign partner appeared to have two objectives. One was obviously the sale of powdered milk; the second was apparently the retention of control over the venture long enough to assure that a major marketing effort was undertaken to expand the demand for milk.

THE HOME GOVERNMENT'S ANALYSIS

Although the manager in the international economy has had to be particularly sensitive to the evaluation of his project on the part of host governments, scrutiny by home governments is becoming more common. The countries from which most foreign investment originates are becoming increasingly concerned over the effects, real or fancied, of the foreign investment activities of multinational enterprises.

Until recent years, the typical analysis in the capital-exporting countries was concerned with the overall effect of the country's foreign investment on the balance of payments. However, increasingly the analysis of the effects of capital outflows is taking on characteristics that are similar to those of project evaluation in countries hosting foreign investment.

Once the manager has mastered the principles that govern the analysis of his projects from the host government's point of view, he does not need to grasp any new principles to understand the analysis from the point of view of his home country. Yet, the shift in perspective can be tricky.

The multinational enterprise itself is likely to view the major benefits of a foreign investment as the dividends, interest, royalties, and other receipts, after the payment of foreign and home taxes. The home government of the enterprise, however, will view the benefits differently. As regards foreign exchange inflows, for instance, the home government will count its tax collections from the foreign flows as part of the relevant yield. There may be other benefits as well. If the foreign investment leads to exports from the home country that would not otherwise have been made, the home country may gain. Exports of machinery that would not otherwise have been sold abroad, for instance, may fall in this category.

The home government may view the foreign investment as entailing certain costs as well. If the investment abroad reduces the amount of capital available at home, the project must be charged with the opportunity cost of the capital. If the project places demands on the time of valuable managers or engineers, the project should also be charged with the opportunity cost of that time. If the investment transfers technology abroad that would not otherwise have been available to the foreigner, the capital-exporting country could lose the benefits associated with exports that would have occurred if the technology had remained solely in the hands of the home country. In that case, the costs of the project as seen through the eyes of the government must be increased accordingly.

The calculations from the home country's point of view involve complexities of the same sort as those involved in the host country analysis. It may prove necessary to adjust distorted prices and distorted exchange rates in the calculation, to adjust for the timing of the costs and benefits, and to deal with multiple objectives. In spite of the problems, these calculations are also likely to play an important role in the future of the manager in the international economy. To deal effectively with governments, the multinational manager must understand the viewpoints of both his host and home governments.

SUGGESTED READING

HIRSCHMAN, ALBERT O., "How to Divest in Latin America, and Why," *Essays in International Finance,* No. 76 (Princeton, N.J.: Princeton University Press, 1969).

LITTLE, IAN M. D., and JAMES A. MIRRLEES, *Manual of Industrial Project Analysis in Developing Countries,* Volumes I and II (Paris: OECD, 1969).

SEN, A. K., *Methods of Evaluating the Economic Effects of Private Foreign Investment,* a report prepared for the Fifth Session of the UNCTAD Committee on Invisibles and Financing Related to Trade (TD/B/C.3/94/Add. I).

UNITED NATIONS INDUSTRIAL DEVELOPMENT ORGANIZATION, *Guidelines on Project Evaluation,* Vienna, 1970.

VERNON, RAYMOND, "Multinational Enterprises in Developing Countries: An Analysis of National Goals and National Policies," Harvard Institute for International Development, Working Paper No. 4, June 1975.

The Developing
Economies

chapter seven

In Chapter 6 we pointed out some of the differences in the ways a manager
and a government might view a particular project. Those differences are
usually particularly apparent when the multinational manager finds himself dealing with the government of a developing country.

To understand the points of view of the developing nations, the manager
must have some understanding of the process of development itself and
some grasp of the relations among the trade, payments, and investment
aspects of the process. He must have some feeling for the speed of
structural change and for the perhaps unfamiliar role of government in the
development process. Without this understanding, the manager's capacity
for projecting himself into the position of officials and businessmen in the
developing country may be dangerously limited.

The multinational manager doing business in a developing country is
very dependent on the goodwill of his host government. To speed economic
development, most such governments exert a much greater degree of
control over decisions that affect the businessman's profits than do the
governments in the industrialized areas. Governmental measures such as
tariffs, import licenses, exchange rates, industrial licenses, and subsidies
determine the level of profits to a much greater degree. Hence, a rather
thorough understanding of the goals and concerns that determine these
policies on the part of government is critical to the success of the manager
in such an environment.

Although the policies of developing countries go through rapid cycles of change, certain underlying objectives and beliefs appear to be long lived. The objectives of increasing the national standard of living and decreasing the sense of dependence on the industrialized countries, for instance, seem enduring.

FACT AND THEORY

Today, the economies of all countries are changing, and most of the change is accompanied by growing per capita output of goods and services. There are few areas of the world that do not now enjoy higher living standards than in the past. Most of the areas of the world that the casual observer might think of as changeless, such as the interior of Borneo, the highlands of New Guinea, or the altiplano of South America, are in fact in the throes of fundamental change. Travelers from the wealthier countries, viewing the miserable living conditions of these regions, are quite naturally more conscious of the low level of living than of the marked change toward higher standards. But that change is swift and presents important opportunities and risks for the multinational firm.

Although change in the developing countries is occurring rapidly, the differences between these countries and the advanced nations remains marked, as Table 7-1 shows.

The figures in Table 7–1 ought not to be taken too literally. Few countries, especially in the developing world, have really good measures of income. The measurement problems are particularly difficult when a significant portion of income takes the form of food and shelter produced and consumed within the family. And there are major conceptual problems with drawing conclusions about welfare levels from data on per capita income. (Is the Mexican farmer, who needs only a little shelter against the weather, really worse off than a Korean farmer, who needs a higher income to provide much-needed shelter?) Despite the measurement problems, there is no doubt that world incomes are highly concentrated in a few advanced countries. And the differences in incomes are paralleled by other measures of welfare, such as life expectancy and infant mortality.

The data in Table 7-1 help to explain some of the convictions of the poorer countries about national development policies. For example, high income appears to be associated with high rates of investment. Also, high income appears to be associated with a relatively modest emphasis on agriculture and with high rates of literacy. Not surprisingly, the policies of many developing countries aim at generating more investment, creating growth in the industrial sector, and increasing the skills of the population.

There are many theories about how development occurs or can be made to occur. In some cases, the theories proceed from significantly different assumptions concerning the facts. Some theories assume, for ex-

TABLE 7-1 Selected Characteristics of Representative Countries, 1972[a]

COUNTRY	GROSS NATIONAL PRODUCT PER CAPITA ($)	GROSS INVESTMENT AS PERCENTAGE OF GROSS DOMESTIC PRODUCT	LABOR FORCE IN AGRICULTURE, FORESTRY, FISHING AS PERCENTAGE OF TOTAL LABOR FORCE	ADULT LITERACY AS PERCENTAGE OF ADULT POPULATION	INFANT MORTALITY PER 1,000 LIVE BIRTHS	LIFE EXPECTANCY AT BIRTH
Industrialized						
United States	5,532	18	4	99	19	71 years
Canada	4,696	21	8	85	18	72
Federal Republic of Germany	4,633	26	8	99	23	71
Denmark	4,557	22	11	99	14	74
France	4,213	26	13	97	13	73
Japan	3,165	34	16	98	13	72
United Kingcom	2,714	18	3	99	18	71
Less developed						
Kuwait	5,280	11	—	53	39	64
Greece	1,400	28	37	80	27	69
Venezuela	1,166	25	—	76	49	64
Portugal	1,021	17	31	63	50	68
Saudi Arabia	920	17	—	15	152	42
Chile	795	14	26	84	88	61
Mexico	753	19	48	76	69	63
Costa Rica	623	25	49	84	67	66
Iran	542	23	—	23	139	51
Brazil	495	16	52	67	94	61
Iraq	465	14	48	14	104	52
Turkey	459	17	72	46	120	54
Morocco	286	14	56	14	149	51
Ghana	266	10	58	25	156	46
Arab Republic of Egypt	243	11	50	26	118	53
Sri Lanka	165	17	49	75	48	62
India	98	15	73	34	139	51
Indonesia	84	17	67	12	229	48

[a]Where 1972 data are not available, the latest data are used.

Sources: Unitec States Agency for International Development, *Estimates of Gross National Product*.
United Nations Department of Economic and Social Affairs, *Statistical Yearbook, 1973*.
Organization for Economic Cooperation and Development, *Economic Surveys: United States, July 1974, Statistical Annex*.
James W. Howe et al., *U.S. and the Developing World*, 1974.

ample, that peasants are not "economic men" who respond rationally to price increases or other economic inducements; other theories assume the opposite.

More important, theories differ in their emphasis on different objectives. Most are concerned with what makes income grow, but some also place a heavy emphasis on how income is distributed within the country as well as on the trade off between the growth of total income and the achievement of an egalitarian distribution of income.

Many of the differences among development theories stem from questions of emphasis. Acknowledging that economic growth involves movement on many fronts, different theorists concentrate on different links in the process. Many theories, therefore, tend more to be additive than contradictory. In the pages that follow, the emphasis is on some of those concepts and convictions that are widely held and have a major influence on policy in the field of international trade and foreign investment.

CAPITAL AS THE SCARCE RESOURCE

Economic growth in a developing country depends upon the availability of many elements: on productive facilities, skilled labor, materials, and effective organizations. Many current policies of the less-developed countries are based on the view that, of all these requirements, the one that is most needed to resolve the critical bottleneck to further growth is the increased availability of productive facilities.

In an economy without foreign trade and investment, if all resources are employed in producing something and if there are no stored-up reserves on which to draw, productive facilities can be increased only by sacrificing current consumption. Consider a simple economy on an isolated island in which everyone is busy growing rice. All the rice is eaten immediately and none is stored. The only way to increase rice yields, let us assume, is by creating a system of irrigation. The yield could perhaps be increased if dams and canals were built so the fields could be flooded as needed. To increase income (in the form of more rice) the task of the development-oriented chief of the island is to make an investment in productive facilities, in this case, dams and canals. The only way the island can accomplish this investment in productive facilities is to take workers away from rice production and use them to dig the canals and build the dams. But that investment will come at a cost in rice available for immediate consumption (unless some rice has been stored up in previous years), since the same workers will no longer produce rice while they are building dams and canals. In fact, these workers will have to be fed with rice produced by other farmers. For the present, total rice production and consumption will fall while the dams and canals are under construction. But if the investment is successful, there will be more rice available in the future. Economists call the process just described *capital accumulation*.

Of course, it is now widely recognized that capital consists of more than dams, canals, and machinery. The idea of "capital" has been broadened to include "human capital," that is, knowledge and skills. Accordingly, a large part of expenditures on research, education, and training is regarded as capital accumulation.

The relationship between capital and growth is often expressed in the form of a simple set of equations. Begin with an economy cut off from the rest of the world, such as the island just described. In a given year, the economy produces a bundle of goods and services, its gross national product or GNP. Some of the economy's stock of plant and equipment is used up in the productive process. This is "depreciation," in the manager's terms; it is a cost of operation and may be subtracted from the total output of goods and services to yield a net national product (NNP). Thus, the net national product is composed of two things: rice for current consumption (C) and dams and canals over and above those that were currently used up (I). For year 1 (represented by subscript 1),

$$NNP_1 = C_1 + I_1$$

The scarce capital theory of growth considers investment as a necessary and sufficient condition for subsequent growth in NNP. Accordingly, we can calculate NNP of year 2 if we only know the relationship between investment and output. In other words, we need to know what a given increase in the investment in dams and canals will add to rice production in the succeeding year. Assume, for the hypothetical country, that for every $3 of net investment in year 1 we can expect a resulting $1 increase in NNP in year 2. Economists call this relationship between added investment and added output the incremental capital-output ratio. If the incremental capital-output ratio is assumed to be 3:1, then

$$NNP_2 = (C_1 + I_1) + \frac{I_1}{3} = C_2 + I_2$$

Observe the sources of NNP_2. $C_1 + I_1$ is what was produced in year 1. $I_1/3$, is the increment in output in year 2, arising out of the net investment in year 1.

If investment is so important for economic growth, how can a nation increase the amount of its investment? One way, it appears to policy makers, may be to suppress consumption, thus increasing the output available for investment.

This simple logic has provided the basis for national policy. The Soviet

Union's neglect of consumer goods output in the first decades of its existence, for instance, very likely was connected with the high output of investment goods, which, in turn, was probably part of the reason for the rapid growth rate at that time.

However, there are dangers in policies based on such strings of seemingly simple logic. To take the policy leap, one has to assume that the size of net national product is relatively fixed for any given year and will not be dramatically reduced in that year by efforts to shift output from consumption to investment goods. Yet, it is easy to picture the possibility that efforts to control consumption (such as through the application of a high excise tax on consumer goods) might fail to increase investment. Conceivably, the existence of the tax might discourage entrepreneurs, who might then be unwilling to invest in expansion of their productive facilities.

A number of governments have taken steps to assure that suppression of consumption does lead to investment. In some cases, governments themselves have provided finance for private investment projects, especially through development banks. In other cases, governments have provided funds to state-owned enterprises that would make the required investments.

The funds for such government-sponsored investments may be raised through taxes. In some cases, the consumption of those being taxed is thereby reduced. In other cases, however, the increased taxes may come out of the savings of those being taxed, not out of their consumption. When institutional or political factors make taxes a particularly difficult way to reduce consumption, governments have turned to the printing presses. By printing money and spending that money for investment goods, the government can increase the amount of investment. Of course, when most resources are fully employed in the economy, the result of running the printing presses is likely to be inflation. That inflation provides the vehicle for decreasing real consumption; those in the country who are unable to increase their incomes along with the increase in prices find they have to reduce their consumption. Of course, the use of inflation as a tool to increase savings has its dangers. One is that the inflation itself may discourage individuals from saving and lead them to spend a larger portion of their current income on consumption. In spite of the risks, the policy has proved attractive and has been successfully used. In the 1880s, when Japan was a poor country, it relied considerably on the printing presses and channeled a good part of the funds it created into industrial firms. In recent years, similar policies have been evident in several developing countries.

FOREIGN CAPITAL AS THE ENGINE OF GROWTH

Squeezing the capital needed for investment out of the local populace by reducing consumption has proved politically difficult for many governments. The difficulties are enhanced in the modern world of television, the transistor radio, and the presence of the ubiquitous tourist, all of which suggest to even the remote peasant the living standards to which he might aspire. Efforts to reduce the peasant's consumption meet quick resistance.

There is an alternative way of obtaining the capital needed for economic growth, that is, by borrowing from abroad. Consider again the rice-producing island. Let us assume that the island suddenly realizes it has a relatively wealthy neighboring island, which has managed to store up a supply of rice. Our poor island, island A, decides to borrow some rice from its wealthy neighbor, island B. Thus, island A can continue its rate of consumption of rice and still free some workers for the construction of dams and canals. Of course, island A will probably have to repay island B in the future. But island A can pay out of the increased rice production that results from the added dams and canals, if that investment is a successful one.

The presentation used earlier can be employed to express the relationships just described. If an economy permits imports (M) and exports (E), its exports reduce the bundle of goods and services available for local consumption and investment, but its imports add to the bundle. Thus,

$$C_1 + I_1 = NNP_1 - E_1 + M_1$$

The reader should realize that the relationship between imports and exports in any year is tied directly to the flow of capital into and out of the country in that year. When imports and exports are exactly equal, no net capital flows into or out of the country. When imports exceed exports, however, the balance on the current account, $M - E$, must be financed by some kind of capital movements. The capital movements may be in the form of loans (short or long term) or equity. Another possibility is that the "financing" simply takes the form of a gift. In the island case, island B might conceivably have given island A the rice outright. Alternatively, island A might have incurred a short- or long-term debt to island B, with a corresponding obligation to repay principal with added interest in the future. Island A might even have allowed island B to own the dams and canals. In this case, island B would receive dividends on its equity holdings. These would be paid out of profits from the fees that the owners of the dam and canal project might charge farmers for water usage.

All these forms of capital movements have provided important financing to the developing countries, as Table 7–2 indicates.

When developing countries have borrowed from outside their own borders, they have usually had strong preferences in their choices of the means of financing. Some countries make a major distinction between raising funds through debt and raising funds by allowing foreign equity investment. Debt has certain technical advantages over equity in the view of

TABLE 7-2   Flow of Financial Resources to Developing Countries and Multilateral
Institutions in 1972 (billions of U.S. dollars)

Total official and private	18.82	
Total from governments	10.25	
Grants and loans on concessional terms, for promotion of development		8.67
Other; including loans at market rates and loans to finance exports from industrialized countries		1.58
Total from private sector	8.58	
Direct investment		4.41
Portfolio investment		2.74
Export credits		1.43

Source: World Bank, *Annual Report,* 1974, Table 3.

policy makers in many developing countries. One advantage is that debt repayment is generally on a predictable schedule with a certain terminal date. In contrast, equity investments generate dividends and other payments that may be variable, and that appear to continue indefinitely into the future. Moreover, policy makers generally assume that the cost of borrowing under a debt alternative is considerably lower than that of the equity route.

The preferences of developing countries are much influenced by the degree of control that is granted to the foreigner who provides the finance. Certain kinds of debt, it is widely assumed, come without interference in domestic affairs. If the government or private firms of the developing country can borrow by issuing bonds in the private capital markets of the advanced countries, the individual lenders presumably have relatively little direct say in the affairs of the borrowing country. If loans are provided by the governments of the advanced countries, some interference in internal policy matters is possible, of course.

However, when capital comes from a foreign firm to a closely related enterprise in the developing country as private direct investment, the foreigner gains many more rights of control over decisions that affect the local investment. In such direct investment, part of the capital contribution is labeled as equity and a part may well be labeled as debt. Whatever the label, the foreign control is viewed as an important cost by most governments, as we pointed out in Chapter 6.

In fact, elaborate theories have been developed about the problems inherent in accepting the control that goes with foreign direct investment. Some theories stress the degree to which the developing country becomes dependent on others when it accepts such investment. As foreign investors control an increasing percentage of jobs, income, exports, and tax payments, the basis is laid for foreigners to dictate local government policies.

According to the *dependencia* school, the foreign investor encourages reliance on outsiders for critical imports and the know-how needed for development. Once this reliance is established, the implicit or explicit threat that the investor may withdraw his investment, and thus the benefits, enables the foreigner to have a major impact on government decisions.

The foreign investor, according to some theories, aligns himself with the existing elite of the host country. The association may be based on the relatively subtle ties that go with common views and interests; or it may be based on outright bribery, including cash payments, political campaign contributions, or personal favors. Whatever the form the association takes, the investor's interest is to support those who can maintain the status quo and assure favorable terms for business. The result is a brake on social change in the developing country.

In addition, according to various versions of the dependencia theory, the foreign investor is likely to call on his home government if he needs protection in a developing country. The home government could respond to the investor's appeal with economic sanctions against the developing country or even with the threat of military force.

Although some of those in the dependencia school would apply the arguments against funds raised abroad through other borrowing as well, their fears are greater when foreign direct investment is involved.

Needless to say, direct investment as a source of capital has its advantages as well. First, the governments or the private firms of some countries have only limited access to other forms of financing from abroad. A more important advantage to most developing countries is that direct investment usually brings more than capital in the narrow sense. As we have pointed out in Chapter 6, the direct investor usually contributes not only capital but also technology and managerial skills. And in some cases direct investment brings access to export markets as well.

It is hardly surprising that developing countries have generally relied in part on foreign capital to finance their needs for growth. Few have relied solely on squeezing consumption at home to provide the necessary capital. True, the emphasis has differed greatly from country to country. The People's Republic of China, the Soviet Union, and Japan have relied relatively little on external capital for their investment needs. Liberia and Mexico have both relied heavily on outside sources of investment. Liberia has raised capital almost entirely through debt and equity provided by foreign direct investors. Mexico has drawn heavily on direct investment from abroad in the past, but in recent years the Mexican government and some of the larger Mexican firms have turned more to bonds and debt instruments to obtain capital from the advanced countries to finance growth. Recently, Mexico has restricted foreign equity investment, especially if that investment carries a great deal of foreign control. Still, she has granted exceptions readily when the technology or access to export markets that accompanies the equity is important to Mexico's growth.

THE PROBLEM OF SERVICING

Any foreign lender is concerned about the ability of the borrower to service the debt he has incurred; foreign-held debt requires the payment of interest and principal. A foreign equity investor is in a similar position; one of his aims is to receive dividends and fees. The lender or investor must evaluate not only the particular project he is financing but also the ability of the host country to provide the foreign exchange required for servicing the debt or equity.

For many countries, the servicing of foreign borrowing is a growing burden, as the increase in public sector debt illustrates. Between 1962 and 1972 foreign debt assumed or guaranteed by the public sector in developing countries grew from $20 billion to $99 billion. Annual amortization and interest payments on such debt increased from $2.6 billion to $8.3 billion. By 1972 the annual payments on outstanding debt alone amounted to about four fifths of the foreign aid received in that year. And to this debt servicing must be added payments on equity investments and on debt owed by the private sector.

Under the assumptions of classical economics, the servicing of foreign equity would present no particular difficulty. The servicing of any investment comes out of the value of the product generated by the investment. The value of a product, as determined by the marketplace, includes charges for dividends, interest, and depreciation reserves, as well as labor costs and rent. Stated in other terms, the foreign investor's share includes only a fraction of the total value of the output generated by the investment. Once the foreigner has been paid his due, there is still something left over to compensate the labor and capital that have been contributed from domestic sources. So, to return to the earlier example, when island A allows island B to own dams and canals in its country, the dividends to be remitted to island B cannot exceed the charges paid by the residents of island A for the usage of water from the irrigation facilities. The residents of island A, we can assume, would not pay charges that are greater than the value of the additional rice which the incremental water generates. Accordingly, the dividends remitted to island B cannot exceed the value of the dams and canals to island A. Island A, therefore, is being called upon to service the investment with only a portion of the output that the investment has brought into being.

Policy makers in the less-developed countries, however, are not prepared to accept the simple logic suggested by the two-island economy. Foreigners' claims, they note, must be serviced out of foreign exchange earnings. Even if the foreigners' claims do not exceed the value of goods and services generated by the investment, there is no automatic connection to be assumed between an increase in the local output of goods and services, and an increase in the earnings of foreign exchange.

In a world in which exchange rates were in equilibrium and markets were free of imperfections, the concern of such policy makers would be irrelevant. Incremental output directly or indirectly would generate incremental foreign exchange, either by reducing imports or by increasing exports. And even in a less-than-perfect world, the existence of the added output could open the door to new governmental policies that might bring about a balance between foreign exchange inflows and outflows. There might be a devaluation, for instance, leading to an increase in exports and a reduction of imports; or there might be a tightening of import restrictions, leading to added domestic output that would replace the barred imports. However, policy makers fear that these steps will be ineffective or politically unacceptable.

The servicing of debt presents an additional risk for the governmental policy maker. For equity investments, the payments generally come out of the profits generated by those investments. If the investments are not successful, no dividends and fees are remitted. However, debt usually involves obligations even if the investments that are undertaken turn out to be unproductive. If the debts are undertaken or guaranteed by the borrowing country's government, for example, interest and principal may have to be paid regardless of the success of the project.

In spite of the difficulties, many countries have financed an excess of imports over exports for considerable periods of time through an inflow of foreign investment. Some appear to have supported a higher growth rate than would have been likely from domestic savings alone. More than this, adjustments in import and export patterns have occurred so that the servicing of the accumulated foreign indebtedness in the end has presented no overwhelming problems. As evidence of the possibility of such a transition from a borrowing nation, observers cite the development of a number of countries, including the United States, Canada, Australia, and Venezuela. Nevertheless, most developing nations understandably continue to harbor fears of an excessive reliance on foreign capital.

EFFECTS ON CONSUMPTION AND INVESTMENT

The governments of developing countries have additional fears about the effects of foreign capital, especially foreign equity investment, on consumption and investment within the country. Remember that foreign funds have the effect of adding to the stock of a country's goods by allowing imports to exceed exports. The aim of increasing the imports is to increase net national product in future years by enlarging the current supply of investment goods. But the effect of increasing imports may be to increase consumption, perhaps by even more than the increase in imports. For example, foreign direct investment in consumer products may lead to a round of advertising and selling that increases consumption. When the increased imports lead to increased consumption, the development strategy has misfired. This is the essence of one line of argument against the unrestrained entry of foreign capital. If foreign debt is used to finance consumer imports without a corresponding increase in investment, the result is that the means of repayment are not generated out of a higher national product in the future.

Another argument is that an inflow of foreign capital may lead to an export of capital. The argument is as follows: the appearance of a foreign producer in the country can so frighten his prospective domestic competitors that they curtail some of their own domestic investment. Rather than invest at home, the local entrepreneurs send their savings abroad. As a result, the full effect of the foreign inflow on investment in the country may be much lower than the foreign investment would suggest.

In the debate over the costs of servicing foreign-owned subsidiaries, the less-developed countries often point out that the dividend payments and other payments of foreign-owned subsidiaries to their parents in any recent year are a good deal greater than the fresh inflow of new foreign direct investment in that year. There is no doubt as to the accuracy of this claim; in 1974, for instance, U.S. parents sent about $7 billion in fresh capital to their foreign subsidiaries while receiving about $18 billion in income from such subsidiaries. But the relevance of this fact to the question of servicing is remote. Since the reader is likely to encounter the use of such comparisons more than once, it may pay to understand what comparisons of this sort mean.

Table 7–3 portrays a theoretical flow of foreign direct investment to a less-developed country over a period of ten years. Observe what is being compared in the tenth year: an outflow of $120 is being measured against an inflow of $100 in capital in that year. The near irrelevance of the comparison is indicated by the hypothetical figures in Table 7–3. The $120 of dividends in the tenth year is being generated out of the activities of all

TABLE 7-3   Hypothetical Flows Associated with Foreign Direct Investment in a Less-Developed Country

	YEAR				
	1	2	3	...	10
Annual investment inflow	$100	$100	$100	...	$100
Annual outflow of dividends, other charges	12	24	36	...	120
Net investment, end of year	100	200	300	...	1,000
Net output associated with investment	33	67	100	...	333

the accumulated capital that has come into the country over the prior ten years, that is, $1,000. If that capital generates goods each year equal to, say, one third of its value, that is, if the incremental capital-to-output ratio is 3 : 1, then by the tenth year $333 of added output is being generated in the less-developed country. It is this $333 of output that is the starting point for an exploration of the balance-of-payment effects of the capital inflow.

Once the argument is carried to this point, of course, there is still room for debate. As observed previously, the classical economist sees the servicing charges as no problem, since they are thought to come directly or indirectly out of the $333. But economists with a more eclectic view of the economic process are inclined to demur, invoking the doubts discussed earlier.

Abandoning speculation, a number of empirical studies have tried to measure the balance-of-payment effects of actual direct investments by foreigners in the less-developed countries. There have been studies of foreign-owned aluminum enterprises in Jamaica, diamond investments in Sierra Leone, and even studies covering all the foreign direct investments emanating from the United States and the United Kingdom for various selected years. And there has been a major study of a number of foreign investment projects in a range of developing countries. In general, studies of this sort indicate that foreign direct investments usually improve the balance-of-payment position of less-developed countries, as compared with the situation that would exist if there were no foreign investments at all. Some of these studies, however, point to the possibility that there might be ways of moving the necessary foreign capital into less-developed countries on terms that are even more favorable to these countries. Whatever the conclusion on that score may be, one is no longer engaged in comparing the essentially unrelated quantities of net dividend outflow for a given year and net capital inflow for that year.

Despite the concern with the economic and political effects of foreign borrowing, most developing countries have turned to foreign sources to some extent for their capital needs. And in spite of the common preference for financing that carries a minimum of foreign control, most countries have been willing to accept some foreign direct investment. For some countries, foreign markets for debt issues have hardly been available. For most, the advantages of certain foreign direct investment projects as a way of obtaining skills and access to export markets have outweighed the costs in terms of control and payments.

AN EMPHASIS ON INDUSTRIALIZATION

Although many theories of development have concentrated on how to obtain the resources needed for growth, many have also been very concerned with how those resources are allocated. Most developing countries aim toward a significant shift in their economies from an emphasis on raw material production to an emphasis on manufactured products.

The desire for industrialization is based on various assumptions. Some of these involve the behavior of raw materials in world trade.

One widely-held assumption is that in the long run the *terms-of-trade* are bound to move inexorably against countries that specialize in producing and exporting raw materials. A country that exports coffee, for instance, will find itself exporting more and more bags of coffee over the years in order to match the cost of a single imported automobile.

Stated algebraically, the commodity terms-of-trade for a country in year N can be defined as

$$\frac{\text{export prices in year } N}{\text{export prices in base year}} \div \frac{\text{import prices in year } N}{\text{import prices in base year}}$$

According to the assumption long held in developing countries, the price of raw materials is bound to decline over time in relation to the price of manufactured goods. Hence, the terms-of-trade for a country specializing in raw material exports in any year following the base year will be less than 1.00.

The belief in an inexorable decline in the terms-of-trade for raw material exporters has been shaken periodically by such events as the Korean boom of the 1950s and the raw material shortages of 1973 and 1974. However, the underlying belief remains, buttressed by some rather straight-forward arguments.

First, the world demand for raw materials is sluggish, as compared with the demand for manufactured goods. As incomes rise, usage of raw materials does not rise proportionately. Second, the supply of most raw materials in the developing countries is easily expanded, especially in the medium and long term. Cocoa, coffee, tea, edible oils, and tropical fruits are obvious candidates for generalizations of this sort. As a result, the argument goes, as long as developing areas compete with one another for markets, they are in no position to exploit any expansion in demand that might occur or to cling to any rewards from increases in productivity. The gains are simply passed on to buyers in the industrial countries in the form of lower prices.

The picture of the position of the supplier of manufactured products stands in sharp contrast to the plight of the supplier of raw materials. It is an article of faith among the governments of the developing areas that monopoly factors in the advanced countries are sufficiently strong so that the output of manufactured products is carefully restricted, or, at any rate, that the gains from productivity increases are retained in the advanced economies rather than passed on to buyers through lower prices. One monopoly element in the process consists of the labor unions, which take part of the gains in wage increases. The other monopoly element is represented by cartels and big business.

If a raw material exporting country does suffer from a persistent deterioration in its terms-of-trade, it is obvious that the real income of that country would be constrained. The country must provide increasingly larger physical quantities of exports to command given quantities of imports. There would be less goods and services available for domestic consumption and investment than there would be if the terms-of-trade remained constant or improved.

The facts are difficult to determine and almost certainly vary from one raw material to another. Moreover, even with all the facts available, the measurement problem is formidable. Consider the problem of comparing the price of manufactures over time. The problem requires the analyst to compare the price of, say, a Boeing 747 aircraft with the old DC-3 passenger plane, which was a very different machine. Worse still, most price indexes are made up of such measures as the value of a ton of miscellaneous machinery.

Even though the actual merits of the terms-of-trade argument are difficult to determine, the belief that the terms-of-trade favor industrialized countries is persistent in developing nations and that belief influences the policies of government officials.

The developing nations' fear of excessive dependence on raw materials is based on another belief as well: that the export of primary materials—particularly for a country that relies on the export of only a few such materials—is bound to generate a highly variable flow of export earnings, because the prices or the sales volumes of most raw materials are unstable. Such variability is thought to cause especially large fluctuations in national income, in investment, and in government revenues for the exporting country. Despite the tenacity of this belief, various studies aimed at testing the generalization fail to indicate that any simple and obvious relationship exists between the degree of reliance on raw material exports and the stability of export earnings or the stability of other aspects of national performance.

The desire for industrialization is not based solely, or even principally, on the trade problems associated with raw material specialization, however. A number of other supporting arguments add up to the view that a developing nation will be able to increase its productivity more rapidly if some significant proportion of the nation's labor force is in industry.

One reason for this view is the belief that an industrial environment is more conducive to the upgrading of labor than an agricultural environment. Agriculture in the less-developed countries is usually a tradition-ridden pursuit, rigidly confined to fixed patterns by the constraints of superstition, habit, and institutional structures. Industry, on the other hand, is a tradition breaker, a school in which new skills are taught and innovating attitudes acquired.

Even if agricultural workers in the less-developed countries were potentially rational and productive, there are still other reasons for the stress on industry in these countries. One is the assumption that the opportunities to increase efficiency through economies of scale and through complementary relations among different producers are much greater in a growing industrial economy than in a growing agricultural economy.

Efficiency increases in industry are seen as arising in two ways. One is the familiar process of enlarging plant size and lowering unit cost. When more resources are devoted to agriculture, according to the usual assumption, they can only be expected to increase the output in proportion to the inputs. For modern industry, on the other hand, scale pays off; increased inputs yield disproportionately large increases in outputs. Moreover, the development of large clusters of industrial facilities increases total efficiency by the proximity of one facility to another; the joint use of power plants, repairmen, inventories, or transportation equipment, for example, adds to the rate and efficiency of usage. Besides, investment in one industry is thought to create demand for output from the other sectors nearby, spurring further investment and growth.

Still another argument in favor of industrialization is the assumption that industrialists plough back a considerable part of their profits in additional investment, whereas farmers use up their increased income in higher consumption. Even if the entrepreneurs' saving propensities are not so high, according to some arguments, they can be made so. Industrialists are more easily enticed or coerced to save, either by the carrot of tax concessions or the stick of regulation; but in practical political and administrative terms, farmers are beyond the reach of either the carrot or the stick.

Government policy makers have also supported industrialization as a way of reducing the country's need for imports. Thus, the country could be less dependent on the whims of international markets and the policies of the industrialized countries. Time was, too, when government officials looked to industrialization to provide employment opportunities for expanding populations. Employment opportunities in the traditional sector were, according to this belief, limited by the availability of arable land and other physical resources. On the other hand, until quite recently, industry was thought to be able to absorb large numbers of workers, if only the capital could be made available.

When attempting to foster industrialization, the less-developed countries have used a number of devices. Import restrictions on manufactured goods and tax concessions for industrial investors have been especially common. These efforts seem to have had a certain success. Since the 1950s, industrial output in the less-developed countries has increased at fairly spectacular rates, while agricultural output has grown more slowly. In fact, characteristic rates of annual growth in the output of the manu-facturing sector have been twice as high as those in agriculture.

Although the concentration on industrialization has hardly waned in the developing countries, some of the enchantment with industrialization apparent in the 1950s and early 1960s has disappeared. Policies en-couraging industrialization have created many inefficient factories and have not contributed to employment to the extent originally anticipated by many. At the same time, industrialization has apparently not done much to decrease the countries' dependency on imports. This continued dependency appears to result from several factors: the need for capital goods in the form of machinery made abroad, the continued demand for intermediate industrial products such as feedstocks for plastics and scrap for steel, and the urbanization of the labor force, which generates demand for imports. Disappointment in some of the apparent results of industrialization has led to some shift in policy emphasis.

INWARD-LOOKING VERSUS OUTWARD-LOOKING INDUSTRIALIZATION

According to some theories, continued problems of inefficiency and con-tinued foreign exchange shortages in the developing countries are a result largely of the way such industrialization has been pursued. In most countries, industrialization policies have been *inward-looking;* that is, they have concentrated on developing factories that would serve the domestic market. Imports have been restricted through tariffs or quotas to encourage the local manufacture of products that had previously been imported. But internal demand in many cases has been too little to justify an efficient plant. As a result, factories designed to serve the local market have tended to be inefficient. The problem has been worsened by the fact that in some industries home demand has been served by a number of plants, despite the limited size of the market. The multiplicity of plants was sometimes en-couraged by governments for fear of being dependent on one or two firms. In many cases, foreign firms themselves have been responsible for the multiplicity of plants by being too eager to enter any market a major competitor had threatened to preempt. Thus, in the late 1960s Indonesia found itself suddenly with more than two dozen pharmaceutical plants. Chile in 1969 had fourteen automobile plants. Needless to say, production costs in these plants were high.

Numerous studies have demonstrated the inefficiencies that resulted from what came to be dubbed inward-looking policies. Quite obviously, few of the factories had a fighting chance on the export market. By the mid-1970s, many developing countries were turning to *outward-looking* development policies as holding more promise. The shift was supported by studies that cited the success of Brazil, Korea, and Hong Kong, for example, in de-veloping rapidly by expanding exports of manufactured goods. The key to the success of these countries, according to the new dogma, lay in a minimum of protection for industries to serve the domestic market and strong encouragement for exports. The goal was to support only firms that could attain sufficient scale. Once exports were encouraged, the large markets of the rest of the world would provide the basis for plants of efficient scale. Those firms that were inefficient would not survive under the new policies.

The new theories strongly influenced the policies of many developing countries toward foreign investment. There was a spread of policies designed to encourage those firms that would provide access to foreign markets. At the same time, some countries, especially in Latin America, began efforts to weed out some of the foreign investors at home who were viewed as surplus. Chile, for example, set out to reduce the number of automobile firms from fourteen to two or three.

As is so often the case with broad generalizations in the field of development strategy, faith in outward-looking strategies also had its problems. To be sure, some relatively large countries appeared to be developing rapidly as a result of such a strategy. However, the usual illustrations, including Brazil and Mexico, had already built up a basic industrial structure through earlier import substitution policies before they turned to the export of manufactures in any substantial quantity. It was uncertain whether other large countries without an industrial base, such as Indonesia, could move directly to outward-looking policies. Moreover, the smaller countries that had been successful in this respect tended to present some rather special features. Hong Kong had a unique history that made it an impossible model to duplicate. It had served as a haven for Chinese businessmen from Shanghai and other mainland cities who had fled from the communist takeover of business after World War II. These businessmen, experienced in a scale of manufacture much larger than required for the local Hong Kong market, turned to export markets. Moreover, the industrial structure of Japan lay in ruins and it was easy for the Hong Kong firms to sell to markets that Japan had previously supplied. Korea, another illustration of successful development based on outward-looking policies, also was in a unique situation. One factor was the massive U.S. aid granted after the Korean War. Also, Korea had a special advantage in attracting export-oriented investment from the United States, since the country was well known to many American managers as a result of U.S. military involvement there.

Moreover, countries that have attempted to base development largely on export markets seem to have run special risks. Exports of many products from developing countries, including textiles and shoes, have met resistance in the advanced countries. In several cases, the developing countries have been encouraged to impose *voluntary export quotas* on products that were threatening established industries in the advanced countries. For the larger developing countries, that fact posed a special problem. To make a significant impact on development, a country such as Indonesia with a population of 130 million would have to have many times the exports of, say, Singapore, with a population of only about 2 million. The larger developing countries, therefore, were bound to rely heavily on import substitution to provide a considerable part of the base for industrialization.

POLICIES TO INCREASE EMPLOYMENT

One basic problem which industrialization seemed to exacerbate in the developing countries was that of employment. Underemployment in the countryside, suppressed and dispersed, was often converted to open unemployment in city slums as peasants moved into the cities in response to the lures of factory work. The cities offered hope for a comparatively high paying job, the attraction of sharing the wealth of a relative who had a job, or the excitement of lights and movies. As a result, throughout the developing world there was a significant movement from the land into the cities. Even though industrial output was growing rapidly, the number of industrial jobs rarely kept pace with the output, much less with the numbers of persons that presented themselves for work.

In some of the countries concerned with the employment problem, the special attraction that big modern plants had held for policy makers began to be shaken slightly. Officials and development experts began to ask whether there were not more appropriate industries and more appropriate technologies that would employ a large number of people and use less capital. Certain countries grew interested in promoting labor-intensive technologies. At the same time, business managers, especially those in the multinational firms, were criticized for not responding to the low wage rates of the developing countries by substituting more labor for capital.

Explanations for the resistance of firms to more labor-intensive technologies are numerous. One popular concern has been that the prices of labor and capital in the developing countries are wrong. Wage rates are kept high because of the power of labor unions or because of minimum-wage legislation. Capital costs are held low through government programs that subsidize borrowers. Thus, according to this view, the investor responds rationally, according to his interests, in not substituting labor for capital. Based on these beliefs, some countries have experimented with programs to reduce the cost of labor or to raise capital costs. However, these programs rarely touch the costs that may be of particular importance to management. Labor-intensive technologies often require more managers and foremen, which are scarce and expensive to train in most developing countries.

Other observers have argued that the technology problem arises out of the sheer unavailability of labor-intensive techniques in many industries.

According to these analysts, most technologies have been developed in the advanced countries where wage rates are high and capital cheap. Techniques for using more labor and less capital either have not been developed or have long been forgotten. On that assumption, governments and international agencies have supported special institutes charged with developing alternative techniques to be used by firms in developing countries.

Still other observers have argued that the fault lies in the noncompetitive markets that are common in developing countries. If the manager does not confront strong price competition, he will not be vigilant to the need to choose the least costly means of operation. He may try to reduce the management headaches associated with employing large numbers of workers by using more capital; he may let his engineers install sophisticated plants for the pleasure it gives them; or he may adopt a capital-intensive process if he thinks it will reduce the problem of quality control.

Moreover, there is a case for the view that capital-intensive plants allow for a quicker adjustment to higher or lower levels of demand. If a good many workers are involved, a cutback requires layoffs or slowdowns in worker speed. In many developing countries, labor unions or government regulations make layoffs difficult or costly. And if slowdowns are used to adjust output, there are problems in getting workers back to speed when demand picks up. On the other hand, machines can be slowed or run part-time with fewer unfavorable consequences.

These concerns of the manager must take a backseat when price competition is severe. Under such a situation, the manager is forced to choose the technology that leads to the lowest production costs. He cannot indulge his noneconomic goals nor is he likely to be able to afford the higher production costs of capital-intensive technologies, even though the technology provides some insurance against certain risks.

There are policies that affect the level of competition and thus the technology. To the extent that the lack of price competition in developing countries stems from protected markets, policies associated with outward-looking development strategies may also lead to the use of technologies that employ more workers. Indeed, it has been observed that the plants in Mexico along the Texas border which supply export markets generally use a more labor-intensive technology than plants in the interior making similar products for the Mexican market. Apparently, the price competition on the world market imposes a discipline on the border plants that requires them to minimize costs. In low-wage-rate countries, such pressure means that more labor and less capital will be used than in an advanced country.

The fact that a firm does not face severe price competition can derive from sources other than the developing country's protective policies. For example, the firm may have a well-advertised trade name that gives it some immunity from competition. The task of the host government is more complex if it desires to discourage the capital-intensive technology that such a firm is likely to use. Some alternatives encountered in developing countries include the imposition of a high excise tax on the output of capital-intensive firms and restrictions on the activities of businesses with well-known trade names.

Although the concern with technology is likely to remain strong in the developing countries, shifts in manufacturing technique appear to offer little hope of making a major dent in the unemployment problems of the most pressed countries. Nevertheless, the manager is sure to confront the problem as a major issue in many areas of the developing world.

SUGGESTED READING

HAGEN, EVERETT E., *The Economics of Development* (Homewood, Ill.: Irwin, 1968).

LITTLE, IAN M., TIBOR SCITOVSKY, and MAURICE SCOTT, *Industry and Trade in Some Developing Countries* (New York: Oxford University Press, 1970).

REUBER, GRANT L., et al., *Private Foreign Investment in Development* (New York: Oxford University Press, 1973).

UNITED NATIONS, *Multinational Corporations in World Development* (New York: United Nations Department of Economic and Social Affairs, 1973).

The Command
Economies

chapter eight

About one fifth of the world's output is produced today in countries which operate "command" economies, that is, economies in which the state directly controls productive enterprise and foreign trade, and in which the state therefore pretty well prescribes the bundle of goods that the economy is to produce and consume. At times, economies of this sort offer special opportunities to enterprises located in other countries.

Of course, the notion of a command economy is something of an over-simplification. Although the communist countries provide most of the world's examples of national economies of this sort, they are enormously varied in their internal methods and degrees of "command." Yugoslavia's managers of industry, although operating in an economy with a professed communist ideology, have considerable freedom in setting outputs, fixing prices, and choosing markets—as much freedom, indeed, as managers in many "capitalist" countries. Even Soviet managers, while clearly operating in a command economy, have nevertheless begun to acquire a limited amount of freedom in their domestic markets, although not in foreign trade.

Still, the idea of a command economy is quite real. Unlike the economies in which Western managers ordinarily operate, the purpose of foreign trade is directly to serve the state, not simply to widen the opportunities of the enterprise. That difference is not trivial; for the reader to grasp its implications, it helps to begin with a vignette of the internal structure and control system of the command economy.

THE INTERNAL SYSTEM

The system that prevails in the USSR is perhaps the clearest illustration of the command economy in operation. Picture a system that figuratively (and in recent years, literally) is being run by a giant bank of computers organized at some central point in Moscow. Under the system, as ideally conceived, each plant is assigned a production target for any month and year, which is specified in physical units—so many pairs of shoes or tons of steel or television sets. Each plant is entitled to receive from other plants, duly designated and identified, the quantities of leather, iron ore, coal, or copper wire that will be required to fulfill its target. All the labor, machinery, and buildings in place at the beginning of the year are expected to be fully employed by the planned output, and all the capital goods needed for the planned expansion of the economy will be fully provided by the system. Rewards and punishments for the manager are to be based largely (not quite exclusively) on his ability literally to deliver the goods.

Although profit, as the enterprise economies define it, plays hardly any role in Soviet planning and Soviet operations, the rewards and punishments for the manager and his staff for fulfilling their plan are generally pecuniary in nature. These incentives take the form of a money bonus to be used either communally or individually for the benefit of the managers and workers.

In a system of this sort, ideally conceived, the problem of dealing with the world outside of the national economy does not normally rest on the shoulders of the plant manager. It is the responsibility of another part of the bureaucracy, specialized in foreign trade, to find and import any copper wire, machinery, or technology that may be needed for the execution of the plan. And another bureau arranges for the disposal of the shoes or television sets that are earmarked for markets outside the USSR.

Now, of course, the productive system of the USSR does not work in quite the way that the official descriptions would indicate, nor in quite the way that the Moscow-based computers plan. In the first place, the data available to the planners in the Moscow ministries are often incomplete and even distorted. Machine capacities, labor skills, transport facilities, and other critical resources are not very well inventoried, and their productivity is not easily measured. Besides, it is next to impossible to forecast the rate of breakdowns, accidents, and other sources of variance that will occur at the individual plant level. Accordingly, with the rewards and punishments of the bonus system being dangled before their eyes, the managers and their staffs in the field often try to ensure that the bureaucrats at the center do not develop an overly optimistic view of the plant's productive capacities. Moreover, managers in the field commonly try to maintain a reserve capacity for bridging any gap that might arise as a result of unexpected breakdowns, undelivered supplies, and other such misfortunes. At various times, managers have been known to juggle the facts, engage in unauthorized barter with other plants, trade in the gray market, and stockpile unused machines and materials.

None of these practices, of course, is wholly unknown to managers in multiplant firms located in the capitalist countries. But, by and large, prices, wages, and profits play a vastly stronger role in the enterprise economies in determining both the mission and the behavior of each producing facility. The only point in the Soviet system at which prices do play a major role is at the wholesale and retail levels. Even at those levels, however, prices are not determined by the market; they are fixed by the state. The equilibrium price, from the state's viewpoint, is one that will move the volume of goods which the state has planned should be moved.

The limited function that is played by the price factor in the internal productive patterns of the Soviet economy spills over into the planning, organization, and execution of their foreign trade activities. The overall volume of exports and imports is determined according to the national plan; the selection of specific products is made according to criteria that need not bear a proximate relationship to their internal prices; and the actual execution of the export and import plan, as noted earlier, is in the hands of ministries that are quite distinct from the enterprises that produce the exports and use the imports.

Most of the fifty-odd export–import combines of the Soviet Union are subordinate to the Foreign Trade Ministry. (A handful, specializing in delivering machinery and equipment to developing countries, are subordinate to a State Committee on Foreign Relations, which reflects the predominately political nature of the goals of these particular combines.) The export–import combines are normally the entities that negotiate with foreigners and enter into contracts for the sale of products or on the licensing of technology. In a legal sense, export–import combines buy their exports from and sell their imports to the producing units in the Soviet economy. In reality, however, the producing units ordinarily have very little to say about the quantities or prices of the goods to be bought and sold. In practice, export combines requisition their products from designated suppliers, who are responding to a set of imposed export goals and in accordance with a set of complex rules. Import combines, responding to the commands of a prearranged import plan, deliver to indicated users in the Soviet Union.

In practice, of course, the existence of the combines does not create a total barrier between the foreigner and the Soviet economy. All kinds of informal circuits are created between large Soviet plants and their foreign users or foreign suppliers. This is especially the case, for instance, when major capital installations are being ordered from abroad. On the whole, however, such direct links are fragile and vulnerable.

To understand the business behavior of the export–import combines, it pays to recall that such combines, like the producing plants themselves, measure their success against a specific plan. As far as the export–import combines are concerned, the plan consists of a series of targets that are calibrated in physical units and in foreign exchange units. The rewards and punishments of the combine, therefore, are not directly related to prices in the Soviet Union. So the disarticulation between prices in the domestic economy and prices in the foreign economy is quite pronounced.

That conclusion with respect to the Soviet Union does not apply with quite as much force to other national socialist systems such as Yugoslavia and Hungary. These countries give considerable latitude to individual firms in such matters as investment, production planning, product choice, and pricing. As a corollary, the internal price structure of the country plays a more important role in the operation of the economy. Business is done with foreigners on a basis that resembles capitalist practices. However, the principle still remains that every enterprise must justify itself in terms of its contribution to the purposes of the state.

Moreover, the differences between such command economies and, say, Sweden or Britain remain profound. Thus far, the countries of Eastern Europe have had only a limited tolerance for unplanned changes in the domestic economy and for open-ended exposure to the world economy. Accordingly, even as the national authorities in the socialist states give managers somewhat more leeway in their day-to-day operations, they try to condition the manager's responses so that he follows fairly narrowly defined lines. This is done by means of general directions and priorities issued from government ministries, by the establishment of industry cartels, by the doling out of long-term credits through government banks according to intended use, and by elaborate systems of subsidies and taxes. None of these devices is wholly unknown in capitalist economies, but the difference in degree of importance remains considerable.

OPPORTUNITIES AND RISKS

Since the time when the USSR adopted its present system of economic management about fifty years ago, it has provided Western firms with opportunities for the sale on a large scale of modern plants and modern technologies. In 1930, the Soviet Union sought such help from Ford, General Electric, and International Harvester, among others. Again, immediately after World War II, a second wave of such projects was initiated by the USSR only to be choked off by the period of the cold war. The mounting wave of such projects in the late 1960s marked the beginning of another period of such opportunities for Western firms.

The off-and-on character of the Soviet Union's requirements for industrial plants and industrial technology has not been accidental. It has been hard for the USSR to build industrial change into its system as a regular ongoing aspect of the system. To be sure, the Soviets have been able without much difficulty to build more and more gargantuan versions of their existing plants. They also have been able to put together elite teams of brilliant scientists and engineers to tackle an explicit task of extraordinary importance to them, such as designing a moon shot or an intercontinental ballistics missile. But the routine development and introduction of industrial technology as a continuous activity has been much harder. There have been various reasons for this difficulty:

1. The planners at the center of the Soviet system have resisted a nonstop process of industrial innovation because it introduced added uncertainties into the system.
2. With rewards and punishments based mainly on output as measured in physical units, plant managers have had every reason to avoid the disruptions that normally go with innovation and change in products or processes.
3. The Soviet labor force has been chronically starved for middle-level engineers and technicians, the kind of men that are most needed in the normal innovational process.

Accordingly, the introduction of new products and processes in the USSR has tended to take place in a lumpy, discontinuous pattern. From time to time, when Soviet industry has fallen badly behind, Soviet planners have invited the West to provide a new wave of processes and products, creating a basis for a Soviet advance on a broad front. In some cases, a simple massive installation has been involved, such as the electric generators and turbines for the Dneprostroi dam in the 1930s and the Kama Truck Plant in the 1970s; in other cases, a number of prototype plants have been purchased, such as the fertilizer plant program in the 1950s. As a rule, such projects have been so large that the financing of the equipment has commonly involved public funds from the exporting countries. Governmental banks, such as the U.S. Export–Import Bank, the Japan Export–Import Bank, the British Export Credits Guarantee Department, and similar organizations in other countries have made loans to their national suppliers to help finance such deals. In the middle 1970s, it was still too early to tell if the sporadic quality of Soviet demands had been greatly modified. Italian Fiat, for instance, had managed over a number of years to move from its first huge commitment to build the Togliatti automobile plant to a number of other projects. Still, the fundamental factors that had given the Soviet demand for Western technology its sporadic off-and-on quality still remained.

Apart from capital goods imports, another major type of Soviet import also has appeared on a sporadic basis; these are imports intended to make up for unplanned shortfalls in internal Soviet production. The problem of unplanned shortfalls has arisen most commonly in agriculture, since so much of Soviet agricultural production is highly vulnerable to weather variations. In cases of this sort, the Soviet export–import combines have often used their advantage of secrecy in implementing their buying strategies. After being out of the international market in a given product for several seasons, the reappearance of the Soviet import combines as buyers has generally been unexpected and its impact underestimated. In that sort of situation, Soviet buyers have naturally tried to conceal the full extent of their needs as long as possible in order to get the best possible price.

From the Soviet point of view, exports generally have no purpose except to provide the foreign exchange needed for imports. In the past, that has been one of the factors which has deterred the USSR from establishing any elaborate selling or servicing facilities for its products outside the Soviet Union. Another factor, of course, has been the long-standing tendency of the USSR to avoid situations that made its economy interdependent with noncommunist countries. Inhibiting factors of this sort, it can be assumed, will limit what the USSR is prepared to do to promote its exports. Bulk sales of standard products such as oil and chrome will presumably continue, perhaps even grow. But the possibility seems slight, for instance, that the USSR will establish the facilities, such as market-based servicing centers and technical advisory staffs, that are generally required for the sustained sale of advanced industrial products in the West.

Another aspect of Soviet export trade that needs to be understood by Western managers is the way in which products are chosen for export. In capitalist economies, the goods that are exported tend to be those that can be relatively cheaply produced, compared with the offerings of competitors. In the USSR, however, the international ruble costs of a product say little or nothing about its cheapness relative to foreign sources. This is no problem as far as the USSR planners are concerned, since the internal ruble costs of a product are not a determining factor in its selection for export. One consideration that can lead to exports is the existence of an unplanned surplus in the product; in the past, when petroleum was discovered in amounts exceeding the needs of the national economy, for instance, the USSR exported the surplus. Another kind of product that is commonly exported by the Soviet Union is the timber and furs produced in the empty eastern areas of Siberia; since these settlements would presumably be maintained for strategic reasons even if they produced nothing, the foreign exchange that they fetch on foreign markets can be seen as a windfall from the perspective of overall Soviet planning.

In summary, from the viewpoint of Western managers, both the risks and the opportunities that go with Soviet trade are very much out of the ordinary. Soviet imports and exports have tended to have a sporadic episodic quality for the reasons already described. Moreover, neither on the import nor export side has the selection of products depended directly upon costs of production or prices in the Soviet Union. Indeed, the nature of the system is such that costs of production cannot be calculated in ways meaningful to the West.

The relations between capitalist enterprises and Soviet enterprises, however, have not been confined to trade alone. Some of these relations, such as that of Fiat mentioned earlier, have been of a more enduring character, akin to a joint venture. In fact, the term "joint venture" is commonly used to describe many of the relations between Western firms and socialist countries, especially relations with the countries of Eastern Europe. On closer inspection, however, it turns out that the term is being applied to a variety of different arrangements involving a wide range of commitments and horizons on the part of the participants.

1. Among the "joint ventures" are one-shot purchase and sale agreements, usually of large capital installations, as described earlier. These often involve provisions that oblige the Western partner to accept payment for the facilities in the form of goods produced over a long period of time. Proposals to foreign firms for the development of new petrochemicals installations in the Soviet Union are ordinarily of this kind.

2. Another type of joint venture involves the Western partner in continuous rather than a one-shot relationship, such as the installation, run-in, and operation of a major plant. Again, payment to the Western partner may be made partly from the plant's output; but the partners retain their separate identity throughout, even in the operation of the plant. This typifies some of the constraints associated with the Kama Truck Plant.

3. Finally, there are cases in which the partners actually merge their identity in a unitary organization and management, akin to joint ventures of the Western type.

Ventures of the sort described in paragraphs 1 and 2 make up practically all the joint ventures. The cases falling under 3 are comparatively rare anywhere, and are nonexistent in the USSR.

In any case, whatever the form of the arrangement, the objectives of the Western partners have been clear. Their aim has been to sell large-scale capital equipment or technical information, to have privileged access to the communist country's raw materials, and to be able to tap a disciplined, cheap labor force. An occasional arrangement has been premised partly on the hope of participating in the internal growth of the communist economy, such as Control Data's joint venture with Romania covering some products in computer hardware. But this objective realistically must be thought of as exceptional in form and purpose.

SUGGESTED READING

BORNSTEIN, MORRIS, ed., *Plan and Market: Economic Reform in Eastern Europe* (New Haven, Conn.: Yale University Press, 1973).

GOLDMAN, MARSHALL I., *Detente and Dollars* (New York: Basic Books, 1975).

HOLZMAN, FRANKLYN D., *Foreign Trade Under Central Planning* (Cambridge, Mass.: Harvard University Press, 1974).

MASNATA, ALBERT, *East–West Economic Co-operation: Problems and Solutions* (Lexington, Mass.: Lexington Books, 1974).

MCMILLAN, C. H., and D. P. ST. CHARLES, *Joint Ventures in Eastern Europe: A Three-Country Comparison* (Montreal: C. D. Howe Research Institute, 1973).

QUIGLEY, JOHN B., *The Soviet Foreign Trade Monopoly* (Columbus, Ohio: Ohio State University Press, 1974).

WILCZYNSKI, JOZEF, "Multinational Corporations and East-West Economic Co-operation," *Journal of World Trade Law,* May–June 1975, pp. 266–286.

PART THREE

THE
INTERNATIONAL
ENVIRONMENT

Foreign Exchange
and the
National Economy

chapter nine

In Chapters 1 to 4, the reader was invited to look at the world through the eyes of a manager who confronts the risks and opportunities that exist in the international economy. In Chapters 5 to 8, the reader was exposed to the views of others, especially of those in the national economies in which the manager operates.

Now we are prepared to enter a third stage. Stepping outside of the perspective of either the multinational manager or the national representative, the objective of the next few chapters is to project some of the central characteristics of the international economic system itself.

From the viewpoint of the manager, a general understanding of this sort is indispensable. Without it, each individual event—a devaluation, an inflation, a tariff negotiation, or a commodity agreement—runs the risk of seeming episodic, unrelated to an ongoing process. With a more general understanding, there is at least a chance that these individual events can be put into a larger context.

Our experience suggests that those readers who have had no prior exposure to economic concepts in any formal way may find on first impact that the next few pages seem like rough going. Experience also suggests, however, that in the end the mastery of these pages will prove a lot less difficult than the first impression, and that the effort to master the ideas will pay off in terms of increased understanding of the problems to be encountered in international business.

MATCHING PAYMENTS TO OUTPUT

THE ISOLATED ECONOMY.   One way to begin to gain an understanding of
the relation between the internal economy of a nation and the stability of
its currency is to explore a few simple ideas of how an economy works when
it is totally isolated from the world, that is, when there is no international
economy to worry about.

Picture an economy that has no international transactions whatever.
Each year it produces a variety of goods and services. For our present
purposes, we can say that there are only two possible types of use for the
goods and services that finally emerge. Some, such as fuel, clothing, and
recreation, are for consumption by the households and governmental
agencies of the country; these will hereafter be called consumer goods and
services (C). Others, such as industrial plants, roads, and structures are
for investment in the productive facilities of the country; these are dubbed
investment goods and services (I). The reader will recall from Chapter 7
that the sum of C and I is the net national product.

In the course of the production of all these goods and services, those
who make a contribution to the process are paid for that contribution. Who
is it that gets paid in this way? The answer is labor, capital, and government.

	Outputs	=		Payments	=	Product
(C)	consumer goods		(W)	payments to labor		(NNP) net
	and services			+		national
	+		(P)	payments to		product
(I)	investment goods			capital (rent,		
	and services			interest, profit)		
				+		
			(T)	taxes		

In short,

$$C + I = W + P + T = \text{NNP}$$

There are a few awkward definitional problems in the identity stated above.
For instance, indirect business taxes (such as sales taxes) figure in the final
price of the goods and services, even though they do not purport to represent a payment for something that the government actually has provided in
the way of service. But technicalities of this sort need not bother us here.

Now the preceding relationship looks easier at first than it may appear
on reflection. Remember that all we have been talking about so far is *final*
goods and services, that is, products elaborated to the stage at which they
are ready for consumption or for productive use. But where does one fit
into the picture all the goods and services that pass as intermediates

between business firms: the steel that goes to make refrigerators, the fuel that goes to make electricity, and so on?

The answer is that, insofar as the output of one industry gets used up to generate another's output, the aggregate value of output of the second industry reflects that fact. The final value of a refrigerator, in short, includes the value of all the steel, copper, and paint that went into it. Each industry's output, therefore, incorporates all the payments for all the inputs that have preceded it. In the end, as one traces back every input, price is eventually accounted for by a payment to labor or capital or government; and the value of all the final output is an accumulation of all such payments. Accordingly, intermediate goods and services do not have to be taken into account when justifying the basic statement made earlier: the value of all output is equal to all the payments to labor, capital, and government in the making of that output.

How stable are prices in the isolated economy likely to be? One might suppose that an economy of this isolated variety could operate with completely stable prices forever. The income placed in the hands of buyers of goods and services—that is, of consumers or government—is exactly equal to the goods and services that are being produced. To be sure, the mix may not be quite right; there may be too much of one good and too little of another to suit the marketplace. But if small shifts in prices could be counted on to restore equilibrium, the price level in general might well be stable.

But, of course, for various reasons, any hope for perpetual stability is chimerical. For instance, consumers may hoard part of their income and refuse to spend it; if they did that, the income they had would not all be put back in the market to bid for the available goods and services. Or consumers might buy big consumer items such as automobiles; when they did that, they would likely be drawing on past savings and not on current income alone. So goods and money can get out of balance.

Besides, the money supply can be increased or reduced by governmental acts. Although governments may acquire the money they spend by means of taxes, they also have the sovereign right to manufacture money with a printing press. Banks have the right under most regulatory systems to vary the volume of their loans outstanding, thus affecting the money supply. These variations in the quantities of money, when placed in the hands of government agencies, individuals, or business, can mean that the amount of money bidding for goods and services is different for the time being from the amount of goods and services being produced.

When that happens, prices can rise or fall. If money exceeds output, bidders in the country compete for the limited available goods; if output exceeds money, sellers compete for the money available. Eventually, the output and the money flow may come back into equilibrium. But for a time even the closed economy may be unstable.

THE OPEN ECONOMY. So far, our illustrations have assumed a closed economy that produced all its own consumer goods and investment goods; it paid all its wages, profits, and taxes to entities inside the country; and all investment decisions and savings decisions affecting the country were made from within.

Now we open up the borders. Suddenly, a number of new alternatives present themselves. Goods and services produced inside the country can be exported; goods and services produced outside can be imported. Entities inside the country can receive income from without; entities outside the country can receive income from within. Decisions to invest in the country can be made from without; decisions to invest outside the country can be made from within. Obviously, all the old identities between national production and national payments are destroyed. Can any shreds of the old identity be restored?

The answer is yes. Equilibrium is a bit more complex to achieve. But it is not wholly out of reach.

Begin with a simple country that involves only one or two of the complexities suggested above. The country produces consumer goods and services for use in the country (C_d), investment goods and services for use in the country (I_d), and materials for exports (E). This permits the statement of one identity, at any rate; as before, the value of all the output of the country is equal to the value of all the payments made to the productive factors involved in turning out those goods. That is,

$$\text{Outputs} \qquad \text{Payments}$$
$$C_d + I_d + E = W + P + T$$

There is one trouble with the identity, however; we cannot be sure of an equilibrium between the country's output and the payments that are to remain in the country. If E is to be shipped out of the country, there will be only $C_d + I_d$ in output to match a larger sum of money; so disequilibrium could result. The possibility of equilibrium is reintroduced, however, by allowing for imports, M. If imports equal exports so that M equals E, equilibrium is restored. The total of goods and services offered on the market is equal to the total of payments made in the economy.

A few more complexities can be introduced at this point; some transactions can change the money supply in the country without changing the supply of goods. Assume, for instance, that a country "exports" itinerant labor to other countries and that the workers send home some of their earnings; also, the country receives money contributions from charitable organizations overseas. Both sources add to the money supply; but they do not add to output, at least not right away. Or assume that dividends are being remitted to foreigners as a result of their prior investments in the country; this reduces the money supply without reducing the output.

As long as items that leave the country and items that come into the country balance in amount, the changes in money supply and the changes in the supply of goods and services will be of equal magnitude; equilibrium will be within reach.

But, of course, the magnitudes may not be equal. Remember that in a closed economy, with the production of goods and services equal to the money received by labor, capital, and government, the threats to equilibrium were principally of three sorts: (1) the government's capability to alter the money supply, (2) the domestic banks' varying the amount of credit for use by the rest of the economy, and (3) domestic businessmen or individuals hoarding savings from their current income or dishoarding savings that had been put by in an earlier period. With the borders open, however, one has also to worry about the possibility that added money generated outside the borders of the country may be shipped in for investment, or, conversely, that added money generated inside the borders may be used to buy goods or investments outside.

The object of the next few pages will be to demonstrate that when an open economy gets out of equilibrium in the sense that payments and output become unequal, several basic things happen:

1. A series of forces are launched in the economy that tend to push the economy back toward balance.
2. In the process, these forces make themselves felt at the nation's boundaries, moving goods or money or both across the border in directions that help to bring the national situation back in balance.
3. As adjustment proceeds, there is an impact on the country's foreign exchange position that affects the supply of the country's currency.

Some of these effects can be traced through the country's income and some through the country's price structure.

INCOME EQUILIBRATING EFFECTS.   In the closed economy, the infusion of new money could lead to more production, higher prices, or both. In the open economy, the possibilities are more complex. Step by step, let us trace through the consequences of injecting $100 into the country's economy. The first illustration of the process might well begin by injecting money from some inside source, such as the use of the government printing press.

Having endowed itself with $100 more of currency of the realm, the government of the open economy sets about spending those funds on labor and goods. To trace out the consequences, one has to make a few simple assumptions about the behavior of the mythical country of our example. Assume that whenever a national of that country receives an added dollar of income, he spends 60 cents on local goods and 20 cents on imported goods, and he fails to spend the other 20 cents. Then, if the increase in money supply is $100, Table 9–1 suggests what would happen.

TABLE 9-1   Result of Injecting $100 of Excess Funds into the Local Economy—Model 1

	INCREASE IN INCOME	INCREASE IN IMPORTS	INCREASE IN SAVING	BALANCE RESPENT DOMESTICALLY
Injection	$100.00	$20.00	$20.00	$60.00
1st respending	60.00	12.00	12.00	36.00
2nd respending	36.00	7.20	7.20	21.60
3rd respending	21.60	4.32	4.32	12.96
·	·	·	·	·
·	·	·	·	·
·	·	·	·	·
Total	$250.00	$50.00	$50.00	$150.00

The first line of Table 9–1 shows how the recipients of the original $100 dispose of their new income: $20 is paid out to foreigners through payments for imports, another $20 will drop out of circulation through hoarding, and only $60 will be respent in the domestic economy. In the next line of Table 9–1, the distribution course of the $60 is followed, and so on, line by line, until the original $100 have all "leaked away."

As a result of the process, nothing in the country would be the same. According to the totals shown in the table, the excess $100 would have generated a total of $250 of added domestic sales and added money income before its effects were dissipated. Of every $100 of injected money, $50 would leak out of foreigners to pay for increased imports, while $50 would be neutralized by remaining unspent.

The government's decision to manufacture $100, therefore, will drain its foreign exchange by $50, according to this simple model, before its effects are dissipated. If nothing further happened to the economy, its income flows and its goods flows would be back in equilibrium. (At this point, the reader may wish to try his hand at the converse possibility. Assume that the government withdraws $100 from circulation through a special tax, then trace the results for income, imports, and savings.)

Now let us change the illustration in one small but critical way. Assume this time that the injection of added money into the economy comes from outside the country. A foreigner sends $100 to a bank inside the country for deposit and receives a credit for the equivalent in the local currency. The foreigner then proceeds to spend the money in the local economy to purchase local labor and local goods for investment. For the moment, the country has made a solid gain in foreign exchange reserves.

But can the country hold on to all its gain? The answer is no. Once the $100 is being used in the country, its effects, according to our simple model, ought to be exactly like that of the government-generated money; before these effects are dissipated, they will have generated $50 of added imports to be offset against the original $100 gain in reserves.

Although the exercise in Table 9–1 is simple in concept, its lessons are very real. When excess funds are turned loose in an economy, a series of forces get to work to dissipate their unsettling effect. In the illustrations used so far, it was assumed that the excess funds came into the country by way of international capital movements or by way of government deficit spending. But one could picture their coming into a country from other directions: by way of foreign aid or export surpluses, or even by way of individuals dishoarding currency previously stuffed into the country's mattresses.

However the funds may be generated, the channels by which they are withdrawn are imports and savings. Just how much of each depends on the economy's characteristics. In a country in which the marginal propensity to import was high, the release of new funds in the economy obviously would place comparatively heavy pressures on imports. On the other hand, if the marginal rate of imports was low and that of savings was high, new funds could be injected into the system with only moderate concern about increasing the country's imports.

These close ties between money injections, imports, and savings explain a great many aspects of monetary policy. They explain why countries that are receiving large infusions of foreign capital, although grateful for the apparent contribution to their balance of payments, still worry about the consequent pressure on their internal incomes, which may then generate new strains on their supplies of foreign exchange. They also explain why countries in balance-of-payment difficulties are urged to reduce their money supply and to increase their savings. Both measures, it is assumed, will reduce the pressure on the balance of payments.

PRICE EQUILIBRATING EFFECTS.   But something has still to be added to the process. In a closed economy, it will be recalled, an infusion of new money could lead to price increases. That possibility exists for a country with open borders as well. It was observed earlier that the money income of the country would be pushed upward by the spending and respending of the $100 excess that its economy was trying to absorb. But the emphasis in the exposition was always on money values, not necessarily on real goods. To be sure, if more goods could somehow be squeezed out of the domestic economy, the increased supplies of money might go to purchase increased supplies of goods in real terms. But if the domestic economy were pressed to the limit and could not produce another pound of rice or another yard of textiles, the money churning around in the country could raise the country's prices without increasing its real income.

Accordingly, if new money were injected into the economy, the first effect might be a sharp rise in prices. If that occurred, Table 9–1 might prove to be a poor predictor of how the country would bring itself back into balance. For inflation could lead its nationals to behave quite differently from the initial assumptions incorporated in Table 9–1. Influenced by the increased prices at home, they might feel disposed to import more. Let us reflect these changed assumptions in Table 9–2. Here, with each respending, the import propensity of the economy is assumed to have risen a little, from 20 to 25 per cent and so on, until a ceiling of 40 per cent is reached; at the same time, savings are assumed to have fallen by an amount equal to the increased spending on imports.

TABLE 9-2   Result of Injecting $100 of Excess Funds
into the Local Economy—Model 2

	INCREASE IN INCOME	INCREASE IN IMPORTS	INCREASE IN SAVING	BALANCE RESPENT DOMESTICALLY
Injection	$100.00	$20.00	$20.00	$60.00
1st respending	60.00	15.00	9.00	36.00
2nd respending	36.00	10.80	3.60	21.60
3rd respending	21.60	8.64	0.	12.96
.	.	.	.	.
.	.	.	.	.
.	.	.	.	.
Total	$250.00	$67.40	$32.60	$150.00

As Table 9–2 indicates, the balance-of-payment drain is greater in the new model, $67.40 against $50.00. Equilibrium is restored in the sense that the injection of new money eventually fritters itself away through imports and saving. But the restoration of equilibrium is accompanied by more imports and, hence, more demands for foreign exchange to pay for these imports. If a country's supply of foreign exchange is limited, the increased import demand will increase the risk of imperiling the country's balance-of-payment position.

At this point in the exposition, let us look back at the structure of the ideas that have been crammed into the last few pages. The basic structure is relatively simple:

1. When the money supply of a country increases, adjustments begin to take place. Some of these adjustments take place through changes in *income,* some through changes in *prices.*

2. The income adjustments lead in the first instance to increased savings and increased imports (or reduced exports); just how much of each depends on the economy's structure. If there is a very high propensity to save, the balance-of-payment strain generated by the adjustment need not be high; if there is a low propensity, the strain will be greater.

3. How much will prices rise as incomes rise? This depends in part on

whether the local economy is capable of increasing its output in response to the increased income. If not, prices may well rise considerably.

4. The price adjustments that ensue may lead to an increase in imports (or a decline in exports). Just how these work out depends on the sensitivity of the country's economy to increases in national costs. Should these reactions be very strong, the price increases would change the country's trade balance; that, in turn, would eventually reduce income and dampen prices, and equilibrium could well be restored.

EXCHANGE RATES AND NATIONAL GOALS

FIXED RATES AND FLEXIBLE RATES.   The discussion so far has been based on the important, yet unspoken, assumption that governments were committed to maintaining the value of their currencies at some fixed rate: that, for instance, the French franc would be held at four francs per U.S. dollar throughout the equilibrating process. Since the early 1970s, however, many governments have been quite prepared, as a matter of course, to allow their exchange rates to vary in value. Before that time, of course, exchange rates had normally been allowed to vary a little around their declared value, up to about one per cent in either direction. But under the new policy, many governments removed such limits. The fact that exchange rates now have no declared value and may vary without limit adds a new variable to an already complex mix.

One way of describing the reason why many governments have abandoned the responsibility of maintaining a fixed exchange rate is that the responsibility has interfered with other obligations which they considered even more important. A system of fixed rates cannot be maintained unless a government decides to maintain it. If governments stay out of the franc-dollar market, the price of the franc in relation to the dollar will vary according to the requirements of the buyers and sellers that are in the market. Thus, if the government of France is determined to maintain the franc at a rate of four to the U.S. dollar and if the bids for francs do not equal the offers of francs at that rate, it is up to the government to make up the difference.

The moment an economy's exchange rate is allowed to vary significantly, the simple models that were offered in Tables 9–1 and 9–2 take on greater complexity. The prices of imports and exports are likely to be affected; the price changes will affect their volumes; those changes, in turn, will alter savings and investment in the country, as well as interest rates and price levels. The effects in the short-run may differ from those in the long-run; the effects in small countries may differ from those in large; the effects on trade movements may differ from those on capital movements. No simple model is capable of picking up more than a fraction of the complex process. The manager in the international economy, confronted with the problem of projecting likely future developments associated with a change in exchange rates, is thrown back on a case-by-case approach, without a very efficient conceptual structure for organizing his ideas.

Still, there are a few generalizations that may help. One of these has to do with the motivation of governments that abandon their commitment to a fixed rate and allow the value of their national currency to vary.

AN INDEPENDENT MONETARY POLICY. Under modern conditions, governments generally find themselves trying to accomplish half a dozen different tasks at once: maintain full employment, avoid inflation, encourage saving and investment, hold down the extremes of poverty among their populations, control environmental pollution, and so on. Working on all these fronts simultaneously, governments constantly find themselves in difficulties. Some of these objectives may demand measures that seem to be working at cross-purposes with other objectives; to maintain full employment, for example, governments may sometimes have to take the risk of encouraging inflation.

In those circumstances, governments often see the obligation to maintain a system of fixed exchange rates as one more onerous constraint that limits their flexibility of action on other fronts. To see why that may be so, let us turn back to the model in Table 9–1, which traces the course of $100 injected into the economy. Suppose that it was the U.S. government which injected the $100 via the printing press, and that the object of the interjection was to stimulate U.S. employment. In a fixed exchange rate regime such as is assumed in Table 9–1, the money eventually leaks away, as $50 are paid to foreigners and $50 are hoarded.

Now it may sound reasonable that money paid to foreigners is money that has leaked away, but when considered more closely, it is evident that a link is missing. If a Frenchman receives a dollar check drawn on a U.S. bank, the money has not yet left the United States. It is only if the Frenchman wants to take the money home that the question of a decline in the U.S. money supply arises. The leakage occurs when the French holder of dollars tenders those dollars for francs, and when governments are obliged to take the dollars and provide the francs. Bypassing some rather complex intervening steps, assume that the Federal Reserve Bank of New York, as agent of the U.S. government, provides the francs. In effect, the U.S. government has taken over the Frenchman's dollar claim on a U.S. bank and has provided a claim on a French bank in return.

Note the significance of the U.S. government's acquisition of U.S. dollars. By that act, the U.S. government is reacquiring some of the funds it once let loose in order to stimulate the economy. The reacquired money has gone through a chain from the U.S. government to the U.S. public to a French exporter back to the U.S. government. The reason for the reacquisition by the U.S. government is its commitment of fixed exchange rates. At the same time, the intended stimulating effect of the expenditure has been partly achieved, but also partly aborted.

Many governments have drawn a moral from the illustration. If they were not obliged to intervene in the foreign exchange market, the buyers and sellers of foreign exchange would have to rely on one another for their funds. Accordingly, since purchases must always equal sales in any market, the amount of money leaving the country and the amount entering the country would perforce be equal. Thus, the money injected into the national economy by the government would remain in the economy, continuing to play its part in stimulating income and employment.

The point acquires vastly increased weight in a modern economy, of course, because of the special role that is played by the central bank in the operation of a nation's commercial banking system. Under a fractional reserve system, any increase in the net claims of the banking system upon the central bank creates the condition for a manifold increase in the total money supply; and any decrease in the banking system's claims on the central bank can force a multiple reduction in the money supply. As a result, the foreign exchange operations of the central banks often introduce a disturbing element of some magnitude in the national money supply. When these operations are a by-product of a government's commitment to maintain a fixed rate, the government sees itself as hobbled in the use of an independent monetary policy.

STIFLING CAPITAL FLOWS. The problem of maintaining an independent monetary policy, as the preceding pages indicate, turns in part on whether foreigners will move their liquid funds in and out of the country in response to a change in national policy. The argument for flexible rates is that the problem is contained: the outflow of foreign exchange must equal the inflow. Besides, flexible exchange rates are thought to avoid other problems that in a fixed-rate regime imperiled an independent national monetary policy.

In carrying out an independent national monetary policy, a government can take various measures that affect the supply of and the demand for money. If a government wants to stimulate the economy, for example, the standard maneuver is to try to lower the short-term interest rate for money, on the assumption that a lower rate will lead managers to build up inventories, consumers to buy household appliances, and so on. By running the printing press, figuratively speaking, the government not only increases the supply of money but also lowers the cost of borrowing.

But in a system of fixed exchange rates, what happens to the supply of money when the short-term interest rate is reduced? For a Frenchman who has money on deposit in a New York bank, a reduction in the short-term money rate in New York precipitates a withdrawal of funds. With fixed rates, that withdrawal not only reduces the money supply but also pushes interest rates upward again. So the government's initial intentions of stimulating the economy tend to be thwarted.

The problem in reverse could be seen in the German economy throughout the 1960s and early 1970s. There, the root problem was a persistent inflow of foreign capital. Under an obligation to maintain a fixed exchange rate, the German government found itself constantly supplying new deutschemarks to the economy, thereby contributing to inflationary pressures. To dampen the inflationary pressures, the German central bank from time to time tried increasing the interest rate, hoping thereby to discourage internal borrowing and internal buying. But all that it succeeded in doing was encouraging foreigners to invest their short-term funds even more heavily in Germany, thereby increasing the German money supply.

The assumption of the early 1970s was that under a system of flexible exchange rates, capital would not be so ready to move across international borders. The added risks of a flexible rate, it was thought, would discourage such responses. According to conventional wisdom, non-German speculators would be less and less willing to buy deutschemark assets as the cost of the deutschemark rose. (According to a less conventional school, the increase in the value of the deutschemark would simply whet the appetite of non-German speculators for more purchases of deutschemark assets.) Leaning toward the conventional assumption, governments proved even more willing to experiment with flexible rates.

By the mid-1970s, it was already beginning to be clear that the hope for a diminution in short-term capital movements was illusory. Whether in spite of the flexible rates or because of them, money continued to move swiftly across international borders. Sometimes the stimulus seemed to be a change in interest rates, sometimes some other factor. But the disappointment of early hopes did not obliterate all the attractions of flexible rates.

STIMULATING EXPORTS. The disposition to allow exchange rates to vary rather than to maintain them on some fixed basis also stems out of another consideration, namely, the encouragement of exports and the suppression of imports. Consider a country that has been losing out in world markets. At current exchange rates, its exports are priced too high for easy sale. At the same time, at current rates, the goods offered to its residents by foreign sellers seem cheap. The government is distressed by that situation for many reasons, including its depressing effects on the country's industries that produce exports and compete with imports.

In a situation of that sort, the amount of foreign currency being earned by exporters and being brought home for exchange into the national currency declines. At the same time, the amount of foreign currency being bid for by importers rises. As long as the government is committed to a fixed rate, the government must fill the gap by providing increasing amounts of foreign currency. But what if it abandons its role as balance wheel? Then the importers bidding for a unit of foreign currency will have to pay more local currency to acquire what they need, while those offering a unit of foreign currency that they have earned through exports will get more local currency for what they offer. The outcome would be a devaluation, a decline in the value of the local currency.

To see what a devaluation may mean for imports and exports, consider the Israeli devaluation of 1974. In this case, Israel devalued her currency from IL4.2 per U.S. dollar to IL6.0. Israel was anxious to encourage exports and to discourage imports. Oranges were one important export and machinery an important import. Table 9–3 sets up hypothetical unit values for oranges and machinery before and after devaluation in dollars and in Israeli pounds.

TABLE 9-3   Hypothetical Prices of Oranges and Machinery
Before and After Devaluation

	BEFORE (IL.4.2 = $1.00)		AFTER (IL.6.0 = $1.00)	
	ORANGE EXPORT	MACHINERY IMPORT	ORANGE EXPORT	MACHINERY IMPORT
In Israeli pounds	IL.4.20	IL.420	IL.6.00	IL.600
In U.S. dollars	$1.00	$100	$1.00	$100

On the export side, after devaluation, the orange exporters of Israel continue to sell their oranges to the New York market at $1 per box, because there is no reason to do otherwise; the demand for oranges in New York has not changed as a result of the Israeli devaluation, so there is no immediate reason to change the price. Observe, however, that Israel's exporters are getting much more for their oranges in Israeli pounds than before the devaluation. For them, it makes sense to produce and sell more oranges to the foreign market, perhaps by taking steps to increase the productivity of their trees.

On the import side, analogous price effects take place. The dollar price of machinery imports continues to be just what it was before devaluation, $100. But the Israeli price is sharply increased. There is a new opportunity for Israel's producers of machinery to sell their output within the home economy.

Accordingly, if the Israeli economy is capable of providing more oranges for export or of providing more machinery to replace imports, or both, production and employment in Israel may be increased and the government's objectives will have been met.

CONTROLLING INFLATION.   With all the seeming advantages that accompany flexible exchange rates, the reader is entitled to ask why governments ever applied a system of fixed rates, as many had done in the 1950s and 1960s. The question is of considerable importance to the manager, since it suggests the factors that could lead governments to return to a fixed rate system.

One reason was the fear of repeating the experiences of the 1930s, when governments were engaged in a race to devalue their currencies so that each could gain an advantage over its neighbor in the promotion of its export industries and in the defense of industries that competed with imports. With flexible rates, a race of this sort could easily develop. To be sure, devaluations may occur from time to time in a regime of fixed rates. But where fixed rates exist, the act of devaluing is a discrete and visible event, and the risk of slipping into a series of competitive devaluations is thought less likely.

Now that the world has had a few years' experience with flexible rates, however, still another worry has surfaced. Remember that governments have adopted flexible rate systems, among other things, in order to be free to pursue an independent monetary policy. The fear is that, in the course of exercising their freedom, governments may increase their national money supply more than they might under the discipline of a fixed rate system. With the supply of money increasing faster all over the world, prices may also be expected to increase faster; so the risk of world-wide inflation is increased. There are cases, of course, in which a regime of flexible rates may permit governments to reduce the money supply as compared to the situation under fixed rates. But the propensity of governments to take measures that reduce the supply of money is much weaker than the propensity to increase the money supply. Accordingly, in the mid-1970s many economists were beginning to fear that the removal of the discipline of the fixed rate had given an extra impetus to world inflation.

PRODUCTIVITY: A KEY VARIABLE

So far, our eye has been on the balance between output and payments as the main determinant of stability and instability in the foreign exchange situation. According to this view, when the money supply is increased without a commensurate growth in output, the excess demand spills over, eventually to be absorbed by imports or by saving.

There is nothing wrong with this sort of generalization. But it is only a part of the story. In the conditions of the modern state, other forces besides the money supply can have profound effects on the balance of payments. Among those other forces are changes in productivity.

WHEN WAGES OUTSTRIP LABOR PRODUCTIVITY. In the process of moving up toward full utilization of the labor force, nations from time to time have run into balance-of-payment difficulties. Some of these difficulties are best understood by thinking in terms of productivity rather than in terms of money supply.

Picture a modern state, such as France or Britain, at a time when most of its labor force is already at work. An increase occurs in the demand for goods and services—an increase induced, perhaps, by the injection of an added supply of money into the system. Managers look about for the labor force necessary to fill the added demand. Experience suggests that in situations of this sort the added labor which they find will prove less productive than the labor already at work. Part of the labor is likely to be provided by extra factory shifts, with the characteristic patterns of poorer supervision and higher spoilage in production. Part will be provided by less productive workers operating under handicaps of inadequate education or insufficient training. Part will be provided by housewives or students working part-time to the extent that the competing demands on their time allow.

If the added labor could be paid according to its lesser level of productivity, there might be little need to anticipate any new strain on the economy. The incremental labor would be providing the means of its own payment without any direct disturbance to the balance that had existed in the economy before its introduction. In the wage-setting conditions of the modern state, however, added labor of this sort is likely to be paid at the prevailing rates, not at a rate reflecting a lower level of productivity. In fact, the wage rates for extra shifts are likely to include a premium, not a discount.

Nothing said so far disturbs the immutable identity:

$$C_d + I_d + E = W + P + T$$

The fact still remains that the goods produced are equal to the payments made on their production. But now the number of chips placed in the hands of each principal player has changed. Aggregate wage payments (W) have increased both relatively and absolutely.

Nothing can be said with certainty about the consequences of an increase in W. In the conditions of most modern states, however, a relative increase in W is likely to lead to a relative increase in C_d, leaving less for I_d and E. In simple words, smaller relative quantities will be available out of domestic production either for investment or for exports. If the shortfall shows up in exports, the balance of payments will be hurt or the value of the currency will decline. If it shows up in investment, the basis for further growth in the economy will be undermined. If the lack of goods for some purpose leads to more imports, once more the burden will show up in the balance of payments.

As a matter of fact, the risk that wages may outrun productivity in the wage-setting conditions of the modern state is not confined to cases in which labor is scarce. The risk exists even when there is genuine unemployment and when fully competent labor is available. If wage bargaining included all producers in the country for a given product or service, if the product or service cannot easily be imported from outside the bargaining area, and if the industry's total sales of the product or service are not very sensitive to higher prices, the freedom of labor to demand higher wages and the willingness of employers to respond can be fairly strong. Boeing can take a relatively accommodating view toward the wage demands of its skilled workers, for instance, if it feels sure that Lockheed and McDonnell Douglas will follow its lead. On the other hand, just to demonstrate that labor's power is not unlimited, the New England textile mills are obliged to stand fairly firm against the wage demands of the local textile unions, having in mind the competition from Southern textile mills as well as the competition from overseas producers.

The record shows unmistakably that, under modern conditions of wage bargaining and wage formation, the money costs of labor have risen steadily in practically every major country of the world. All sorts of factors can affect such a figure, of course. But it is fairly clear that one major force pushing the money costs of labor upward has been the modern process of wage determination.

Of course, if the wage-setting process could be counted on to produce about the same increase in money costs in every country, the pressure on cost levels generated by rising wage costs might not add greatly to the uncertainties of any single country's foreign exchange position. Inflation might be stronger everywhere. A country like Britain, for instance, might find itself paying more foreign currency for machinery imported from Germany, but it would also find itself earning more foreign currency for machinery exported to Denmark.

The fact is, however, that wage increases have raised labor costs per unit much more in some countries than in others. In some countries, such as Japan, labor has been comparatively docile, so wages could be held in check. In others, such as Spain, labor has been poorly organized. In still other countries, such as Switzerland, the labor supply has been supplemented by large quantities of "temporary" foreign workers whose availability has reduced the bargaining power of the permanent labor force. In Britain, on the other hand, labor has not been greatly restrained by conditions that might limit its capacity or disposition to press wages upward. Skilled labor has been scarce and immigration limited. If the increase in wages and prices encouraged imports and impaired the balance of payments, that was of little concern to labor, as long as the problem did not lead to local unemployment. The United Kingdom, therefore, seemed vulnerable to wage-push inflation rather more than some of the countries with which it competed. This was an added source of weakness for the pound sterling, a source that the logic of Table 9–1 would not have revealed.

WHEN LABOR PRODUCTIVITY OUTSTRIPS WAGES.   When projecting the sources of the strength and weakness of a currency, however, it is not always safe to assume that payments of labor represent a force on the side of rising prices and weakening currencies. There have been cases in recent history when exactly the opposite proposition could have been made, and it would be rash to assume that the manager will not encounter other such cases in the years ahead. The outstanding cases so far have been Japan and Germany. In the two decades following 1950, additional units of labor or capital brought into the economy appeared to be producing higher and higher increments of output, generating an added source of strength for these economies.

Those accustomed to thinking in terms of the economies of modern plants will not find this phenomenon very surprising. It is taken for granted that if 1 hour of labor is needed to produce 100 units in a plant of a given size, there are ways of increasing labor's hourly output to 150 or 200 units in a plant of larger size. One such way is to increase the specialization of tasks. An increase in productivity also is to be expected for the capital itself. For instance, applying a rough rule of thumb, designers of modern chemical plants calculate the increase in plant capacity associated with a one-unit increase in capital by the same formula that would be used to calculate the increase in the area of a circle generated by a one-unit increase in its circumference.

The fact that increased output may yield lower real costs per unit is not solely due to principles of engineering efficiency, however. It stems from other forces as well, especially from a reduction in the cost of providing for various risks that are encountered in the process of production. As output grows, the inventories and spare parts needed to cover interruptions in the supply pipeline need not be increased as fast; so capital is economized. As the economy becomes larger, specialized services such as repair services can be searched out and secured with lesser delays; so downtime is reduced. And so on.

All these factors seem to have been at work in Japan and Germany during the years after 1950. In Japan, in particular, an important sector of the economy made up of small plants was systematically liquidated and replaced by the expansion of the modern sector made up of larger and more efficient plants.

When a national economy is in a position to increase the productivity of its labor and capital by expanding its output, the added units of labor brought into play probably will not be paid at their marginal productivity, at least not right away. If the payments to labor are determined at any given time by the prevailing wage of the labor that is already at work, for a while the added unit of labor may be paid less than the value of the added product it has generated. Naturally, that discrepancy could hardly go on forever, since anyone capable of hiring more labor would be eager to do so and to gain a special windfall. But the difference could exist for a time, and the situation could be prolonged if added increases in output continued to raise the productivity of the average unit of labor even further. As long as labor can be hired at less than its marginal productivity, interesting sources of strength can be brought into play in an economy. Let us see what some of these may be.

Our earlier discussion, covering the opposite kind of case, lays the groundwork for the present case. Once again, it is evident that the arithmetical identity between output and payments cannot be breached. But when W is not increasing very fast, C_d can generally be expected not to increase very fast either. After all, sales of consumer goods cannot depart very far from the amounts that are paid out in wages, unless wage earners are willing to tap their past savings or borrow in order to add to their current purchases. If they simply live on current wages, more of the country's goods are available for investment or to increase exports or reduce imports. In other words, I_d grows, a possibility that may increase productivity. Or E begins to exceed M, a possibility that strengthens the currency. Or both occur simultaneously.

Exactly which of these various things happens depends on many variables. With business gaining windfall profits and governments presumably acquiring added taxes, the mood for higher investment in the country may be strong. Still, investment will increase only to the extent that businessmen or government decide to increase it. Exports will increase in measure as the price and availability of supply make the goods attractive to outsiders. A decline in imports will depend partly on the extent to which domestic production can substitute for foreign goods. But one or the other response, or several in combination, are likely to occur.

These responses in turn may well set the stage for their own prolongation. With foreign exchange being piled up through export balances and with investment increasing, an economy can try to plan for constantly increasing total output. And with increasing output, it can hope to exploit the remaining opportunities, if any exist, for reducing its average real cost of production.

It may not be laboring the obvious to point out that the phenomenon just described can work in both directions. Just as a rise in national output may lead to a decline in costs and an improvement in foreign exchange earnings, so also a decline in national output could produce the opposite result. Shrinkage in the level of output in an economy could reduce the average productivity of the units of labor and capital that were still at work after the shrinkage.

This outcome seems to have appeared at times in Argentina and Brazil during the 1960s when governments tried to cope with their foreign exchange problems by cutting down the money supply, that is, by following the prescriptions suggested by the model in Table 9–1. Having that model in mind, these governments sharply reduced the amounts of funds in the economy, mainly by reducing bank credits.

What the governments did not reckon on was that the cutting off of bank credit could, in the end, raise the costs of production rather than lower them. The curtailment could reduce the ability of business to finance its accounts receivables and its inventories; this, in turn, could lead to reduced output; and reduced output could lead to lower efficiency in the use of capital and labor.

Of course, if the payments to capital and labor could be reduced to reflect the change in their efficiency, some kind of equilibrium between payments and output could eventually be restored. But that possibility often proves chimerical in a world where contractual obligations, including interest payments and wage agreements, must be honored. Using their "excessive" income, wage earners and other consumers are almost certain to satisfy their consumption demands either by forcing a reduction in investment goods, I_d, or by bringing about a decline in exports or an increase in imports. In this case, the balance-of-payment difficulties of the country will grow, while its ability to improve its economy by way of investment will decline. In this situation prices need not decline—they can even go up.

So in a world in which economies of scale exist and in which wage rates and capital charges are a bit sticky, the outcome projected by the money-supply model with which this chapter began may be turned upside down by the forces of productivity change.

This conclusion does not mean that one model is right and the other wrong. Each of them depicts forces that are at work in national economies, often at work side by side within the same economy. All the models are right, therefore, within their own premises. The art of projection involves the need to be able to sense which of these sets of forces is the stronger at a given time in a given nation.

SUGGESTED READING

KINDLEBERGER, CHARLES P., *International Economics, 5th ed.* (Homewood, Ill.: Irwin, 1973), pp. 322–430.

ROOT, FRANKLIN R., *International Trade and Investment, 3rd ed.* (Cincinnati, Ohio: South-Western Publishing Co., 1973), pp. 207–250.

Foreign Exchange
Problems
and Policies

chapter ten

As a result of the processes outlined in Chapter 9, currency values are constantly changing in relation to one another. That contingency is obviously something the manager would like to know well in advance of the actual event. How, then, does the manager attempt to keep track of existing or potential pressures on a currency in which he has an interest?

This is a question most managers of international enterprise like to leave to experts; but the problem is too important for such uncertain handling. Even a general manager must be aware of the nature of the problem and the diagnostic process that his experts are likely to use.

THE FOREIGN EXCHANGE NETWORK

We begin at the level of two nations, observing the foreign exchange links that connect, say, Brazil and Germany. The demand for foreign exchange by the residents in any country can come from numerous sources. For example, the residents of Brazil may need deutschemarks to pay for imports from Germany, to finance a trip to Germany, or to remit interest or rent or dividends to German investors who own assets in Brazil. Brazilians also may need deutschemarks to set up bank accounts in Germany as a prelude to doing business there, or to buy German real estate or German securities. In such cases, the Brazilians that want to acquire deutschemarks ordinarily present a check in cruzeiros to a bank that specializes in foreign exchange trading and in return receive a deutschemark claim on a German bank.

The demand of the Brazilians for deutschemarks confronts a supply of deutschemarks previously acquired by Brazilians. The supply may arise from Brazil's sale of coffee to Germany or from Volkswagen's purchase of a plant site in Brazil or from other transactions that put deutschemarks into the hands of Brazilians. As the Brazilians convert their deutschemarks into cruzeiros, the supply of deutschemarks and the demand for deutschemarks create a market.

If the government of Brazil is committed to a given rate of exchange between the deutschemark and the cruzeiro, the government is also in the market. Its special task is to bring about a balance at the specified price—offering deutschemarks where not enough have been offered by others and buying deutschemarks where deutschemarks are in excess supply.

The Brazilians, of course, are buying and selling not only deutschemarks but also dollars, sterling, lire, pesos, yen, and other currencies. The sources and uses of these currencies arise in much the same way as the sources and uses of deutschemarks. Accordingly, rates of exchange between the cruzeiro and each of these other currencies are also being recorded in the market. However, the prices for the various currencies, expressed in cruzeiros, do not depend solely on the balance of Brazil's needs in each of these currencies. Say that in New York one deutschemark is worth about 40 cents in U.S. money. One can be sure that in São Paolo the U.S. dollar and the German mark will bear about the same relationship to each other, when expressed in cruzeiros. If the U.S. dollar is worth 6 cruzeiros, the deutschemark will prove to be worth about 2.4 cruzeiros.

The reason why these relationships work out so neatly as a rule is that the trading banks are constantly looking for opportunities to exploit any inconsistencies that might emerge in the rates among the various currencies. A bank that has a demand for deutschemarks from Brazil may in effect find that it can acquire deutschemarks in two steps: by buying U.S. dollars at the existing rate between cruzeiros and dollars, then using the dollars to buy deutschemarks at the deutschemark-dollar rate. With enough traders operating in the market, transactions such as these tend to hold the international market together, making the rates in the different currencies in any market more or less consistent with the rates in any other market.

When a government is maintaining a fixed rate for its currency in relation to other currencies, other governments are on notice as to the pattern that the declaring government proposes to follow when intervening in the market for its currency. For instance, the Mexican government's decision to maintain a value for the Mexico peso equivalent to 8 U.S. cents means that the Bank of Mexico will offer pesos on the market whenever the price of the peso rises one per cent above the 8-cent level, and will buy pesos whenever its price falls one per cent below the 8-cent level. With flexible rates, however, the problems of government intervention in the foreign exchange market become much more complex.

If governments felt able and willing to stay out of the foreign exchange market altogether under a system of flexible exchange rates, there would be no need for governments to keep in touch with respect to their interventions in the foreign exchange market. In fact, however, governments intervene massively in the foreign exchange market even when their rates are flexible. The incentive to keep in touch, therefore, is very strong, lest the objectives of one government prove to be at cross-purposes with the objectives of another. If the German central bank is selling deutschemarks to hold down the deutschemark-cruzeiro rate while the Brazilian central bank is buying deutschemarks to hold the rate up, their actions could conceivably cancel one another out.

Paradoxically, therefore, the institution of a flexible rate system has required the principal central banks all over the world to communicate with one another far more continuously than they were wont to do before. In some cases, the need for consultation is simply to avoid operating at cross-purposes. In other cases, the need arises from more specific commitments to one another, such as commitments to keep the value of two or more currencies aligned in some agreed relationship. In Chapter 12, for instance, we shall be referring to an agreement among some of the European countries to link their currencies together in an arrangement known as "the snake." According to the agreement, each central bank is obliged to see to it that its national currency remains in a fixed relationship to the others in the group. Small variations are allowed, enough to permit the rate for any pair of currencies to vary by as much as 2¼ per cent. Bound together in a 2¼ per cent band, yet free to undulate collectively in relation to other currencies such as the dollar or the yen, the group's currencies can be pictured as a monetary snake.

KEEPING TRACK OF THE PRESSURES

Anyone interested in the future movement of a national currency must take numerous factors into account: the behavior of the national economy, the commitments to international arrangements such as the snake, access to international credit facilities, and so on. But he must also have access to some basic data, such as data on the foreign transactions of the national economy.

In response to widespread demand, most governments periodically publish a record that reports the transactions between its residents and the outside world. This record is generally referred to as the country's balance-of-payment accounts. For the major countries, most key figures in the accounts are available quarterly and a few key figures can even be obtained monthly.

To understand better how the figures are usually arranged and what they purport, it is useful to pretend that every transaction between a resident of the country concerned and the rest of the world was recorded in the first instance by the conventions of double-entry bookkeeping. In standard double-entry bookkeeping, every transaction is recorded as if it consisted of an exchange of something for something else, that is, as both a debit and a credit.

In the case of merchandise imports, for instance, goods are ordinarily acquired for money or for debt; according to bookkeeping convention, the imports are recorded as a debit and the payment as a credit. In the case of merchandise exports, the exports are recorded as a credit and the receipts as a debit. Debits consist principally of (1) imports of goods and services, (2) increases in assets, or (3) reductions in liabilities. Credits consist principally of (1) exports of goods and services, (2) increases in liabilities, or (3) reductions in assets. The principal categories of debits and credits are shown in Table 10–1.

TABLE 10-1   Principal Balance-of-Payment Accounts

	DEBITS		CREDITS
	Current Items		
D-1	Imports of goods and services, and foreign tourism of residents	C-1	Exports of goods and services, and tourism of foreigners
D-2	Interest, dividends, rents, and royalties to foreign entities	C-2	Interest, dividends, rents, and royalties from foreign entities
D-3	Gifts to foreign entities	C-3	Gifts from foreign entities
	Capital Items		
D-4	Increase in private short-term claims on foreign entities (such as private holdings of foreign bank deposits and foreign short-term paper)	C-4	Decrease in private short-term claims on foreign entities
D-5	Increase in long-term claims on foreign entities (such as foreign stocks, bonds, and real estate)	C-5	Decrease in long-term claims on foreign entities
D-6	Decrease in foreigners' short-term claims on domestic entities	C-6	Increase in foreigners' short-term claims on domestic entities
D-7	Decrease in foreigners' long-term claims on domestic entities	C-7	Increase in foreigners' long-term claims on domestic entities
	Reserve Items		
D-8	Increase in official short-term claims on foreign entities (such as public holdings of foreign bank deposits and short-term paper)	C-8	Decrease in official short-term claims on foreign entities
D-9	Increase in gold stock	C-9	Decrease in gold stock

The reader may already have recognized a certain similarity between the credits and debits of balance-of-payment accounting and the double-entry accounts of the business firm. The parallel is summarized in Table 10–2.

In actual practice, of course, no government actually knows enough

TABLE 10-2   Corporate Accounts and Balance-of-Payment Accounts Compared

CORPORATE ACCOUNTS		BALANCE-OF-PAYMENT ACCOUNTS		
DEBITS	CREDITS	DEBITS	CREDITS	RELATION TO TABLE 10-1
Profit and Loss Items		*Current Items*		
	Sales		Exports	C-1
	Other income		Other current account income	C-2 and C-3
Cost of goods sold		Imports		D-1
Other costs (except depreciation), taxes, and dividends		Other current account expenditures		D-2 and D-3
	Net retained profit before depreciation		Current account balance	C-1 to C-3 minus D-1 to D-3
Balance Sheet Items		*Capital and Reserve Items*		
	Increase in current liabilities		Net increase in foreigners' short-term claims	C-6 minus D-6
	Increase in long-term liabilities and equity		Net increase in foreigners' long-term claims	C-7 minus D-7
Increase in current assets except cash		Increase in private short-term foreign assets		D-4 minus C-4
Increase in fixed assets		Increase in long-term foreign assets		D-5 minus C-5
Increase in cash		Increase in official holdings of gold and foreign exchange		D-8 and D-9 minus C-8 and C-9

about each foreign transaction to be able to record the transaction according to the entries required in double-entry bookkeeping. Instead, each category of debit and credit is laboriously estimated from separate sources, such as customs house records and special questionnaire returns. In theory, the debits and credits should balance. In fact, they never do. So, an artificial balancing item, "net errors and omissions," is introduced to bring about balance. If clandestine transactions are important, or if the reporting system is weak for other reasons, "net errors and omissions" can be a very sizable item.

A little practice in the recording of typical transactions helps to clinch the relationships between the items. Even without such exercises, however, a number of points will be apparent almost at once.

1. Just as in the case of a corporate statement, no item of the balance-of-payment accounts taken by itself indicates very much about the strengths or weaknesses that may be affecting a nation's capacity to defend its foreign exchange position. What is needed is the whole record.

2. An analysis of the future supply of the government's foreign currencies has certain striking parallels to that of the corporation's cash-flow analysis. In both instances, it is necessary to rearrange the items listed in Table 10–2 into a conventional "sources and uses of funds" analysis. The national economy counts the following items as its sources of foreign exchange: the excess of credits over debits in its current items, the increase in foreigners' short-term claims, and the increase in foreigners' long-term claims. An economy's uses of foreign exchange appear in various categories, including the increase in its short-term foreign assets, the increase in its long-term foreign assets, and the increase in official holdings of gold and foreign exchange. (Of course, any of these items can decrease as well as increase, in which case they shift their classification from "source" to "use" or from "use" to "source.")

When an effort is made to project the likely sources and uses of foreign exchange by a national economy, however, it begins to be evident that the projection involves dimensions that have no obvious analogue in corporate fund flows. As we saw in an earlier chapter, exports and imports of a national economy are an intimate function of the internal demand of an economy. If the domestic demand for goods is very strong, the economy can suck up potential exports and pull in excessive imports. Although some developments inside a business entity can be thought of as a parallel phenomenon, the parallel begins to be a little strained when pushed very far.

In efforts to detect future trends in national liquidity, analysts are constantly reviewing the behavior of the balance-of-payment accounts, looking for added light. In the process, certain measures have tended to be given special weight. One is the *merchandise balance,* often calculated as the difference between exports and imports (C-1 minus D-1). Another is the *current account balance* (the sum of C-1 to C-3 minus the sum of D-1 to D-3). Others are various combinations of the payment accounts.

Of the various payment account balances, the simplest, of course, is the change in the gold stock and foreign currencies held by the government. Since no country that wishes to intervene in the foreign exchange market dares to run out of convertible foreign currencies, all analysts watch with exquisite attention the changes in supplies of such currencies (D-8 and C-8). The sum of these changes plus changes in gold holdings in a given period is sometimes called the *payments balance* of the country for that period.

United States government authorities, however, feel that the payments problem of the United States is of a very special kind, requiring somewhat different measures of payments balance. As they see it, a decline in gold or convertible currencies is not the only type of bad news for the United States; also bad is a rise in foreigners' holdings of short-term claims on the United States, such as bank accounts or Treasury bills (C-6). True, the rise in foreigners' holdings may have been the result of a series of transactions that simultaneously increased U.S. short-term assets abroad (D-4). That would happen, for instance, if a U.S. businessman made a deposit in an Italian bank with a check drawn on a U.S. bank. It would also happen if the reverse occurred—if an Italian businessman made a deposit in a U.S. bank with a check drawn on an Italian bank. Either way, foreigners' short-term claims on the United States have increased; and this increase has come so close to representing a claim on the United States that U.S. officials have thought it wise to count it so. Accordingly, U.S. officials add changes in foreigners' short-term claims to the payments balance to obtain a *liquidity balance*.

Having broadcast this rather extreme measure of the U.S. position, U.S. government authorities have thought it best to propagate another conception of "balance" as well. This calculation prunes back the scope of the payments balance to the official world only, that is, to the changes found in the U.S. government holdings of foreign exchange and foreign government holdings of dollars or of paper easily converted into dollars. The *official balance,* then, covers (1) changes in U.S. government holdings of gold and convertible currencies (D-8 and C-8, and D-9 and C-9) plus (2) changes in the liquid and near-liquid dollar holdings of foreign official agencies. (This last item will not be found in the table of debit and credit items, but it consists of portions of D-6 and C-6, and D-7 and C-7.) The rationale for this pruning back is in part the view that the dollar holdings of private foreigners could well represent indispensable working balances, and therefore should not be thought of as short-term claims on the United States.

Finally, to prepare the reader for the full panoply of balances that he is likely to encounter, still another balance is worth describing. This conception reflects the view that the *basic balance* of the United States should be measured only by the net result of certain kinds of transactions, that is, transactions in goods and services, in foreign aid, and in long-term investments; or, to invert the proposition, that changes in short-term holdings by foreigners in the United States and by U.S. entities overseas, being responsive to very ephemeral and impermanent forces, should be omitted from any measure of "basic" change in the United States. The basic balance, therefore, is computed as the net of all the current items listed in Table 10–1 plus the net of all the long-term capital items (together with a few technical adjustments intended to eliminate the effects of extraordinary international transactions); it omits, therefore, the influence of short-term capital movements if these were not tied to some long-term investment or trade or aid transaction.

These compilations of balance-of-payment data have changed in the past, and they will change again in the future. The important point to remember is that no single account or limited group of accounts can tell the story. The data are a reflection of a series of underlying processes. The processes have to be understood if any useful projections are to be made. The data can make some small contribution to that understanding.

THE PETRODOLLAR ISSUE

In the mid-1970s, one overwhelming factor dominated the international payment system: oil-exporting countries had succeeded in increasing the price of oil about 300 per cent over the levels of the early 1970s, adding something like $70 billion to $80 billion annually to the importing costs of other countries. Suddenly, by one means or another, importing countries would have to find a way of dealing with these increased costs.

To get a sense of the choices available to the importing countries, it is helpful to return to the basic identity that was presented in Chapter 9:

$$C_d + I_d + E = W + P + T$$

Goods produced equals payments made. As long as E (exports) are replaced by an equal amount of M (imports), goods and payments in the economy are in balance. Then suddenly M is increased vastly in money value. There are two effects to worry about: (1) the risk of imbalances inside the national economy, and (2) the risk of foreign exchange imbalances.

First, let us see what can happen inside the economy. By examining the equation, one can identify a number of possibilities. With M increased drastically, a portion of the wages, profits, and taxes will have to leave the country in payment. As the means of payment leave the country, there is less to be spent on C_d or I_d, at least out of current payments. The decline in living standards or in domestic involvement that this shift implies may be accompanied by an increase in E, which balances the increase in M.

Possibilities of this sort entail internal adjustment for the oil-importing countries. Some are more painful than others. For example, if the imbalance were taken up simply by increasing the *prices* of exports, the pain of internal adjustment would not be very great. On the other hand, other adjustments generally entail internal pain in one shape or another.

What about the second problem, that of foreign exchange imbalance induced by the increased cost of foreign oil? Here, adjustment might eventually be possible pursuant to the processes described in Tables 9–1 and 9–2 of Chapter 9. The possibility would be especially real if the importing country had enough foreign exchange reserves so that an interim period of disequilibrium could be financed out of a pool of existing foreign exchange reserves. In that case, during a period in which M exceeded E, the country could draw down on its reserves to finance the excess. Meanwhile, increases in E and reductions in C_d and I_d could gradually close the gap.

The difficulty with this solution to the foreign exchange gap, of course, is that the sum of $70 billion or $80 billion annually is a formidable quantity. Although not of overwhelming magnitude in relation to the $4 trillion of world product, that sum does represent a very large amount in relation to the world's foreign exchange reserves. More to the point, the excess of M over E, when distributed among the individual countries concerned, turns out to hit some countries with much greater force than others. The manageability of the problem for any country depends on how rapidly the country can restore itself to external equilibrium and how large its foreign exchange reserves may be for financing the interim gap.

Of course, even in the absence of stored-up foreign exchange reserves, there are still other ways for a nation to handle the foreign exchange gap created by the sudden increase in M. One possibility is for a nation to induce others to invest their funds inside its economy, whether on a long- or short-term basis, thus adding to the foreign exchange reserves of the nation so favored. In that case, the favored nation will have "borrowed" its foreign exchange reserves from the rest of the world, anticipating that eventually the processes of adjustment inside its economy will generate enough slack to permit the nation to repay the reserves to the lending source.

In this context, the reader should remember that the word "borrow" has a very broad meaning. Turn back to Table 10–1 which portrays a schedule of balance-of-payment accounts. Recall that these accounts are the result of double-entry bookkeeping; every transaction leads to a debit and a credit, and all the accounts inescapably balance. Accordingly, when a nation has "borrowed" to finance an increase in its imports, the manifestation of its borrowing is to be found in its capital accounts, notably in an increase in foreigners' short- or long-term claims upon the nation, or in a reduction of the nation's claims on foreigners. "Borrowing" by a country in that sort of situation may consist merely of the building up of bank accounts by foreigners or the buying of assets by foreigners.

To bring these abstract concepts down to everyday practice, consider the case of Italy confronted with a vast increase in its import bill for oil. Assume that the Italian government has very little foreign exchange reserves, and that Italy has done what it can to reduce other imports and increase exports to restore equilibrium to its balance of payments. One way or another, the gap must be closed. What are Italy's remaining options?

1. Italy can try to compel its residents to surrender their private claims on foreign entities (such as Swiss bank accounts or shares of General Motors) to the Italian central bank, to be paid for by the Italian government in lire and used for the payment of oil imports. In that improbable case, the maneuver would be reflected in a decrease in private claims on foreign entities (C-5 and C-6 in Table 10–1).

2. Italy can try to buy oil on credit; if successful, the increase in imports (D-1 in Table 10–1) will be offset by an increase in foreigners' short-term claims on Italy (C-6).

3. Italy can borrow from third parties, such as the International Monetary Fund or the German government, to pay for oil; in that case, the accounts will be affected as in paragraph 2, above.

4. Italy can invite the oil-exporting countries to buy into Italian industry or to buy Italian government bonds. In that case, foreigners' long-term claims on Italy (C-7 or C-8) would increase.

All these possibilities can be thought of as part of the process of *recycling,* that is, of shifting the availability of foreign exchange reserves among countries in such a way as to bridge the gap occasioned by the increase in oil-import costs.

The recycling issue, however, has another aspect. Although the problems of closing the gap seem difficult, the adjustments that are needed by most nations to close the gap are not so vast that they entail major changes in the critical magnitudes, that is, in C_d, I_d, E, W, P, or T. (An important exception to this generalization is found in a group of poor oil-importing countries, notably India, Pakistan, Bangladesh, and Sri Lanka.) The problems of closing the gap, however, relate not only to its size but also to the limited capabilities of some of the institutions that are involved in the process. For instance, the private and public institutions that would be expected to perform the various intermediary tasks associated with shifting reserves from country A to country B simply may not have the legal or institutional capacity for handling the transactions involved.

A major institutional bottleneck exists, for instance, in the commercial banking system. The oil-exporting countries in the ordinary course are paid for their oil with checks drawn on foreign banks in dollars or sterling or deutschemarks. As a rule, a considerable part of those funds have been siphoned out of the accounts of buyers in the local economy, funneled through the major oil companies, and eventually passed on to institutions in the United States and Europe. For the banking institutions that accept the oil-exporting countries' funds, the liabilities they represent are disconcerting. Liabilities of this sort, controlled by a few large depositors, are subject to more than the usual risks of sudden withdrawal; a lack of liquidity would be perilous for the banks' solvency. The banks grow nervous and fearful lest a sudden withdrawal of the huge sums will force them to scramble for liquid funds.

Of course, a large proportion of the funds acquired by the oil-exporting countries is not allowed to rest in bank accounts but is placed instead in investments such as securities and real estate. In that case, the problem shifts from one of bank liquidity to one of market liquidity. Securities markets and real estate markets cannot absorb unlimited amounts of funds without experiencing violent movements in price. So institutional problems persist, although their character changes.

The problems of institutional limitations are seen even more visibly in the process of transferring foreign exchange reserves from countries that have too much to countries that have too little. Here, the limitations are of various kinds. Organizations such as the International Monetary Fund, as noted below, can only lend in limited amounts in accordance with their articles and their internal regulations. The central banks of national governments also are restrained in lending to other central banks. Even if they were not, there is a limit to how much any of them are prepared to accept the risks of making large open-ended loans to another government that seems to face substantial long-term difficulties.

The net effect is, therefore, that the closing of the gap through the recycling process can easily be blocked by institutional limitations. After that, what is left of the gap must be bridged by adjustments that hurt—by reductions in C_d or I_d or nonoil M, or by increases in E.

INTERNATIONAL COOPERATION

The joint stake of the leading nations in maintaining a workable system of international payments has led to all sorts of cooperative arrangements among them. Commonly, the cooperative arrangements consist of providing short-term funds to bolster the foreign exchange position of a country whose currency is under pressure.

The largest and most global of the many arrangements to bolster the foreign exchange position of nations is the International Monetary Fund (IMF). The fund plays two rather different roles in the provision of foreign exchange reserves. One role relates to the long-run problem of matching the expansion in international transactions with a like expansion in "international money." How can the means of payment that countries are prepared to accept from one another be made to keep pace with the swift growth in the volume of international transactions?

Until the 1971 currency crisis, gold had been one medium for international payment. For several years before the crisis, the gold supply available for use in international settlements had almost ceased to grow.

With gold fixed at 35 U.S. dollars per ounce, production of the precious metal had been limited. What was produced tended to disappear from time to time into the lockboxes of the gold hoarders, who were gambling on the possibility that the price of gold might be increased. The major governments, for their part, tried to quench these outbursts of gold fever by making solemn side agreements that none of them would buy or sell gold at any price other than $35 an ounce, however tempting it might be to join the ranks of the speculators or profit from their speculation. As a result, although the amount of gold that was in the hands of governments in the late 1940s came to about $33 billion, it had barely reached $40 billion by the early 1970s.

If the central banks of the major countries were willing to accept U.S. dollars or British sterling from one another and to hold the dollars or sterling as if those currencies were the equivalent of gold, the lack of gold would create no serious problem. But well before 1971, the disposition of central banks to hold dollars or pounds proved to have its limits. To hold another country's currency without limit, after all, is to expose one's reserves to the decisions of that other country, such as the decision to devalue. The need, therefore, was to find some other medium of exchange.

In January 1970, the member governments of the IMF agreed to create a supply of "paper gold" out of thin air. The new international currency, dubbed Special Drawing Rights, or SDR's, consisted of credits set up on the books of the IMF by agreement among its members and distributed to the members in proportion to their basic participation in the IMF. Members were entitled to redeem their own currency from one another simply by paying out of these accounts, as if the accounts were gold. There were some agreed limits on members' use of the accounts, but the limits are of only technical interest. It was understood among the major countries that, as the need arose, more SDR's would be created by agreement through the IMF. By mid-1974 about 9 billion SDR's (worth roughly 11 billion U.S. dollars at the prevailing exchange rates) were outstanding.

The second role of the IMF in providing foreign exchange reserves is of a very different sort and—so far, at any rate—much more important. The IMF maintains a pool of national currencies from which its members may "buy" the currencies they need to meet a "temporary" disequilibrium in their balance of payments. Members actually "buy" such currencies by paying with their own, and eventually they have to repay the currencies originally bought. So perhaps it is more accurate to think of their purchases from the IMF's supply of foreign exchange as if they were borrowings rather than purchases.

The IMF's pool of foreign currencies is created by the contributions of its members. On joining the organization, each member negotiates a quota. The size of the quota serves three functions at once: it determines (1) how much the member must contribute to the common pool, (2) how much he may borrow from the common pool, and (3) his voting power in the organization.

Out of its pool of money, the IMF is in a position to sell the currency of any one member to any other member. It has in fact exercised that power extensively. In the first 27 years of its existence, the IMF sold the equivalent of $26 billion of currencies to its members, of which $17 billion had been repaid at the end of 1974.

The IMF's sale of currencies to member countries by now follows some well-developed patterns. If Argentina needs sterling to meet a temporary crisis, the IMF has supplies of sterling available for sale to Argentina, to be paid for by Argentina in pesos. Under IMF policy, Argentina will be required "as a general rule" to return the sterling and retrieve its pesos within a three- to five-year period; meanwhile, it has added elbowroom in pursuing its national policies.

Argentina's right to buy the needed sterling from the IMF is not always automatic. It depends on the state of Argentina's financial position with the IMF and upon the circumstances that have created the foreign exchange need. The manager, when confronted with an impending crisis in the national currency, may well need to know how the country concerned stands in its capacity to buy currencies from the IMF. Each month, the IMF publishes that information in its regular *International Financial Statistics* series. What the manager will discover from such a source is that a member country's right of access to the IMF's pool of currencies is graduated: the more a country has already borrowed, the greater are the difficulties and conditions that attach to further borrowing.

Apart from its general funds, the IMF also has funds that can be used for special purposes. One such fund, created by borrowing from the oil-exporting countries, is devoted especially to the financing of oil imports. By 1974, that fund had reached 5 billion SDR's and seemed likely to grow more.

By the early 1970s, many of the operating principles and assumptions on which the IMF had originally been established were being abandoned. In August 1971, for instance, the U.S. government abandoned its commitment to buy and sell gold at $35 an ounce in transactions with the central banks of other governments. Unique among IMF members, the U.S. government had previously accepted this obligation as its way of pegging the U.S. dollar to a stated value in world markets. But its dwindling supply of gold in the summer of 1971 made such an obligation no longer tenable.

Meanwhile, other governments with important currencies were abandoning analogous commitments—commitments that took the form of maintaining the market value of their currencies at a declared value in relation to the U.S. dollar. Some fixed relationships did continue to exist; many smaller countries continued to tie their national currency to that of their major trading partner. Latin American countries, for example, continued to tie their currencies to the U.S. dollar; French-speaking African countries linked their currencies to the French franc.

The abandonment of fixed parities in the early 1970s produced a period in which the value of various major currencies underwent considerable change. The abandonment of the commitment to maintain fixed parities did not mean, of course, that governments would refrain from trying to influence the value of their national currencies through their purchases and sales of foreign exchange. Governments continued to be deeply concerned about the price at which their currencies were being exchanged for the currencies of other countries. They continued, therefore, to buy and sell their currencies to influence the prevailing price. But they no longer considered themselves committed to an explicit value. As a result the U.S. dollar lost a considerable part of its value in relation to other leading currencies, while the yen and deutschemark gained in relative strength.

The latitude of governments in influencing their exchange rates created obvious dangers. During the 1930s, in the depths of world depression, governments had been unable to resist the temptation to lower their exchange rates as a means of promoting their exports. Although that possibility was apparently being resisted by the major countries at least up to the mid-1970s, the specter of a repetition of the 1930s was deeply troubling. As some Europeans saw it, the decline in the relative value of the dollar, even though seemingly brought about by market forces, threatened eventually to place U.S. exporters in a powerful position in international markets. This might require European governments to depress the value of their own currencies to restore the position of their own exporters. Accordingly, with fixed rates abandoned, the IMF was engaged in an urgent effort to try to develop rules of the game that would restrain governments from slipping into the use of competitive devaluation policies. The main deterrent to competitive devaluations up to that time appeared to be the collective realization of governments that the tactic invited retaliation and threatened destruction of what was left of an orderly international payments system. The possibility that effective rules might be developed to fortify the restraint did not seem very strong.

REGULATING FOREIGN EXCHANGE TRANSACTIONS

In the last resort, one way for a country to handle its foreign exchange problems is to try to curb its residents' use of foreign goods or services; to the extent that these needs can be curbed, fewer offers will be made by the country's residents to sell the country's currency in return for foreign exchange. Indeed, one main purpose of restrictions imposed by countries on imports of foreign goods, on the use of foreign services, and on the freedom of its residents to tour abroad has been to reduce the demand of residents for foreign currencies.

In the years immediately following World War II, there were few countries that did not maintain such restrictions. By the mid-1960s, most advanced countries felt secure enough in balance-of-payment terms to lift most restrictions of this sort, although practically all the underdeveloped countries still had such restrictions extensively in force.

Although most of the advanced countries have lifted the bulk of their restrictions on current transactions—that is, on the purchase of foreign goods and services and on travel abroad—many continued to restrict capital transactions. Capital transactions could generate balance-of-payment strains just as certainly as current transactions; indeed, the effects of capital movements could be much more mercurial and dramatic. For that reason, many countries have maintained controls over foreigners' use of their capital markets and over their own residents' access to foreign capital markets.

The persistence of controls on capital transactions has been due not only to the high danger potential of capital movements, but also to the related fact that capital controls are traditionally tolerated in international agreements. For instance, the Articles of Agreement of the International Monetary Fund are clear in prohibiting restrictions on payments in connection with current account transactions unless the IMF's permission is obtained; but nations may strictly regulate capital account transactions without running afoul of IMF provisions.

At times, the efforts of countries to keep their foreign exchange situation under control leads them to enter into bilateral trade agreements with other countries. In fact, in the extreme case, that of the Soviet Union, the bilateral trade agreement is the normal rather than the exceptional arrangement for the conduct of trade. Countries need not conduct a command economy, however, to see advantages in such an agreement. Whenever countries maintain a tight control over the use of foreign exchange, it does not take long for them to realize that, through the use of such bilateral agreements, there may be possibilities for expanding the volume of their imports without increasing their expenditures of foreign exchange.

In the mid-1970s, bilateral agreements of this sort were prominent in the trade of sixty or seventy countries. In most such arrangements, at least one of the partners was a country committed to a system in which the state itself did the trading. But the raw material and foreign exchange shortages of the 1970s were leading other countries to develop arrangements that had elements of such bilateral agreements. Arrangements that involved a swap of oil for machinery, for instance, were beginning to attract various countries in Western Europe.

The core of a typical bilateral trade agreement is usually an undertaking by each of the two signatory countries that they will allow their importers to bring in goods and services in such quantities as to ensure an equal flow in both directions. The agreement may be set out in great particularity, specifying the products that are to be permitted as imports and exports; or it may be more general. In any case, if such an agreement exists, it becomes possible for the central banks of the two countries to agree concurrently upon the setting up of some sort of clearing account. The central bank of country B extends sufficient credit to the central bank of country A so that A can sell its residents the necessary exchange to import goods and services from country B; and A does the same for B. When residents of country A import a product, the money flows are those shown in Figure 10–1. When country B imports, the flows are reversed. Since

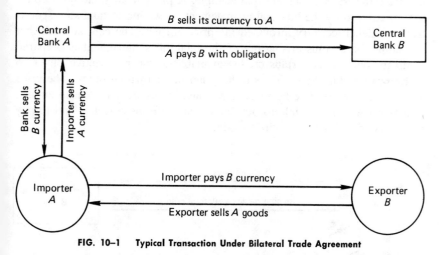

FIG. 10–1 Typical Transaction Under Bilateral Trade Agreement

trade controls and capital controls are usually being manipulated to force a balance in the period of the trade agreement, the central banks can be assured that the flows in both directions will balance out as far as they are concerned, and that no precious convertible currencies will be needed to finance the trade.

Of course, the best laid plans of central banks can go awry. Wherever bilateral agreements have existed, therefore, there have always been problems of what to do with unplanned balances, that is, with excess credits accumulated by one of the two parties. That kind of problem has been quite common in the operation of bilateral arrangements between the Communist countries and the countries of Western Europe, especially before the sharp increases of the 1970s in the prices of raw materials. As a rule, the Communist buyers have eagerly bought up all they could afford in Western Europe, while the Europeans have encountered difficulty finding goods in the Communist countries at a price and of a quality worth buying. To be sure, the Western countries could restore balance in the account by clamping down on exports to the Communist buyers. But they have been loathe to do this for fear of losing a market. So they allowed the surpluses to develop.

Whenever situations of this sort have arisen in international trade, they have led to the spontaneous generation of institutions designed to deal with them. Specialists in *swap transactions* have appeared, men who make a living by arranging for the disposal of the credits accumulated by the surplus country in bilateral arrangements. (This is not to be confused with the swap loan arrangements described in Chapter 5.)

Swap transactions can take many different forms and can appear extraordinarily complex. Basically, however, despite the complex details involved, the transactions are quite simple. A party from some third country not covered by the bilateral arrangements is willing to take some goods from the deficit country, provided the price is right. The central bank that is holding the surplus arising out of the bilateral arrangement is prepared to make some of its surplus credits available to the prospective buyer so that he can pay in these credits rather than in his own currency. The price at which the prospective buyer acquires the surplus credits is cheap enough to make it worth his while to buy the credits with his currency and to pay for the goods with the acquired credits.

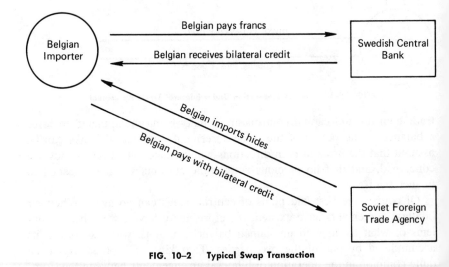

FIG. 10-2   Typical Swap Transaction

In Figure 10-2, a typical swap transaction is diagrammed. In this case, a Belgian acquires surplus ruble credits that the Swedes have accumulated in transactions with the Soviet Union, and he uses these credits to buy Russian hides. The price at which the credits were acquired is presumably sufficiently attractive so that it is cheaper for the Belgian to buy his hides by this indirect route than by direct purchase.

The difficulty with bilateral agreements of this sort is that they narrow the opportunities of the importing countries by forcing them to buy from sources that would not be favored if the choice were free. Accordingly, nations tend to move away from these agreements as fast as they dare. In doing so, they have created various halfway houses—multinational payments arrangements confined to a limited group of countries—in which the participants are exposed neither to the full risks of losing convertible currencies nor to the full losses of discriminatory bilateral trade. Arrangements of this sort permit the countries concerned to offer their nationals a wider range of sources for imports and wider access to markets.

The prototype of such multinational payment arrangements is a system now defunct, that devised by the European Payments Union (EPU). The union was instituted in Western Europe in 1950 and was maintained, in one active form or another, until 1959. Its seventeen members had already been joined together in the European Recovery Program and had already subscribed to an elaborate Code of Trade Liberalization. Under the code, the countries concerned had undertaken to open their markets to one another (although not necessarily to outsiders) and to expand the size of the opening as their individual positions permitted. The means existed, therefore, by which the member countries could keep their trade with one another in balance, or, at least, could hold the size of any imbalances well in check.

There were two basic principles of the EPU. First, all the current account transactions of any member with the other members were to be settled collectively in a monthly clearing operation that lumped together all the transactions of each member inside the system. A consequence of this principle was that in the licensing of imports no member had any financial reason to discriminate among any of the other members. The second principle was that, in the clearance, net debtors would have to pay a part of their debt in gold or dollars but would receive a credit for the rest. The fact that credit would be available for part of the bill gave debtors a special incentive to channel their imports away from outside sources, such as the United States, where payment had to be made by normal international means.

It is unlikely that the manager has seen the last of such arrangements in the international economy. The pressures to conserve on the use of foreign exchange are so great that arrangements of this sort are sure to appear again. When they appear, they are likely to contain the two basic features of such arrangements: mutual extensions of foreign exchange credits, coupled with systematic discrimination against those that do not belong.

SUGGESTED READING

HODGMAN, DONALD R., *National Monetary Policies and International Monetary Cooperation* (Boston: Little, Brown, 1974).

KINDLEBERGER, CHARLES P., *International Economics,* 5th ed. (Homewood, Ill.: Irwin, 1973), Chapters 23–27, pp. 389–457.

MAYER, HELMUT W., *The Anatomy of Official Exchange-Rate Intervention Systems,* Essays in International Finance, No. 104, International Finance Section, Princeton University, Princeton, N.J., May 1974.

MCKINNON, RONALD I., and WARREN E. OATES, *The Implications of International Economic Integration for Monetary, Fiscal and Exchange-Rate Policy,* Essays in International Finance, No. 16, International Finance Section, Princeton University, Princeton, N.J., January 1966.

MEIER, GERALD M., *Problems of World Monetary Order* (New York: Oxford University Press, 1974).

POLLACK, GERALD A., "The Economic Consequences of the Energy Crisis," *Foreign Affairs,* April 1974, p. 452.

Underlying Forces
in International
Trade

chapter eleven

For the manager in the international economy, any concept that will help to analyze and predict the directions of world trade is an obvious boon. Judgments on where to locate future plants and on the prospects for international competition usually require, implicitly, or explicitly, predictions as to the future patterns of world trade. For instance, the decision to place a new television assembly factory in Britain is likely to be a mistake if large volumes of competing imports from the low-wage areas of southeast Asia are on the immediate horizon. Some of the concepts developed by trade theorists offer a starting point for the manager who desires to organize his analysis on a systematic basis.

Even if the theories were not valuable in providing a base for prediction, the manager would still find it useful to know something about the main theories concerning international trade. The manager operates his enterprise in a ferment of government ideas about the role of exports and imports. The ideas find their concrete manifestations in all kinds of helpful or unpleasant acts of government—changes in tariff rates, imposition of requirements for import licenses, application of import taxes, and so on. The underlying rationale is often best expressed in the economic theories to which the government officials claim allegiance.

Obviously, no economic theory is powerful enough to provide complete "answers" to the manager's problems in international trade. One does not leap from a product-cycle model or from the doctrine of comparative advantage to a decision on where to locate a television assembly plant.

But such theories can help the manager to organize his analysis somewhat more efficiently, to identify the questions to which more attention must be given, and to reject some positions outright.

INNOVATION AND TRADE PATTERNS

The reader who has followed the discussion of the origins and strategies of multinational enterprises as presented in Chapter 1 can hardly be surprised to find that innovations influence trade patterns as well as investment patterns. The technological lead generated by a firm may give it an edge in exports. Accordingly, Germany may find itself with an advantage for a time in the export of certain plastics innovated there, while the United States benefits for a time from the exports of Polaroid and Instamatic cameras.

If a particular innovation were as likely to occur in one country as in another, there would be little basis for predicting trade patterns that are associated with innovative activity. Fortunately, for the analyst, the patterns of innovation, and thus certain patterns of international trade, do seem to be somewhat predictable. The chances are not equal that a particular type of innovation will take place in Germany, Britain, Japan, or the United States. Although numerous innovations occur in each of these countries, various studies indicate that the innovations in a particular country are likely to have special characteristics associated with the conditions that exist in that country.

Consider the United States. For some time the United States has been the country in which a very large proportion of the world's new products have first been produced on a commercial basis. This is not to say that the ideas behind the products were first generated in the United States; there are too many illustrations to the contrary, from antibiotics to jet engines. But there are great leaps from a test-tube idea to a pilot-plant project to a commercial production line.

One reason why the first commercial production line so frequently appears in the United States has to do principally with market conditions there. The manager who is most likely to take the risks and make the investment associated with the commercial introduction of a new product is the one who has the greatest assurance that a market will exist for his products. The manager physically located in a particular market is likely to be more aware of the risks and opportunities it presents than he is of more distant markets.

In Chapter 1, we suggested that certain features of the U.S. market lead its firms to develop the technology for particular products. The sheer size of the U.S. market is one important feature that reduces the perceived risk in the introduction of new products. Another has been the high income per head of U.S. consumers, a condition which increases the probability of a market for certain new consumer products. Still another has been the relatively high cost of labor, which creates a continuous demand for innovations that substitute capital for labor. These conditions have led to the introduction of a wide range of rather special products in the U.S. market. Sixty to one hundred years ago, the response could be seen in the introduction of mass-produced automobiles, sewing machines, and pistols with interchangeable parts. In more recent years, it was seen in television, video tape equipment, instant cameras, forklift trucks, automatic controls, and other products that appealed to high-income consumers or conserved on labor.

The fact that a market exists in the United States, however, may not appear sufficient in a modern world of multinational enterprises to explain why production should first be located there. In Chapter 1, we explored some of the reasons why a firm with a technological lead might produce near its largest market at the outset, even if that site might not be the one with the lowest costs. One cannot assume that the innovating producer, on detecting the opportunity to introduce a new product, then diligently searches out the lowest-cost location for production and distribution. More likely, the risk and uncertainty of the undertaking will lead him to take a different approach. They will encourage him to hold down his commitments to the production of the new product, as well as to locate its facilities close to the decision-making center of the enterprise, wherever that may be. For products that appeal to high-income consumers or which save on expensive labor, that site is likely to be the United States.

A U.S. location might well be indicated for still other reasons. During the uncertain and risky stage in the launching of a new product, the manager usually sees no great need to hold down production costs. New products for consumers, such as video tapes and metal skis, are not highly price elastic in their early stages. The need to hold down production costs comes later, when standardization develops and competition appears. In the sale of new products for industrial use, the needs are similar. The first buyers also are comparatively price insensitive; if the products are real innovations and not small variants on existing products, they must be able to demonstrate very large prospective savings to the buyer, not just trivial gains.

Besides, even a cost-conscious producer contemplating the production of a new product may have a strong preference for a U.S. location, given the country's industrial characteristics. At the early stage of a product's life, it would be unwise to commit the firm to the use of given materials, given processes, or even to a given scale; hence the need exists for easy and flexible employment of a changing mix of factors hired piecemeal out of the industrial environment. Such a producer is likely to prefer an industrial environment in which facilities, equipment, and skills could easily be drawn in from outside the firm. These requirements may rule out less familiar areas or less industrialized areas, even though labor or other factors appear cheap in those areas.

Once the early producers decide to locate in a given country, it is likely that the country will retain its lead for some time. Late-starting producers elsewhere, without much of a domestic market of their own as yet, would feel disinclined to compete with the established producers for their own market; the uncertainties of serving a remote, unknown market in a comparatively new product against competitors who already had achieved certain scale economies generally would seem too great.

Accordingly, with little or no foreign competition for their new products, innovating producers commonly begin developing a modest export market for those products. In the case of consumer goods, high-income groups in other countries seek out the new goods about as quickly as buyers in the United States. In the case of labor-substituting industrial goods, producers in other countries often find the substitution of capital for labor to be economical in their own countries, even if the cost savings are not quite as large as in the United States.

In time, foreign markets for both the consumer and the industrial goods grow as incomes abroad rise and as labor costs increase. Concurrently, U.S. exports of products resulting from U.S. innovations tend to grow. Figure 11–1 shows this pattern in the first stage of what has sometimes been dubbed the *product cycle*.

In time, however, two new factors set in: (1) the demand in some non-U.S. markets grows sufficiently large to support a local production facility that can exploit the existing scale economies, and (2) the product becomes sufficiently standardized that price competition begins to be important. Thus, cost considerations start to play a significant role in locational decisions.

At this point, late in the "New Product" stage of Figure 11–1, the international manager may well confront a new problem. As tariffs, shipping costs, and perhaps even lower labor rates tip the scale in favor of foreign locations for sales abroad, production spurts sharply upward in industrialized countries other than the United States, and the rate of growth of U.S. production begins to fall. That foreign production will often be undertaken by the overseas subsidiary of a U.S. firm, as the U.S. firm ventures abroad out of fear that a foreign producer will preempt his export market.

If labor costs are sufficiently important in the cost structure of the product, and if transport costs and tariffs do not constitute blocking obstacles, there are further changes in trade flows. Producers in countries like Italy or Spain may have sufficiently low labor costs that they can compete with U.S. exports to third countries. In fact, their output may eventually become competitive in the United States. Accordingly, the position of the

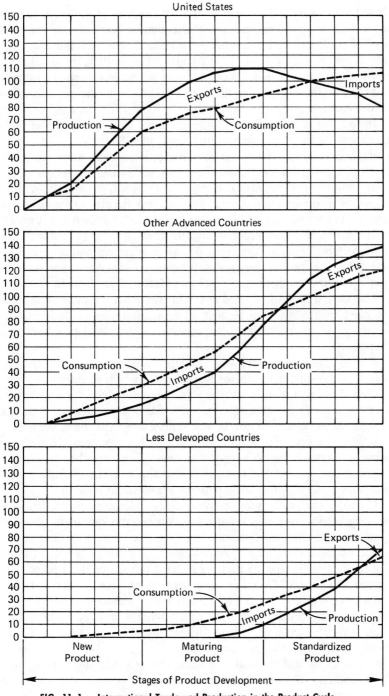

FIG. 11-1   **International Trade and Production in the Product Cycle**

United States may shift from that of a net exporter of the particular product to that of a net importer, as other countries become competitive. The possible trade pattern for another industrialized country is illustrated in the second part of Figure 11–1. That country which initially imported the new product from the United States produces later for its own consumption, and then begins to export to the U.S. market and to the markets of some third countries.

In fact, for some products the international manager may confront still another problem. The cycle by which the United States has lost its absolute advantage to Europe or Japan may be repeated once more, as the less-developed countries eventually acquire a producing advantage over the more industrialized countries. Here, too, the facilities may be under the control of a foreign multinational firm that has decided to move its operations to an area where unskilled labor is plentiful and cheap; or it may be a local entrepreneur who accounts for the threat. Figure 11–1 illustrates the trade patterns of some developing countries in certain manufactured products. Although the emergence of developing countries as exporters of electronic products, clothing, and other manufactured products in recent years can be viewed as the last stage in the international life cycle of a product, the phenomenon also can be seen as a manifestation of the comparative advantage of the developing countries, a subject developed later in this chapter.

Although U.S. firms have a particularly strong reputation for innovation, they hold no monopoly on innovative activity. There have been several studies of the nature of innovations in other countries. Although the manager can feel fairly confident about the kinds of innovations that are likely to occur in the United States, he confronts a somewhat more complex pattern when he proceeds to innovations in other countries. However, evidence is accumulating to suggest that innovations in other countries also follow rather predictable patterns. Once the patterns of innovation are understood, the resulting trade patterns are easier to forecast.

Consider the patterns of innovation first. Germany, in particular, has been inclined toward innovations that conserve on raw materials—rayon, synthetic dyestuffs, and synthetic fertilizer. The strength of Germany rests in part on the chronic scarcity of raw materials inside its borders. Germany, like the rest of Europe, had few of its hard raw materials at home. Unlike Britain and France, Germany never had many colonies, and it had even fewer after World War I. Thus, it did not have seemingly secure sources of raw materials abroad, as did the other major European industrial countries. This shortcoming was underlined by the blockades of Germany during the Napoleonic Wars and World War I. In a country with possible shortages of natural materials, an entrepreneur would find a ready market for a synthetic substitute. German firms have responded with a wide range of innovations to conserve on scarce raw materials.

In contrast, Britain seems to have emphasized innovations that saved on labor, especially on labor in manufacturing operations. On the surface, this may seem to be an aberration from the usual pattern according to which innovation responds to market forces. But given the propensity for labor disputes in Britain, such innovations may be a response to the high real costs of British labor, once its productivity is taken into account.

Japan also has its own special fields of innovative activity. Miniaturization seems to be one such area, possibly partly in response to the premium placed on space in that crowded country. Another area appears to be emerging, the field of antipollution devices.

In a number of cases, innovations in Europe have given rise to new products that could be exported. German ingenuity in synthetics led to the export of plastics. But a large portion of the innovations in Europe have been process rather than product oriented. In some cases, new processes lower the cost of products and thereby encourage their export. In other cases, however, process innovations only enable the innovating country to hold its own against imports from another country. Moreover, process innovations are more easily licensed than product innovations. Accordingly, the innovating firm may license the process to enterprises in other countries, thereby reducing the likely impact on international trade patterns.

The exports and imports of both the United States and the European countries still appear to reflect the historical differences in costs and availability of factors such as labor, capital, and raw material in the two regions. However, in recent years, Europe's labor costs have moved much closer to those of the United States. And both areas have become increasingly dependent on raw materials from third countries. At the same time, the European Economic Community provides an opportunity for European firms to innovate for a home market roughly as large as the U.S. market. As firms respond to these shifts in opportunities, substantial changes may occur in innovative activities in various countries and in the resulting trade patterns of the United States and Europe. If those changes do occur, it would lead to rather different generalizations about likely patterns of international trade. At the same time, from the managerial point of view, the mode of analysis used here may still provide a base for projections of patterns in individual products.

COMPARATIVE ADVANTAGE

Although managers usually feel comfortable with the concept of the product cycle as a reflection of some of their own experience, the product-cycle approach leaves a wide area of international trade unexplained. When products are mature and the technologies are well known, the advantages of a country based on its position as an early producer may easily disappear. The shifting patterns of trade associated with the availability of special knowledge and skills may be replaced by a more stable pattern that results from underlying cost factors. The theory of comparative advantage is a useful concept for understanding the patterns of trade that may emerge when the technical ability to produce a product is widely dispersed. It is a theory with a deep hold on the minds of economists and government officials. Although basically a very simple concept, it is also elusive and often imperfectly understood. One way to develop an understanding of the theory is to trace through a simple example.

Picture Argentina and Mexico, each with its supply of land, labor, and capital. Imagine that each is producing only two products, cotton and wheat. Argentina is more fortunate than Mexico, being blessed with a climate and soil that are much more favorable for most agricultural purposes. When a production unit (a given mixture of capital goods, labor, and land) is put to work in Argentina, therefore, it generally produces much more wheat than a production unit would produce in Mexico. The same, we shall assume, is true for cotton: a production unit in Argentina generates more output than a production unit in Mexico.

At this point, one may be tempted to conclude that it makes no sense for Argentina to buy anything from Mexico. The physical superiority of Argentina in the two products is likely to suggest that Argentina would be wise to fall back on its own resources for both cotton and wheat production.

But a moment's reflection will indicate that this is a fallacy. There is a well-known corporation lawyer on Wall Street whose legal skills and legal fees are among the highest in the profession. At the same time, he is a superb house painter, capable of doing interiors far more swiftly and efficiently than any available painter in the business. Like Argentina, therefore, he excels at two lines—at the law and at house painting. Yet he has long since learned that it makes no sense for him to paint his own house. Instead he hires painters, even though they are slower and less efficient than he. In effect, although he is an outstanding painter and an outstanding lawyer, he sells his legal services and buys his painting needs.

This exchange seems to make sense; intuitively one can accept it as wise. Now, let us return to the Argentina–Mexico cotton–wheat case to trace out the arithmetic that supports the intuitive conclusion. In Table 11–1, the assumption is that Argentina and Mexico have not yet discovered each other's existence. Each, in isolation, is producing and consuming its own cotton and wheat. Each country has the same number of production units to begin with, but Argentina is capable of producing more bales of cotton per production unit and more bushels of wheat per production unit than Mexico. One production unit yields 10 bales of cotton in Argentina and 8 in Mexico. Table 11–1 summarizes various production possibilities available to Argentina and Mexico.

The student will observe that one pair of cotton–wheat figures for each

TABLE 11-1 Production Possibilities of Argentina and Mexico (each country contains 10,000 production units)

	ARGENTINA		MEXICO	
USE OF PRODUCTION UNITS	COTTON (000 BALES)	WHEAT (000 BUSHELS)	COTTON (000 BALES)	WHEAT (000 BUSHELS)
10,000 in cotton, 0 in wheat	100	0	80	0
7,500 in cotton, 2,500 in wheat	75	15	60	5
5,000 in cotton, 5,000 in wheat	50	30	40*	10*
2,500 in cotton, 7,500 in wheat	25*	45*	20	15
0 in cotton, 10,000 in wheat	0	60	0	20

country carries an asterisk (*). This is the pair of production possibilities that it is assumed each country has in fact chosen. For their own reasons, the people of Argentina have chosen to produce and consume 25,000 bales of cotton and 45,000 bushels of wheat; the Mexicans have elected a combination of 40,000 bales of cotton and 10,000 bushels of wheat.

Let us now suppose that Argentina, playing the role of the rich lawyer who cannot afford to waste his time on house painting, decides to concentrate all its production units in the activity it does best and to trade off its surplus for the things it needs. What *does* Argentina do best? Table 11–1 suggests the answer. The table not only shows that Argentina produces both wheat and cotton more efficiently than Mexico; it also shows that Argentina's wheat advantage (6:2) is larger than its cotton advantage (10:8). To state the same proposition the other way around, Mexico's cotton disadvantage is less than its wheat disadvantage. *Comparatively* speaking, Argentina's advantage is greater in wheat than in cotton, while Mexico's disadvantage is less in cotton than in wheat.

Then let Argentina specialize fully in wheat and Mexico fully in cotton. If that were to happen, the two countries would have both more cotton and more wheat to divide up between them. In isolation, as Table 11–1 shows, their combined production is only 65,000 bales of cotton and 55,000 bushels of wheat. But with each specializing in what it does best, their combined production will be 80,000 bales of cotton and 60,000 bushels of wheat. Then one can conceive of the pattern of production and trade shown in Table 11–2.

Observe the final consumption patterns now, a result of specialization and trade. Mexico is now consuming 50,000 bales of cotton and 12,000 bushels of wheat, instead of the 40,000 bales and 10,000 bushels consumed when in isolation. Argentina, meanwhile, is also doing better in all products: under the regime of specialization and trade, 30,000 bales of cotton and 48,000 bushels of wheat are consumed, as against only 25,000 bales and 45,000 bushels in isolation.

All that has been illustrated so far is the possibility that, in certain conditions, international trade may turn out to afford benefit to both parties.

TABLE 11-2   Argentina and Mexico in Specialization and Trade

| | ARGENTINA | | |
	PRODUCES	TRADES (IMPORTS +, EXPORTS −)	CONSUMES
Cotton (000 bales)	0	+30	30
Wheat (000 bushels)	60	−12	48

| | MEXICO | | |
	PRODUCES	TRADES (IMPORTS +, EXPORTS −)	CONSUMES
Cotton (000 bales)	80	−30	50
Wheat (000 bushels)	0	+12	12

Although this is a modest conclusion, it is also a powerful one of which all countries are acutely conscious. Neither the most efficient country nor the least efficient feels altogether free to abandon the search for that hypothetical advantage. Accordingly, the impulse to open up the economy to foreign trade is never wholly lacking among government policy makers.

Of course, illustrations have a good deal more meaning for the manager in the international economy when they get away from the assumption of barter exchange and introduce money prices. To introduce prices, one has only to assign some kind of payment to each production unit used in Mexico and Argentina. Obviously, it makes no sense to assign exactly the same payment to production units in both countries. Intuition urges that the Argentine production unit, being more productive, ought to be paid more for its work. An Argentine production unit produces 10 bales of cotton to the Mexican figure of 8; hence, it appears to be valued at 125 per cent of the Mexican unit by this measure. And an Argentine production unit produces 6 bales of wheat to the Mexican output of 2; this suggests a value of 300 per cent for the Argentine unit in comparison to the Mexican.

Suppose, then, we select a value of 250 per cent for the Argentine unit, that is, a figure somewhere between the indicated limits. If Mexican production units are paid the equivalent of $1.00, Argentine units might be paid $2.50. (Let us brush aside the problem of exchange rates for the present and simply state all money in terms of U.S. dollar equivalents.) At those levels of payment, the prices of cotton and wheat prevailing in the two countries, just before they begin to trade, are those shown in the upper half of Table 11-3, which portrays a situation in which two-way trade is possible.

Because Argentina's production units are being paid more than Mexican units, Mexico is able to offer an attractive cotton price to Argentina; but despite the higher payment to Argentine production units, Argentina is still able to offer an attractive wheat price to Mexico. The willingness of

TABLE 11-3   Payments and Prices in Argentina and Mexico Before Trade

	ARGENTINA	MEXICO
In equilibrium		
Payment per production unit	$2.50	$1.00
Cotton—bales per unit	10	8
cost per bale	$0.250	$0.125
Wheat—bushels per unit	6	2
cost per bushel	$0.417	$0.500
In disequilibrium		
Payment per production unit	$2.50	$2.50
Cotton—bales per unit	10	8
cost per bale	$0.250	$0.312
Wheat—bushels per unit	6	2
cost per bushel	$0.417	$1.250

Mexico's production units to accept a price that reflects their relative inefficiency is what keeps Mexico's cotton price competitive; but that willingness is not enough to make Mexico's wheat competitive. So two-way trade can occur. And the pattern suggested in Table 11–2, or something very much like it, is not foreclosed.

Suppose, however, that the owners of Mexico's production units were to find the relatively low payments for their units quite intolerable. Suppose they were to insist upon payment equal to that received by production units in Argentina, that is, $2.50 per unit. In that case, as the lower half of Table 11–3 indicates, the price of both cotton and wheat in Mexico would be higher than in Argentina; that is, Mexico will have priced itself out of the market. Mexico could not export anything and it would want to import everything, a situation that could not be sustained for very long.

This is a point of fundamental importance. Although the theory on which it is based is crude and oversimple, the empirical fact is confirmed repeatedly from experience. In general, the factors of production of any nation tend to be compensated at a rate, relative to other countries, that roughly reflects their efficiency relative to those other countries. The relation is not perfect, nor need it be. But, in general, when a country's performance is grossly out of line, some kind of disequilibrium sets in. If the country attempts to overcompensate its production factors in terms of their international efficiency, the country's prices are likely to rise; this in turn will increase its imports and reduce its exports. Strain on the balance-of-payments can be expected to follow, eventually demanding some form of readjustment to bring payment to the production factors back into line.

The theory of comparative advantage has been extended by economists to a form that makes it particularly useful for the manager seeking a basis for organizing his thinking about trade patterns. The Heckscher–Ohlin theorem concludes that it would be advantageous for a country to export products that use intensively the country's most abundant resources. The country should import those items the production of which uses the country's scarcest resources. Thus, a country with scarce labor and relatively abundant capital might be expected to concentrate on the export of goods whose production processes require large amounts of capital while it imports products whose production processes are labor intensive.

Following this line of reasoning, one might expect the United States to concentrate its production facilities on the manufacture of products that are capital intensive and import those which are labor intensive. In fact, however, a celebrated group of studies by Wassily Leontief, the *éminence grise* of interindustry analysis and input–output techniques in the United States, generates a contrary finding. Leontief demonstrated that U.S. exports as a whole are slightly more labor intensive than are the U.S. products which are subject to the most import competition.

A possible explanation of the "Leontief paradox" will be obvious to some readers by now. If U.S. exports and imports are made up to a large degree of products whose trade patterns reflect the advantages of innovation rather than the sheer supply of and demand for capital, land, and labor, Leontief's findings would be expected. Early in a new product's life, its production processes are likely to be labor intensive. A relatively heavy use of scientists and engineers is typical at this stage. Besides, the processes of manufacture are not yet large scale or standardized, as compared with the processes that later will be developed. Since U.S. exports contain a large number of new products and U.S. imports include many more mature and more standardized products, Leontief's findings are not so surprising. At the same time, however, one must not forget that an important part of U.S. trade—including agricultural products, minerals, and some manufactures—are not influenced so much by innovative activity as by underlying comparative costs based on the availability of certain inputs.

The illustrations of comparative advantage that have been presented so far have rested upon a number of highly simplifying assumptions. One is the assumption of constant returns to scale, that is, the efficiency with which the economy produces added units of a product is always the same, irrespective of the amount produced. For the manager, this assumption is hard to swallow.

In some cases, for instance, efficiency is likely to decline as production increases. If Argentina were to devote every acre of its land to wheat production, it would probably not be using all its land efficiently. The last units of land brought into wheat production, one can assume, would be less suited to that use than the first units. Thus, specialization may result in relatively high costs if it is carried too far.

The opposite sort of problem also exists. To most managers, the problems and opportunities associated with increasing returns to scale are more apparent than those associated with decreasing returns. However, most versions of the theory of comparative advantage pay little attention to the decreasing costs that are so frequently associated with specialization. For some countries, these economies are particularly important. Once the possibility of declining costs is introduced, the argument offered in earlier pages on the advantages of an open and free trading system begins to lose some of its cutting edge. The intellectual basis for justifying systems of protection, subsidy, and preference, especially on the part of developing countries, begins to take shape. As a result of increasing returns to scale, many governments are unwilling to let existing comparative advantage determine their national trade patterns.

Consider the problems of a small country producing manufactured goods. Before world trade opens up, the country's manufacturers produce a large number of products to satisfy the needs of the local market. Faced with a small market, local firms face high costs for most products. If the firms could expand their volume, costs would fall and opportunities to sell abroad would develop.

However, in the real world most firms are hesitant to expand rapidly to supply uncertain export markets. Even though such firms could compete internationally if they could just expand their output to overcome their scale problems, they are usually hesitant to do so if the required expansion is large. As a result, factor costs alone are usually unable to explain the trade patterns of small countries.

To explore adequately the important effects of scale on trade patterns, one has to be clear regarding the different kinds of economies of scale that are encountered. The economies most familiar to the manager are those that can be achieved within a single plant by increasing its size, that is, *internal economies of scale*. The efficiency of certain equipment increases if it is built to handle a larger volume, at least up to a point. Moreover, the efficiency of a group of machines in combination also may rise as the volume of a plant increases. The bigger the plant, the easier it is to find the combination of machines that will keep all units fully occupied.

The trade patterns of countries are influenced not only by economies of scale internal to the firm but also by scale factors that transcend the individual firm, including economies that result from the increased size of the industry to which the plant belongs or even to a complex of interdependent industries.

As a cluster of industrial plants grows, it lays the basis for large, low-cost, common services, such as a large power plant. It also lays the bases for common risk-reducing facilities that no single plant, taken by itself, could easily afford. All producers confront unavoidable contingencies, such as the shutdown of the plant of a major supplier, the failure of an electric power supply, the breakdown of a carrier delivering essential materials, the failure of a piece of critical machinery, the loss of a key repairman, and so on. Risks of this sort can sometimes be hedged, provided the enterprise can afford to pay the price. Unusually large inventories of raw materials may be stocked at the plant site, idle repairmen may be maintained on the payroll, standby generators may be kept on tap, and so on. But risk hedging against unforeseen breakdowns becomes both less necessary and less difficult as industrial complexes grow. If supplies from accustomed sources suddenly dry up, the chance of finding an alternative source is high. If a carrier breaks down, the possibility of arranging another source of transportation is very real. Repairmen can be borrowed or hired for emergencies. And so on.

Considerations of this sort suggest that declining cost situations may well be of great importance in any analysis of the forces that make for international trade. When the economies of scale derived from larger plants are added to those derived from larger industrial complexes, the declining cost case becomes one of real practical interest.

Governments often follow policies to ensure that the problems of scale are not overwhelming to their manufacturers. Small countries sometimes band together in an effort to provide local industries with a large enough market so that they can manufacture efficiently. In arrangements such as the Central American Common Market, certain firms are granted "integration status" to encourage large-scale production. The hope is that these firms will be able to compete with imports and may eventually succeed in export markets.

Although some governments institute policies to exploit their underlying comparative advantage, other governments are eager to take steps that will change their comparative advantage. Their goals are twofold: to gain more from international trade, and to concentrate on activities that will enable the country to produce more with the resources it has on hand. Efforts to gain more from trade are especially apparent in developing countries, which fear the implications of specialization in raw materials if that is where their comparative advantage seems to lie. Their concern with declining terms-of-trade, discussed in Chapter 7, is one of the reasons they prefer manufacturing industries over raw material activities. Another factor is the opportunity to benefit from increasing returns to scale in manufacturing. It is widely assumed that an increase in resources devoted to the production of raw materials results in only a proportional increase in output. On the other hand, more resources allocated to manufacturing leads to a more than proportional increase in production.

Developing countries have still another fear that makes them hesitant to rely completely on their apparent comparative advantage, even when the result of that reliance is more manufacturing activity. They fear that concentration on labor-intensive industries will leave them with little more than assembly operations to supply the markets of the advanced countries. These assembly operations, it is widely assumed, bring few skills and impart little technology, thus limiting the country's ability to improve its efficiency in the future. Moreover, developing countries are concerned about being dependent on the industrialized nations that provide the market for their output.

THE MULTINATIONAL ENTERPRISE IN INTERNATIONAL TRADE

Most theories of international trade, such as that of comparative advantage, assume that transactions take place between two unrelated parties. A product exported from the United States, according to the usual assumption, is sold by an American firm to an unrelated German importer. In fact, an increasing portion of international trade takes place between parties that are related to each other. The U.S. export may be a component sold to its German subsidiary for local assembly, or it may be a finished product sold to its German subsidiary to fill out the line of products which that subsidiary manufactures in Germany. In 1970, about one quarter of U.S. manufactured exports were accounted for by sales of American firms to their foreign affiliates.

There are a number of reasons why trade among affiliated companies may depart from the patterns predicted by the theories described thus far. First, scale factors are important in influencing the trade patterns of multinational enterprises. Consider a multinational firm with a facility in Japan that is supplying a certain component to affiliates located in other countries. At a point in time, the parent, with its capability of scanning the international environment, discovers that a devaluation, say, has changed the costs of production factors in another country. As a result, it would cost less to manufacture the components in that country. Nevertheless, the multinational enterprise may well decide not to shift production from Japan to the newly attractive site. From the viewpoint of the multinational enterprise, the decision to continue to source the component in Japan may make sense if the Japanese facilities involve a large element of fixed costs that would not be recoverable if the plant were closed down. In the calculation of the relevant costs of components from the Japanese plant, the manager of the multinational enterprise considers only the marginal costs, once the facility is in place. However, new facilities in the low-cost country involve increasing the fixed costs all over again. Thus, the manager ends up comparing the marginal costs of his Japanese operations to the average costs of facilities in the prospective site. The decision may be to continue the old sourcing patterns for some time, even though average costs are lower outside Japan.

The same outcome is possible, of course, even if the Japanese supplier is not part of a multinational firm. If the Japanese supplier, as an independent firm, offers its components on the world market at marginal costs, no one is likely to undertake the new investment in the lower-cost site. However, it is much more likely in the real world that the independent Japanese firm will set his prices at a level higher than marginal costs, in order to recoup some of his overhead. The result, in the absence of multinational ties, is likely to be a shift in trade patterns as the low-cost supplier takes an increasing share of the market.

Second, the trade patterns of a multinational firm are influenced not only by the question of relative cost but also by the desire for control. In Chapter 1, it was pointed out that some firms venture abroad to gain control over raw material sources for use in a vertically integrated structure. Once that control is established through foreign branches or subsidiaries, the parent firm usually continues to purchase its needs from those affiliates, even if an alternative source offers an advantage in costs. The comparison of average and marginal costs may play a role in the decision. But other factors are usually important. A parent firm might consider selling the output of its sources to another user and buy the output of an unaffiliated supplier whose facilities are closer, saving on transport costs. That alternative may not in fact be feasible. In industries for which firms are eager to control sources of raw materials, the markets for such transactions are usually poorly developed. In the absence of markets, it is difficult to arrange the swap of raw materials that would minimize costs. Thus, ownership ties may determine trade patterns as much as do relative costs.

The spread of multinational firms causes still other deviations from the trade patterns that the usual trade theories predict. Earlier in this chapter it was suggested that a developing country might become an exporter of a product at a late stage in the product's development. According to the doctrine of comparative advantage, that is likely to happen only if the production process requires a good deal of labor and little capital, since most developing countries have abundant labor but relatively little capital. Nevertheless, multinational enterprises sometimes are responsible for locating the production of relatively capital intensive products in developing countries. This may occur because the relevant cost of capital, as far as the multinational enterprise is concerned, is not the cost that exists in the developing country. Multinational enterprises often acquire low-cost capital in the advanced countries and combine it with the cheap labor of a developing country. Even though labor may be only a small percentage of costs, the firm can thereby gain an advantage over some of its competitors. The slight edge provided by the lower wage rates is important once price becomes the critical element of success, as it often does in the mature stages of a product's development. Accordingly, the ability of some multinational enterprises to scan international markets affords a special advantage in combining the lowest factor costs for the production of some products.

A few multinational firms that have developed the required scanning ability have begun to "short-circuit" some of the stages of the product cycle. Once they have established manufacturing subsidiaries in low-wage countries, they may be particularly quick in recognizing the opportunities. These firms sometimes find that the seeming drawbacks of such areas have been exaggerated by communications problems and ignorance. Accordingly, rather than starting the manufacture of new products in an advanced country and waiting for competition to force them to move production sites to lower-cost countries, some firms anticipate the pattern and skip some of the early stages. As a result, in industries dominated by experienced multinational firms, the locational shifts suggested by the product-cycle sequence can be rather short. For example, some new electronics products that were introduced in the United States have been manufactured by U.S. firms in their Southeast Asian plants within a very few years.

The multinational enterprise influences trade patterns in still other ways. Although most trade theories emphasize production costs and skills as the factors determining trade patterns, a major barrier to the export of a wide range of manufactured goods from the developing countries lies in the field of marketing. In spite of an apparent production advantage in certain labor-intensive products, some developing countries have had difficulties in obtaining export markets for such products.

To be sure, low production costs may be sufficient to allow a manufacturer to sell gray cloth, copra, or other standardized, undifferentiated products in world markets. In such cases, the job of distribution is taken off his hands by highly specialized marketing facilities that respond mainly to questions of price. However, when products are unstandardized and differentiated, the potential exporter must make an initial investment to determine the size of the foreign market and the nature of its distribution channels. The Argentine producer who thinks of selling canned beef to Japan, for instance, has to know something about Japanese tastes and sales channels, or else he has to find someone who does. At the outset, the Argentine producer who is ignorant of foreign market conditions is trapped in a logical cul-de-sac to which economic theory offers no solution. His problem is to guess how much he can appropriately gamble on the acquisition of knowledge, even though he may be unable to judge the value of the knowledge in advance. Confronted with this dilemma, many producers simply do not act for long periods of time.

In many instances, the multinational firm overcomes the problem. With its own subsidiaries in Argentina and in Japan, it can provide the information that is needed with little risk and low cost. The Argentine subsidiary receives through its affiliates the quality standards, specifications, packaging requirements, and delivery schedules that are required for Japan. And the Japanese subsidiary takes over the distribution task once delivery is made from Argentina.

Factors such as ignorance of market opportunities may have an important impact on trade patterns, but they are not yet systematically handled by theory. Nevertheless, trade theory does have much to offer the manager in the international economy. It permits him to organize and classify some of his problems in systematic ways and to isolate and define many of the questions that demand an answer. It offers him a glimpse of how governments think and react and of the kinds of considerations to which governments might be responsive.

SUGGESTED READING

BHAGWATI, JAGDISH, "The Pure Theory of International Trade: A Survey," *Economic Journal,* March 1964.

TILTON, JOHN E., "Choice of Trading Partners: An Analysis of International Trade in Aluminum, Bauxite, Copper, Lead, Manganese, Tin, and Zinc," *Yale Economic Essays,* Fall 1966.

VERNON, RAYMOND, "International Investment and International Trade in the Product Cycle," *Quarterly Journal of Economics,* February 1967.

VERNON, RAYMOND, "The Location of Economic Activity," in John H. Dunning (ed.), *Economic Analysis and the Multinational Enterprise* (London: Allen & Unwin, 1974).

WELLS, LOUIS T., JR., (ed.), *The Product Life Cycle and International Trade* (Boston: Division of Research, Harvard Business School, 1972).

Intergovernmental

Agreements

on International Trade

chapter twelve

Nations have a habit of imposing such restrictions on trade as their own national interests seem to require, without much regard for the effects of such restrictions on others. When shortages exist, exports of scarce items are commonly restricted; when surpluses develop, imports of overabundant items are often curtailed. However, the disregard of nations for outsider interests is not total. Through painful experience, nations have learned that unilateral action harmful to another's interests can provoke retaliation that can more than cancel out the seeming gains of the triggering action. As a result, many nations have subscribed to intergovernmental agreements in the field of international trade, even though the agreements have set limits on their freedom of action.

MAIN TRENDS

Intergovernmental agreements in the field of trade surely go back as far as governments and trade. The tradition, principles, and convictions that affect nations in the negotiation of such agreements generally are fairly strong. This is a field, therefore, in which the manager with a sense of history may have an advantage in predicting governmental behavior.

To gain a historical perspective, it is enough to go back to the late eighteenth or early nineteenth century, when nations began to accept and articulate the view that international trade could be what game theorists now call a "plus-sum game," that is, an international exchange from which both parties could gain something. Once that concept was accepted, nations set about trying to develop an international system in which trade would not be blocked by uncooperative action. In the nineteenth century, a number of different patterns developed. One pattern, exemplified from time to time by Great Britain, was for a nation simply to eliminate import restrictions without regard to the action of its trading partners.

Most countries were more cautious, however. The policy of the United States, committed to the Hamiltonian principle of protecting its infant industries, was to enter into a series of bilateral agreements with other countries requiring the selective reduction of import barriers. In the U.S. agreements, each country bound itself not to apply tariff rates in excess of a stated amount on the importation of specified products from the other party. The products on which one party bound its tariff rates were not necessarily the same as those on which the other party undertook commitments. Commitments on both sides simply had to be "equal" or "reciprocal" in effect.

In time, however, nations found that attempting to apply different tariff rates to a given product coming from different sources was administratively difficult and politically irritating. By the 1920s the principle of nondiscrimination had come to be regarded as the "normal" rule of trade relations; under this principle, a single tariff rate applied to the importation of any product, irrespective of its source. At the same time, however, certain deviations from nondiscrimination were beginning to be generally accepted. Mother countries, for instance, could continue to receive and extend preferential treatment in trade with their colonies. Isolated frontier areas of a particular country could trade freely with neighboring countries, granting and receiving duty-free treatment for their goods. But the most important exceptions struggling for international acceptance were those in which a number of countries, acting as a group, sought the right to grant preferences systematically to one another without granting the same preferences to third parties.

The details of the efforts in the period before World War II are of no particular importance today. It is enough to know that some kinds of preferential arrangements were looked on by outside countries with a greater degree of tolerance than others. Arrangements that were nonselective with regard to different products, for instance, were looked on with less disfavor by outsiders than those that were selective by products. Accordingly, agreements among a group of countries to form a customs union or a free trade area by eliminating all restrictions on trade among their members were generally accepted by outsiders. The Imperial Preference System, on the other hand, was wholly unpalatable, because the preferences extended by the United Kingdom to others in the system and the preferences extended by the others to the United Kingdom seemed to have been carefully selected, product by product.

After World War II, unremitting efforts were made to reconcile the widespread desire for nondiscrimination with the equally pervasive urge for preferences. By the mid 1970s these efforts still had not been fully harmonized. One can gain a sense of the nature of the conflict by considering the characteristics of two groups of postwar institutions: (1) global trade agreements, and (2) preferential and regional trade agreements.

GLOBAL TRADE AGREEMENTS

By the 1920s, the dominant view of economists in the developed portions of the world was that open nondiscriminatory trading among nations was the most desirable of global trade regimes. In accordance with comparative advantage analysis, all nations gained from trade, although some gained more than others. Discriminatory tariff barriers interfered with a global trading system more than did nondiscriminatory duties.

Despite this widespread conviction, every restrictive and discriminatory trade device known to man was tried by some country or another during the 1930s. In this period, the use of the bilateral payments agreement described in Chapter 10 and its related discriminatory trade arrangements came into flower. The experience of nations with arrangements of this sort since the 1930s is especially interesting to the manager of the 1970s because of the threatened revival of such arrangements on a large scale.

The countries that entered into *bilateral balancing* agreements were trying to ensure that trade between them over a given period of time would be kept approximately in balance, so that the payment of scarce gold or convertible currencies could be avoided. To keep such trade in balance, the governments involved were usually prepared to administer their import controls on a discriminatory basis, that is, to hold down imports from the countries with which they had no bilateral trade and payment agreements to the extent necessary to make place for imports from agreement countries.

But the efforts of any country to apply bilateral balancing on a large scale usually set up tremendous tensions inside its economy. Enterprises in the country were obliged to buy from designated sources that were more costly and less reliable than the sources they preferred, and were forced to sell in markets that were less profitable or less promising than those they would have chosen. As a result, in countries with market economies, the pressure for more open and less discriminatory systems of international trade usually built up very rapidly.

Besides, there is a well-known argument against bilateral balancing that commands considerable respect in official and technical circles. Bilateral balancing, according to the argument, results in less international trade than global balancing. By *global balancing,* we mean a system of trade by which each country balances its total imports and exports but does not necessarily balance its imports and exports with each trading partner.

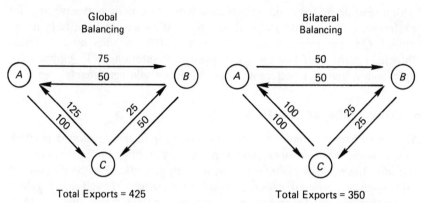

FIG. 12–1   Global Balancing and Bilateral Balancing in International Trade

Figure 12–1, using the case of countries A, B, and C, demonstrates the superiority of global balancing. In the global balancing case, each country's aggregate exports to the other two equals its aggregate imports from the other two; but there is no requirement that the trade of any pair of countries be in balance. In the bilateral balancing case, each country restricts its imports from any partner wherever those imports would otherwise exceed its exports to that partner; so each pair is in balance. Observe that the total trade under global balancing is higher than that under bilateral balancing.

The system of international trade and payments created after World War II was aimed at achieving an open trading world in which the remaining barriers were generally moderate and nondiscriminatory in character. The General Agreement on Tariffs and Trade (GATT), although originally regarded as a temporary, stopgap entity, proved a critical building block in the structure.

Although GATT commenced operations in 1948 with only nineteen member countries, by the early 1970s its membership of about ninety countries included most of the important trading nations outside the Communist world and one or two within. With considerable particularity, the agreement lays down rules aimed at four goals:

1. A reduction in import restrictions, including a gradual reduction in existing tariffs and the ultimate elimination of import-licensing restraints.
2. The adoption of the principle of nondiscrimination by each member country in applying its trade restrictions to the commerce of each other member country.
3. The settlement of trade disputes.
4. The grant of waivers from any GATT commitment upon the basis of an international consensus.

Tariffs have been reduced through a series of giant bargaining sessions arranged under GATT's general aegis. There were six such sessions between 1947 and 1967, and a seventh was in process in the mid-1970s. In each, a complex bargaining process was applied that eventually culminated in a schedule of commitments on tariff rates. The cumulative effect of these negotiations was to reduce the world's tariff levels to a fraction—perhaps one third or one fourth—of what they had been at the end of World War II. Despite the anarchistic trends in international trade that were beginning to appear in the mid-1970s, efforts to bring down tariff rates even further through GATT-sponsored negotiations were still going strongly ahead.

GATT's work in the reduction of import restrictions has been directed not only at tariffs but also at import licensing. The GATT rules on import licensing are quite complex. They begin with the general principle that all restrictive import licensing should be eliminated, but they give wide latitude to countries that are in balance-of-payment difficulties; they take cognizance of the special case of agriculture wherever countries have some domestic scheme to protect their farmers; and they give what amounts to a free hand to the less-developed countries of the world in protecting their infant industries. In effect, therefore, the commitments on import licensing apply principally to the nonagricultural trade of advanced countries, and only for as long as such countries have adequate foreign exchange resources.

Still, the GATT regulations have had obvious effects. By the mid-1960s, the advanced countries had largely dismantled the extensive system of import-licensing restrictions on nonagricultural products that had been instituted in the period immediately following World War II; and although the general system seemed to be losing some of its vitality in the mid-1970s, the licensing of nonagricultural imports had not yet reappeared on a wide scale in the industrialized countries.

The provisions of GATT cover many other subjects besides tariffs and import licensing. They lay down rules on the use of export subsidies and the use of countervailing import duties, that is, duties intended to offset export subsidies. They also prescribe rules and procedures applicable to the use of antidumping import duties, that is, duties intended to offset dumping by foreign suppliers. And so on.

One glaring inadequacy of GATT's rules, as the events of the 1970s were to underline, was its failure to lay down any effective standards on the use of export restrictions. As the extraordinary shortages of 1973 and 1974 surfaced, the prevailing rule proved to be every-man-for-himself. In the field of agriculture, that policy was simply a continuation of the habits of past operations. But as the pattern spread to other basic materials and to industrial products, it soon became clear that the existing structure of intergovernmental agreements had left a major area of potential friction practically uncovered. The point became even more apparent as groups of exporting countries formed selling cartels, aimed at extracting the highest possible prices from buyers. These government-organized cartels among exporting countries appeared during the early 1970s not only in oil, but also in copper, bananas, bauxite, sugar, and various other products. In the mid-1970s, the general direction of future international policies in this field was not clear.

GATT's practices in the settlement of disputes and its grants of waivers from GATT rules have been powerful influences in shaping the world trading system. Before the era of GATT, there was simply no way in which trade deadlocks between any two countries could be resolved. If the parties disagreed on the facts, the disagreement remained; if the interpretation of an agreement was at the bottom of a dispute, it produced an impasse. GATT procedures cut through these Gordian knots by various techniques of interpretation and conciliation. The GATT practice was to convene a group of experts who would receive complaints from any aggrieved country, establish the facts in the case, assess rights and wrongs in light of the GATT provisions, and suggest a way out of the dispute.

The waiver procedures of GATT represent one more device—the device of last resort—for modifying the willful exercise of national power in the trade field. From time to time, nations have applied for waivers of various GATT provisions in order to legitimate a breach of the rules. Waivers have been required to permit the discriminatory trade provisions of various regional arrangements such as the European Coal and Steel Community, to allow the United States and other countries to maintain some of their otherwise illegal restrictions on imports of agricultural products, to permit the continuation of assorted restrictions of industrial imports by various nations, and so on. In each case, the waiver has been wrapped about with conditions, restraints, and time limitations, as the individual countries have been nudged persistently toward greater conformity to the rules.

In appraising the future role of GATT, it should not be assumed that the old objectives of nondiscrimination and an open trading system will continue to represent the principal aims of the organization. In the mid-1970s, the great majority of GATT's members, like the majority of members in most global institutions, consisted of less-developed countries. Even in earlier years, when the influence of such countries was not so strong, special allowance was made for their problems in the implementing of GATT's principles. As these countries came to dominate the organization, however, the fundamental assumption that nondiscrimination and an open trading system were the ultimate aims of an international trade order were questioned more and more. Numerous difficult issues began to be raised. What should be the "normal" state of commercial policy in a less-developed nation? Should the advanced countries grant more favorable treatment to the products of less-developed nations than they were obliged to grant to like products from other advanced countries?

As time went on, the less-developed countries focused more and more on the objective of securing preferential tariff rates from the advanced countries. Like so many other proposals to assist the less-developed countries, the preferential tariff proposal originated in the early 1960s in the first general meeting of the United Nations Conference on Trade and Development (UNCTAD). By the mid-1970s, real progress had been made toward reaching the goal. Many industrial exports from the less-developed countries were being admitted into the markets of the advanced countries on a preferential basis, at very low duties or entirely free of duty. In each advanced country, the system of preferences included numerous exceptions and escape clauses intended to make the approach less unpalatable to particular political interests. Still, managers commonly discovered that products such as bulk chemicals or household furniture manufactured in less-developed countries had access to the markets of the advanced countries at preferential rates.

Apart from the increase in the less-developed countries among the members of GATT, there has also been an increase in the number of state trading members, that is, countries that normally conduct their foreign trade through government trading agencies; Burma, Poland, and Egypt are included in the membership, for instance. Their presence has led to another set of fundamental queries. How does one reconcile trading systems based upon the decentralized acts of individual enterprises with trading systems based upon the centralized business decisions of governments? In systems based upon the existence of widespread state trading monopolies, what is the counterpart of such concepts as discrimination, high tariffs, and import licenses? It was by no means certain how basic questions of this type would be answered. At the same time, it was evident that the form of these answers was of the utmost importance to the future structure of world trade.

REGIONAL TRADING AREAS

Despite the global framework offered by GATT, one finds many intergovernmental arrangements that are regional in scope and that appear to be pulling in a very different direction. The forces responsible for the creation of these arrangements need to be well understood if the manager is to be able to appraise their durability and the likelihood that others may come into being.

Over the past hundred years and more, nations wanting the benefits of more trade or of a larger and more open economic society have found it easier and more natural to explore the possibility with a few close neighbors than to raise the issue in a global forum; the desire to generate the benefits of more international trade, therefore, has sometimes led to the creation of discriminatory regional trade groups. But other motives have sometimes been behind such projects. At times, for instance, a group of countries has felt the need to pool their economic strength and bargaining power against one or more outsiders.

The famous German Zollverein, forerunner of modern Germany, contained all these elements. Fearful of the strength of Russia and France, joined by a common language, and guided by the dominant hand of Prussia, the German states found it relatively easy to form a customs union. The British Imperial Preference System, which came to fruition in 1932 after years of piecemeal development, also contained the necessary elements: the leadership of Britain, the common ties of language and trade, and the common disappointment of its members with the failures of global economic efforts during the period of the Depression.

When GATT was created in 1948, its adoption implied that nations were prepared to abandon their persistent efforts toward the creation of regional trading groups in favor of global organizations. But this was not the case. The European economic integration movements after World War II included many of the leading members of GATT. The strength of propinquity was still powerful. Besides, there was a latent sense in Europe of the need to pool political power to be able to confront the Soviet Union and the United States.

Among the less-developed countries, too, the 1950s and 1960s generated dozens of projects and proposals for regional arrangements. A Central American Common Market, composed of five countries, took form; a Latin American Free Trade Area (LAFTA), eventually comprising eleven countries from Argentina to Mexico, came into being. The Andean Group, composed of five (later six) members of LAFTA, pushed ahead with their own special set of arrangements under the larger umbrella of LAFTA. Numerous groupings, many of them overlapping and inconsistent, were proposed for the African states, the Middle East, and Asia.

The arguments for and against these preferential arrangements have been widely ventilated. It is recognized that such groupings build up trade among themselves partly by the process of trade diversion, that is, by the members' redirecting their imports from outside sources that may be efficient producers to inside sources that may be only second best. At the same time, however, such groupings also create international trade that otherwise would not exist by reducing the protection that their home industry has enjoyed, at least to the extent of allowing the producers in other member countries of the preferential area to compete against their home industry.

The effects of customs unions and other preferential arrangements, however, are much more profound than the simple trade-diversion, trade-creation possibilities usually discussed. Preferential areas, when suitably designed, can sometimes reduce the internal price levels of their members and stimulate internal consumption. Even wider implications are opened up if one introduces the possibility of economies of scale, whether they are economies of the individual plant or "external economies," derived from the clustering of mutually helpful economic activities. One small country, perhaps, cannot provide a sufficient market to sustain a steel mill of effective size; but several small countries, all pledged to buy from one another initially on a preferential basis, may collectively provide the market necessary to support a steel mill of reasonable efficiency. On similar lines, one small country may not be able to provide enough market to justify the cluster of interrelated facilities that are needed directly or indirectly to sustain a modern automobile-producing complex, but several such countries can jointly provide the necessary market.

Another factor that has pushed some groups of countries toward large economic groupings has been the problem of domestic monopolies. Developing countries that have large enough internal markets to sustain a plant or two in a given industry may succeed in substituting local production for imports; but they may find (indeed, they commonly have found) that the local market has fallen under monopoly control.

The economic consequences of a monopoly are exceedingly complex. A monopolist will almost certainly charge comparatively high prices for his product. And he may be less concerned with cost reduction or with innovation than a group of competing firms would be. On the other hand, not all the consequences of monopoly are adverse to economic development. Monopolists may save and reinvest, for instance, at a higher rate than that of a group of competitive enterprises. But for a government that prefers to avoid the adverse consequences of a monopoly, a customs union or a free trade area may be an attractive way out.

The most important force that has been pressing nations toward wider economic arrangements may be a desire to avoid the risks that go with a heavy reliance on foreign trade. Small countries cannot afford to isolate themselves from the effects of world trade for fear of losing its benefits. At the same time, however, small countries are fearful of the risks that go with heavy reliance on outside markets. Preferential trading arrangements seem to offer an answer; guarantees may not be exchanged with the world at large, but at least they are exchanged with a larger group. The trade advantages associated with the arrangement may not be as great as the hypothetical advantages of a global free-trade system, but in a world of the second best they often seem an adequate compromise.

It is one thing to analyze the theoretical basis of regional trade arrangements; it is quite another to examine such arrangements in their day-to-day detail. One such arrangement is of particular importance—the European Economic Community.

THE EUROPEAN ECONOMIC COMMUNITY

The European Economic Community (EEC) is by far the largest of the world's regional trading arrangements and the archtype of modern economic unions. Its institutional organization contains the usual branches of government—executive, quasi-legislative, and judicial. Its mandates run the full gamut of the economic life of its members, including undertakings in the fields of trade, capital, labor, monetary policy, and fiscal affairs. The commitments of the treaty that created it (the Treaty of Rome signed in March 1957) run deep, going to the heart of the economic sovereignty of its participants.

BACKGROUND.   The original version of the treaty created a common market among six members, France, Germany, Italy, Belgium, Holland, and Luxembourg. Over a transitional period of about fifteen years that began in 1959, the following major steps were taken:

1. Customs duties and licensing restrictions affecting the movement of goods and the sale of services among the original six members were eliminated, and a common tariff was applied to imports from the outside world.

2. Obstacles to the free movement of labor among the six were virtually abolished.

3. Obstacles to the movement of business capital were greatly reduced.

4. The national policies of the various countries relating to the protection of agriculture were supplanted by a common community-wide system of pricing, subsidies, and controls.

5. An impressive start was made on the complicated business of merging the transportation policies of the member countries in order eventually to obliterate national distinctions and national discriminations in the use of rails, roads, and waterways.

6. A European Investment Bank and a European Social Fund were put in operation to help workers and employers deal with the economic dislocations and structural adjustments that are always involved when a modern economy sets about changing its industrial structure.

7. A strong economic link was created with less-developed overseas countries that had been related to one or another of the EEC's members (mostly French and Belgian ex-colonies). This link gave these countries favored access to the EEC's markets and set up an extensive system of development assistance for them.

Then, in 1972, the EEC was enlarged from six to nine countries, adding even more to its scope and reach.

Despite these nearly incredible achievements, all undertaken within an action-packed period of about fifteen years, it was not at all clear in the mid-1970s where the European community concept was headed. Were the various arrangements nothing more than a series of ad hoc measures, to be applied function by function, that in the end would still leave each country free to pursue its own vital national interests in international politics and national defense? Or were these measures part of a half-deliberate process of national self-entrapment, aimed in the end at producing a new federal state in Europe?

The prevailing opinion of most Europeans in the mid-1970s was that the EEC arrangements were of only limited functional significance, a series of agreements that left the essential elements of national sovereignty largely unimpaired. The record of the community institutions themselves in the first half of the 1970s seemed to be consistent with that general judgment. Despite that fact, numerous public opinion polls kept affirming the fact that a majority of Europeans thought themselves quite prepared to accept a federal Europe, even if that meant being governed by Europeans of other nationalities. At the same time, however, there were still the signs of deep-seated national attitudes that had a way of surfacing at critical times. Surveys of French opinion still displayed a mistrust of the motives of other nations and an unwillingness to reduce greatly the concept of France as a nation; surveys of German opinion indicated a lack of confidence in the future economic course of the German state, despite its brilliant postwar performance, as well as a desire for continuing close political ties with countries outside the EEC, surveys of Dutch opinion indicated a deep uneasiness over being locked into a political system dominated by Germany and France; and in Britain's case, public mistrust and disaffection toward the European community idea were high.

To place the reader's feet somewhat more solidly on the ground as he confronts this amorphous bundle of prospects, it will be helpful to master a few more details on the achievements of the EEC as well as to identify some of the items on its agenda of unfinished business.

ELIMINATION OF TARIFFS. By the mid-1970s, the elimination of tariffs among the original six members of the EEC had long been completed and the tariffs that were still applied by the three new members were being reduced on schedule. True, the passage of goods between, say, Italy and France was not quite so simple as a movement between New Jersey and New York or between Wales and England. Customs officials still demanded documents attesting to the origin of the goods or collected border taxes that reflected the incomplete and imperfect harmonization of the various nations' internal tax systems. But for the businessman who was bent on marketing his goods in the EEC as if it were a simple national market, these were generally minor annoyances, not major obstacles.

At the outer perimeters of the EEC, confronting the products of other countries, was the EEC's common external tariff. The development by the EEC of a common tariff had not been achieved without a considerable amount of agitation from outside countries. For instance, Austrian steel exporters began to find that their long-established markets in southeast Germany were now being challenged by Italian exporters. Whereas the

Austrians were obliged to pay the EEC duty, the Italians could export to Germany duty free. Numerous other examples of this sort, representing apparent trade diversion, were complained of by exporters in the United States, Sweden, Switzerland, and other areas.

Despite the agitation, exports by outsiders to EEC countries did not decline in the 1960s. On the contrary, the countries outside the EEC increased their exports to that area by larger percentages than they increased their exports to one another. However, EEC members increased their trade with one another even more than with outsiders.

DEVELOPMENT OF AGRICULTURAL POLICY. Title II of the Treaty of Rome consists of ten important articles enunciating the principles for the creation of a common market in agriculture. The regime contemplated by the treaty aims at eliminating all national restraints to the movement of agricultural products in the area. The object is not one of laissez-faire, however. The aim is to stabilize markets, to guarantee regular supplies, and to ensure reasonable prices inside the EEC. To that end, a common agricultural policy is imposed on a community-wide basis, including a system of minimum price guarantees, production and import controls, production and export subsidies, and all the other devices that commonly form a part of the agricultural policies of modern states. By the early 1970s, the program had been fully articulated and put in effect. Yet, in some respects, it was beginning to show signs of unraveling.

Within the EEC area itself there had always been a certain amount of trade across national boundaries in agricultural products. France in particular had exported substantial quantities of wheat and coarse grains to Germany, and the Benelux countries and Germany had exchanged significant quantities of the same products. Much more important, however, were the imports of wheat and coarse grains from Canada, the United States, Australia, and Argentina, which were measured in billions of dollars. Only France had managed to avoid a heavy dependence on imports from those outside areas.

From a political point of view, agriculture was a touchy subject throughout the EEC and promised to remain so through the 1970s. Partly as a result of rapid productivity increases, farm populations were declining; but they still represented a formidable part of the electorate, constituting over 10 per cent of the total population. Despite rapid increases in productivity, much of the agriculture of Europe was a high-cost activity, unlikely to survive for long without heavy protection. This was less true for dairy products than for cereals, and less true for French wheat and coarse grains than for German and Italian production of these products. Still, a real problem existed.

In the circumstances, each country in the EEC that had an agricultural surplus for export tried to find a way of displacing some of the outside suppliers to the European market; the French had a surplus in wheat, the Italians in citrus fruits, and so on. In short, the object of the exporting country was trade diversion.

To achieve the large-scale trade diversion that the EEC members sought, a complex system of protection was put in place for wheat and coarse grains, aimed at ensuring that outside suppliers could not undersell EEC producers in EEC markets. A key device in the protection system was an agreed target price for domestic producers of each commodity, a figure that would theoretically represent a "fair return" to relatively efficient producers in the EEC. To maintain that price, an internal price-support mechanism was developed. A buying authority intervenes in the domestic market with purchases or sales to keep the price close to target; if the price nevertheless falls to a rock-bottom support level—an agreed-upon level, say, 5 to 10 per cent below the target—the price is pegged at that level.

The measures governing agricultural imports were designed to prevent outsiders from offering their products in the EEC market at prices lower than the internal target price. A variable levy was applied to imports, a levy that was calculated to add just enough to world prices to raise them to the internal target price. When world prices fell, the levy was increased; when world prices rose, the levy was reduced; when they rose above the EEC's internal price, as happened from time to time in the early 1970s, the levy was suspended.

The methods described above do not, of course, apply to all agricultural commodities; other methods are also used. For instance, products that were produced from feed grains, such as eggs, pork, and poultry, were safeguarded by formulas that took cognizance of the high prices of feed grains inside the EEC. Producers in the area, obliged to buy at the elevated EEC prices, were protected from outside competition in their final products by enough margin to offset the cheaper feed grains available outside the EEC area.

Variable levy systems such as those of the EEC generate considerable quantities of revenue. Much of the revenue has been used to subsidize the export to various markets outside the EEC of agreed-upon quantities of high-priced agricultural products. Since the exporters concerned are principally in France, French producers have received the lion's share of the funds, even though the bulk of the imports by which the funds were generated has been consumed in Germany.

A vital flaw in these arrangements was beginning to be evident by the latter 1960s, however. It stemmed from the fact that prices in the system had to be set on a common basis which guaranteed farmers in the different countries more or less the same price for their product. That was not difficult to do, as long as the deutschemark, franc, lira, pound, and the other currencies of the EEC retained some fixed and unvarying relationship with one another. But what to do when the deutschemark, for instance, was revalued in relation to the franc? When that happened, the only way to restore a single price inside the EEC was to pay the German farmer fewer deutschemarks or the French farmer more francs, or both. But sporadic adjustments of that sort, it was soon discovered, were grossly upsetting to the system. Various kinds of shock-absorbing devices had to be invented, so that the full impact of the price changes could be spread over longer periods of time. The abandonment during the early 1970s of any pretense at maintaining fixed exchange rates among all the members of the EEC in one sense mitigated the problem; frequent changes in such rates meant frequent adjustments in national prices; the shock of large, step-like changes was accordingly reduced. But the unity of the program seemed to be under heavy pressure, and it was unclear how long the program could be maintained in its existing form.

OTHER INTEGRATION ACHIEVEMENTS.   The goal of the EEC as elaborated in the Treaty of Rome was to achieve much more than a customs union, that is, much more than the elimination of internal tariffs and the application of a common external tariff. The goal was full economic union —the generation of a united internal market in which the national boundaries of the member states would lose their economic meaning. Not only goods but a great many other things would move freely across national boundaries. That concept required among other things that labor and capital should move freely.

Free labor movement inside the EEC has been made possible by various measures. The general limitations that would normally apply to foreign workers, such as quota limitations, exclusions from certain industries, and exclusions from certain areas, have been lifted for EEC nationals. Once in possession of a job, these foreign workers are entitled to nondiscriminatory treatment in such matters as pay scales, fringe benefits, housing facilities, and so on. Although national retirement systems and other national social mechanisms are not organically integrated, the problems that national differences would create are dealt with systematically; frontier workers, in particular, are offered a set of well-defined rights that make it possible for them to live on one side of the border and work on the other side without penalties.

It is hard to distinguish the effects of these measures from other forces that added to labor mobility in Europe during the early 1960s. Migration out of southern Italy into Belgium and Germany, for instance, would almost certainly have been great in any case. But there did seem to be some especially marked labor responses that were attributable to the new regime. For instance, the member governments began to find that, if they attempted to hold down wages inside their own borders, many workers near the frontiers simply took up jobs in neighboring countries and commuted to work across the border. The national unions in Europe were beginning to discover a related phenomenon. It grew clear to many unions that bargaining on a national basis had distinct risks. If a manager faced especially high wages in one country of the EEC, he might well decide to relocate some of his existing production—or more likely to place some of his added production—in another country of the EEC.

Not only had the EEC eliminated many of the restraints on labor's movement by the mid-1970s; it also had eliminated many of the restraints that barred professionals and service industries from pursuing their callings in other countries of the EEC. A steady stream of directives was gradually widening the rights of doctors, lawyers, accountants, banks, and consulting firms to conduct their business outside their home country.

The steps taken by the EEC to facilitate capital movements seem to have been as significant as those in the field of labor and the professions. By the early 1970s, enterprises in the EEC were free to move capital across national boundaries in order to establish subsidiaries in other EEC countries. Considerable freedom also existed for transactions on securities exchanges and for capital transactions in connection with the financing of trade or the movement of labor. Business firms were free to borrow or loan for business purposes across national boundaries. In fact, the only type of capital movements for which tight controls were still legitimate was the kind that might represent flight from a weak currency area in the community or an effort to profit from short-run interest-rate differentials.

Reinforcing the measures to free the movement of capital and labor have been measures to prevent firms in the EEC from carving up national markets by agreement. The EEC has instituted a vigorous program against restrictive business practices that affect the movement of goods inside the EEC. The program is described more fully in Chapter 13.

Finally, as a sign of the possibility that European sovereignty might yet develop by accretion, the EEC was assigned sources of revenue in its own right. According to an agreed timetable that extended through much of the 1970s, the EEC became the direct recipient of an increasing proportion of the proceeds from all import duties and agricultural levies collected in the member countries. It was anticipated that by the end of the 1970s all the duties and levies collected at the perimeter of the EEC would be at the EEC's disposal, as well as a small share of the revenues raised through national value-added taxes.

UNFINISHED BUSINESS.   A recital such as this, listing the dazzling achievements of the EEC, may leave the reader with the impression that an economic union had in fact been as good as achieved. But that impression would be erroneous. The role of the state is so extensive and pervasive in the modern era that, despite the EEC's accomplishments, national boundaries inside the common market still have enormous economic significance.

One area of unfinished business is that of monetary policy. In the early

1970s, each country of the EEC was still maintaining a separate system, with separate central banks, credit policies, and foreign exchange reserves. The implications for disruption arising out of that separateness were demonstrated several times: by the revaluation of the deutschemark and the guilder in 1960, by the second revaluation of the deutschemark in 1968 and the devaluation of the French franc in 1969, by the third deutschemark crisis in the spring of 1971, and by the dollar crisis in the summer of that year. Clearly, a closer linkage of the monetary systems of the member countries was needed. But the road to effective linkage was fairly long and tortuous, one that in the best of circumstances would require eight or ten more years to traverse.

Early in 1971 it appeared that some key agreements had been reached providing for a number of preliminary steps toward monetary merger. One was an undertaking among the member countries to limit variations in the exchange rates existing among their various currencies even more narrowly than their International Monetary Fund commitments required. Another was the decision to develop a common mechanism for joint intervention by the various governments in their foreign exchange markets. An earlier undertaking of the members to provide $2 billion of 90-day money to any member country in order to help the member stabilize its currency would be augmented by another $2 billion of available credit, on terms of up to five years. By 1975, according to the plan, a decision would be made on whether to move to a merger of foreign exchange reserves and to a single credit policy.

These agreements, however, were overwhelmed by the money crises that kept erupting after 1971. When the United States separated the dollar from gold in 1971, the EEC countries found it difficult to generate a common response. Whereas the Germans and the Dutch preferred to let the foreign exchange market determine the price of their respective currencies in relation to the dollar, the French and the Belgians were much more reluctant to do so. Yet any failure to follow a common policy would break the price relationships among the EEC currencies.

An uneasy compromise was reached in 1972, but it could not last for very long. At the time when the new commitment was first taken, in March 1972, the United States and the major European countries had already agreed to keep their exchange rates from straying more than 2¼ per cent on either side of the then-existing relation to the dollar. To emphasize Europe's special monetary ties, the major European countries agreed to link their own currencies even more tightly, by a 1⅛ per cent variation in either direction. The currencies that made up the European group were seen as a snake moving within a wider tunnel.

For a time, therefore, the currencies of these European countries were linked closely to one another. But the pound sterling and the Italian lira proved too weak, and the deutschemark and the guilder proved too strong, to allow the relationship to last. If the currencies were to be held at a common level, the Germans and the Dutch would have to be willing to buy and hold vast quantities of sterling and lire. By early 1974, the lira and sterling had floated away from the snake, to be followed soon after by the French franc. By 1975, the franc had rejoined; but the tenuousness of the tie cast a shadow on EEC efforts at cooperation in the monetary field.

Some of the objectives of agreement on the monetary front required agreement on the fiscal front as well; greatly different tax structures can produce different economic conditions, a situation disturbing to the common market concept. Already by the 1970s, the member countries had agreed to harmonize their tax structures and had set up a timetable for the adoption of the value-added tax in all countries. But there was much more to do before differences in tax structure ceased to be a problem inside the EEC.

Even if the tax problems could be mastered, however, there were other problems still to be met, for example, the question of policies toward state-owned enterprises. Remember that some of the countries of Western Europe have a large state-owned industrial sector. The French government owns railroads, electric power systems, and international oil companies; the Italian government, operating through its Instituto per la Ricostruzione Industriale (IRI), owns enterprises over an even wider range of business activities. One unfinished task of the EEC was to ensure that this motley but powerful group of enterprises derived no special rights from their public status that interfered with the idea of a common market.

Just as formidable was the job of creating a common "industrial policy," an ambiguous phrase that covered various relationships of enterprises with their respective national governments. As matters stood in the mid 1970s, each member state independently promulgated and administered its laws and regulations that governed the creation and operation of enterprises within its national boundaries. At times, these national provisions created formidable obstacles to the operation of a common market. For example, the laws of some member states had the effect of imposing a prohibitive tax on enterprises that were being absorbed by merger, provided one of the parties to the merger was a foreign corporation. In other cases, mergers that involved a foreign corporation could only be effected by the actual liquidation of one entity and the sale of its assets to the other. The need in effect to disclose the actual assets of the liquidating enterprise meant that hidden reserves and undeclared profits of prior years were forced to the surface, thereby generating prohibitive tax liabilities.

Worse still, some nations exercised their national authority by simply refusing to grant permission for some proposed mergers. Unlike the situation in the United States, where obstacles of this sort could eventually be struck down by federal legislation or by decisions of the federal courts, the EEC had not yet acquired the powers to dispose of such obstacles. Although such provisions were not always discriminatory in form against transnational mergers or other transnational initiatives in the EEC, they nevertheless had an especially strong impact in curbing the kind of industrial initiative that the opening of the EEC's markets had stimulated.

Other problems suggestive of the vestigial strength of national jurisdictions also were in evidence. For instance, each nation still maintained its own national patent and trademark system, under which each was in a position to grant legal monopolies applicable to its own territory. In effect, the power to issue national patents gave a continued importance to national boundaries that was inconsistent with the general theory of the EEC. In the mid 1960s, the problem seemed on the way to being solved—or in any event diluted in its impact. The emerging system is described in Chapter 13.

Of all the functions in which the personality of the EEC was underdeveloped, the conduct of foreign affairs was perhaps the most obvious. It goes without saying that the EEC had no powers in matters of national defense. But even in questions of foreign economic policy, the EEC's role was limited. To be sure, the EEC played a major role in tariff negotiations sponsored by the GATT. But in general, the tendency of member countries to deal with outsiders on an independent basis still persisted, even on subjects in which member countries had lost much of their independent freedom of action.

In several ways, events of the mid-1970s seemed to be developing conditions in which the durability of the EEC would be effectively tested. First, the agricultural program, a keystone in the EEC structure, seemed in the process of unravelling. Second, perhaps even more vital, the European nations were building up large quantities of highly volatile funds in the hands of the oil-exporting countries, funds so large as to require some kind of tightly coordinated policy among the monetary authorities of the European states. Whether these threats to the stability of the EEC would be effectively met was not yet clear.

RELATIONS WITH OVERSEAS ASSOCIATED COUNTRIES.   There was one area, however, in which the countries of the EEC acted as a group in their dealings with outside countries. This was in the fashioning of a complex group of ties with forty-six less-developed countries, consisting primarily of the former colonies of member countries.

The basic instrument linking the EEC to the developing countries in the mid-1970s was the Lomé Convention, a five-year undertaking covering various matters of trade and aid.

The trading regime linking the associated overseas states to the EEC is extensive and complex. In principle, the distinctive position of the former mother country has been obliterated, to be replaced by a new relationship in which all the EEC countries shared. The EEC countries, for instance, grant the overseas territories all the trading advantages that they are committed to extend to one another, including the duty-free entry of the overseas areas' exports. Moreover, the EEC has fixed a common external tariff on critical tropical items, such as coffee and bananas, to be applied to exporters other than the associated overseas states. On top of that, the European Development Fund, set up out of contributions by the member states of the EEC, promotes "social" and economic projects, technical assistance programs, and agricultural diversification programs in the forty-six developing countries. These agreements, taken as a whole, represent an attractive bargain for the developing countries, which has served to maintain some economic and cultural ties with their former mother countries.

LATIN AMERICAN INTEGRATION MOVEMENTS

ORIGIN.   Just as the EEC is the archetype of economic unions among the developed nations, so the Latin American integration projects hold a like position among the less-developed countries. These projects constitute a much looser and more disjointed bundle of initiatives than those in Europe. Figure 12–2 is intended to help the reader see some of the interrelationships among the main institutions and projects.

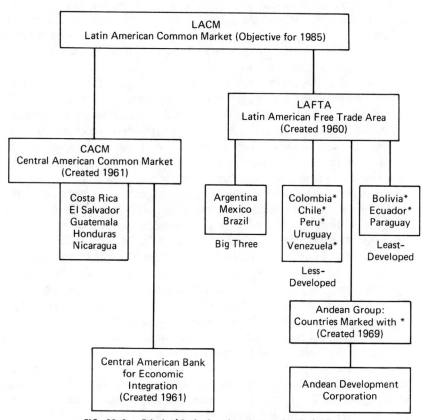

FIG. 12–2   Principal Latin American Integration Projects

The Latin American process of regionalization is similar to that of the EEC in some respects. Just as the EEC had been conceived partly as an exercise in countervailing power against the United States and the Soviet bloc, so Latin America drew its inspiration partly out of the fear of European and United States power. The Latin American response, like that of the EEC, has taken an economic form. The objective has been to achieve a widened market sufficiently large in scale to be capable of developing a modern industrial base. There, however, the similarities between the EEC and the Latin American case end. Both the historical background and the present-day circumstances of Latin America have led to a different set of emphases from those in the European organization.

THE TRADE REGIME. It was inevitable that the larger countries of Latin America should approach any proposals for a free trade area with a certain degree of reserve. In the 1950s, all these countries had been fully engaged in various programs of industrialization. The strategy of these programs was to replace imported manufactured products with those of domestic manufacture, and this strategy involved drastic import restrictions. In Argentina, import duties of 100 to 300 per cent were common. In Mexico, outright prohibitions of imports were the rule for domestically produced items. Brazil, Chile, Venezuela, and Colombia maintained restrictive import regimes that were almost as severe.

The terms of the Latin American Free Trade Area (LAFTA), created in 1960, reflected the preoccupations and uncertainties of its members. In the first place, since LAFTA was a free-trade area rather than a customs union, there was no common external tariff vis-à-vis third countries; each member country remained free to set its own tariff levels applicable to outsiders. In the second place, the aim of LAFTA was something less than total free trade among its members. Various formulas were devised and amended from time to time, all intended to provide a framework that would encourage the gradual reduction of tariffs among the member countries without greatly reducing their freedom to protect their newer industries. The negotiations that took place under these formulas did generate some reductions in the mid-1960s, although of limited importance.

Early in 1967, just as LAFTA's forward movement seemed to be drawing to a slow halt, the U.S. government threw its full weight behind the resumption of a Latin American integration process. Among other things, the United States offered to help finance a continuation of the process. As a result, agreement was reached on new initiatives to be built upon the old. The eleven members of LAFTA would consult with the five other countries that were members of the more advanced Central American Common Market in order to develop the basis for a larger Latin American Common Market. The Latin American Common Market, it was hoped, would be achieved over a transitional period of fifteen years beginning in 1970. To move toward such a market, the LAFTA members would set about developing a common external tariff and eliminating the nontariff restrictions between them, very much on the pattern of the EEC.

With a new fuel added to the integration movement, the process lurched forward into another period of activity. The goals that were to have been achieved by 1973, already quite clearly impossible of achievement by that date, were stretched out to 1980, and the impasse created by seeming failure was avoided.

Meanwhile, however, five of the eleven member countries of LAFTA decided that the pace at which they could move toward economic integration and the depth to which they could push the integration process exceeded that of the LAFTA group as a whole. The five, therefore, moved ahead in 1969 with the formation of the Andean subregional group. In 1974, Venezuela joined the group (in 1975 it appeared that Chile might be withdrawing). The group is devoted to the achievement of a common market among its members by 1980, a market whose ties would be much more organic in nature than those intended among the larger LAFTA group. For instance, a close coordination of industrial strategy was contemplated, and a common external tariff was to be achieved on a timetable more explicit and more rapid than that of LAFTA. Also, a tightly coordinated and highly restrictive policy toward foreign-owned investment and foreign licensing was to be instituted; the process was to be presided over by a high commission and a secretariat endowed with powers on the EEC pattern.

The special initiative of the Andean group was not an accidental aberration. It was a response to one major problem that had dogged LAFTA from its beginnings, the large differences among LAFTA's members in both size and stage of development. The differences at that time between, say, Argentina and Bolivia were so great as to prevent effective integration. The response of the Andean group was to move ahead more rapidly with a more homogeneous set of participants.

DEVELOPMENT ISSUES.   Since the beginning of the Latin American integration process, it has constantly been necessary to recognize the wide disparities in development within the area. These disparities have generated fears that the benefits of any common market in the area might be captured mainly by the more advanced portions of the region, especially by Argentina, Brazil, and Mexico. Accordingly, countries that are notably backward, such as Paraguay, Bolivia, and Ecuador, have received special consideration.

When the five members of the Andean subregional group pooled their economic fortunes, they carried over the same kind of distinction into their internal arrangements. Bolivia and Ecuador were given many privileges and few obligations; they were entitled to access for their products into the markets of the other three without being obliged to open up their own markets on the same rapid timetable.

Another context in which the development concern emerges has to do with the *complementarity agreements,* a type of agreement provided for in the LAFTA and Andean accords as well as in the Central American Common Market. To appreciate the character of these agreements, one has to realize that in Latin American ideology "competition" is not a "good" concept nor "restriction" a "bad" concept. The Latin American regional arrangements are not intended to increase competition, as if competition were an automatic virtue.

As seen by Latin American adherents, the virtue of an enlarged market area is that it opens up new opportunities for coordination and complementarity among different industrial establishments. It offers the opportunity for arranging to have country A specialize in product X, while country B specializes in Y; if both agree to permit the immediate free exchange of the products involved, neither feels obliged to produce a full line for its own needs with all the attendant disadvantages of small scale. The underlying assumption is that, in the absence of some kind of explicit agreement, such a pattern of specialization would be a long time in coming, despite the existence of a free-trade area. (The reader may wish to look back at Chapter 11 to review the problems of specialization in small countries.)

Under the complementarity provisions of the various Latin American accords, a number of agreements have been developed. Some of these agreements, hardly an impressive illustration of the principle, consist essentially of an arrangement among the subsidiaries of a major foreign producer in South America, under which the subsidiaries in different countries specialize to a greater degree and interchange their parts more extensively. But other arrangements are of a more significant character, including an undertaking among the Andean group that parcels out various petrochemicals for production in the different countries and even assigns designated country markets in a few cases. Whether this kind of activity could be expected to contribute much to the development objectives of Latin America remained uncertain.

Among the other problems that the Latin American integration movements have confronted is that of development finance. The number and variety of the institutions that have contributed to Latin American development are slightly staggering. Bilateral aid from the United States has been the largest single source. The World Bank and its satellite agencies have contributed significant amounts. In addition, the Interamerican Development Bank, created in 1959, has added to the flow. On top of these, as Figure 12-2 shows, a special banking institution has been created for the Central American area and another for the Andean group. All these have been busy finding and providing the necessary finances for worthwhile regional projects. By the mid-1970s, the immediate bottleneck in development financing appeared to be the paucity of credit-worthy projects rather than the paucity of funds.

PROBLEMS AND PROSPECTS. Although the 1967 initiative of the United States and the 1969 initiative of the Andean group had the apparent effect of pushing the Latin American integration process over a hump in the road, many difficult problems still confronted the movement. One was to find a common approach toward foreign-owned, especially U.S.-owned, enterprises.

Projects of regional integration that have offered any opportunity for success have usually stirred the interests of foreign enterprises even before they have generated interested responses in businessmen who were nationals within the area. The phenomenon was clearly seen in the case of the European Economic Community; it was repeated again in the development of the Central American Common Market; and it reappeared once more as LAFTA and the Andean group began to take shape.

The reasons for the comparatively rapid response of foreign-owned enterprises are fairly clear. In many cases, such enterprises already were familiar with more than one of the national markets in the area, whereas local businessmen characteristically knew little about any market outside their own. The foreigner, therefore, has found it easy and natural to plan for regional integration, whereas national businessmen have generally been out of their depth in such planning. The consequence has been that the first wave of business response to any initiative in regional integration has been from the foreign-owned business sector. Ford, General Foods, Philips, Olivetti, and IBM have been quicker to recognize the potentialities of an expanded common market than Altos Hornos or Petrobras.

Acutely aware of this fact, the Andean group has been determined to restrain foreign-owned enterprises in order to afford local interests an opportunity to exploit their enlarged horizons. In 1971, therefore, the Andean group agreed on a set of restraints to be applied to foreign-owned subsidiaries in the Andean area. These restraints were unmatched in scope and severity in the history of regional integration movements.

Existing enterprises in the area in which foreigners own 50 per cent or more of the equity are not entitled to the tariff concessions and other trade advantages agreed on by the Andean group, unless the foreigners commit themselves to a divestiture program that will eventually place majority ownership and control in local hands. New foreign-controlled enterprise is not to be admitted into the area unless entry is accompanied by a like divestiture program. Moreover, divestiture must take place in a brief prescribed period—within fifteen years as a rule—and must take place stepwise during the period. In defining the rights, obligations, and opportunities of local partners, state bidders are accorded various advantages over private bidders. For example, state enterprises may be given preference in the purchase of the divested shares.

Especially restrictive rules are applied to foreign investment in certain "sensitive" sectors (although an individual member country has the right explicitly to relax these rules). In the extractive industries, foreigners in effect are barred from stock ownership and are limited to concession contracts that may not exceed twenty years in duration. Foreigners are barred altogether from public utility enterprises, publishing, and radio and television undertakings, and foreign-owned banks are prohibited from accepting local demand and time deposits.

The rules of the Andean group go a step further by regulating some of the business relationships between foreign-owned subsidiaries and their outside affiliates. Technical assistance contracts between affiliates must be free of royalty payments; moreover, such contracts, whether or not between affiliates, must be free of any clauses that tie the local enterprise in terms of its choice of sources for raw materials, technology, or markets. Borrowings by foreign-owned subsidiaries from their affiliates may not carry an interest rate higher than 3 per cent per annum above the prevailing prime rate in the lending market. Borrowing from local credit sources on any terms is sharply limited.

Accompanying the application of the stick to the foreign investor are some proffered bits of carrot. Foreign exchange is guaranteed for remission to the point of earnings up to 14 per cent of the foreign-owned subsidiary's investment. The convertibility of the proceeds from any approved divestiture also is guaranteed; and once the divestiture program has been completed, the right of the foreign owners to withdraw additional amounts of invested capital is assured.

It was not altogether clear in the mid-1970s just what these rules would mean in practice. Responsibility for their implementation lay mainly in the hands of the member states. With varying degrees of formality and explicitness some countries were being less than insistent on the full implementation of the rules. In some cases, notably that of Chile, deviations from the agreed rules were overt. Nonetheless, the rules were not going altogether unheeded. Various countries, including Venezuela, Colombia, and Peru, were engaged in implementing one aspect or another of the agreed rules. As part of the process of limiting profit remissions, national governments were defining and establishing the size of the investment to be imputed to each foreign subsidiary. Interest remissions by subsidiaries to parents were being effectively limited in some countries, and technical assistance contracts were being screened for objectionable provisions. How far and how fast the divestiture provisions would be enforced remained unclear.

In addition to the problem of relations with foreign investors, a second difficult problem facing Latin American integration projects has to do with the nature of the foreign exchange relationships among the participating countries. The currencies of these countries run the gamut, in terms of historical performance, from the Mexican peso to the Chilean escudo. The first has remained fixed at a single value for periods as long as a decade or more; the second has depreciated by over 99 per cent in a recent ten-year period. Such profoundly different patterns suggested disturbing difficulties. Some members in the system might constitute a major source of disruption to trade relations in the region as a result of their repeated changes in currency parities. Even if the parities were not changed, there would be a risk—indeed, a likelihood—that some members of the system might run a heavy deficit in relation to the others and might be unable to finance their deficit balances.

The participants in these Latin American integration projects have been keenly aware of such possible difficulties, of course. But an effective response has not been obvious. Insofar as response has existed, it has taken the form of a modest apparatus for facilitating payments within the region. Under a multilateral compensation arrangement, the central banks of the area are prepared to defer collection of claims on one another arising out of current transactions until given settlement dates. On settlement, each is prepared to extend a line of credit to the others, provided that the credit does not exceed some agreed limit. More than that, each is prepared to pool its claims and counterclaims into a single regional debit or credit. By the mid-1970s, the transferability of debits and credits among the central banks, achieved through a clearing agency in Lima, had become a well-established feature of Latin American payment relationships. Both the volume of clearing transactions and the lines of reciprocal credits among Latin American countries had reached impressive proportions.

The road to a regional market in the Latin American area has been difficult since its beginnings. Still, the movement has been persistent. Of the many uncertainties confronting the movement in the middle 1970s, perhaps the most formidable were the political issues. Could Chile and Brazil with military regimes, Mexico with a bourgeois one-party system, and Colombia with a working democracy hope to find the political means for generating a joint economic arrangement? All that one could count on as a force pushing toward integration was a common concern of the Latin American countries that they must develop a countervailing weight against the great economic power of the United States and Europe.

SUGGESTED READING

BALASSA, BELA, "Tariffs and Trade Policy in the Andean Common Market," *Journal of Common Market Studies*, December 1973, pp. 176–193.

EVANS, JOHN W., *The Kennedy Round in American Trade Policy: The Twilight of GATT?* (Cambridge, Mass.: Harvard University Press, 1971).

MILENKY, EDWARD S., *The Politics of Regional Organization in Latin America:*

The Latin American Free Trade Association (New York: Praeger, 1973).

MORAWETZ, DAVID, *The Andean Group; a Case Study in Economic Integration Among Developing Countries* (Cambridge, Mass.: MIT Press, 1974).

PREEG, ERNEST H., *Traders and Diplomats; an Analysis of the Kennedy Round of Negotiations Under the General Agreement on Trade and Tariffs* (Washington, D.C.: Brookings Institution, 1970).

SWANN, DENNIS, *The Economics of the Common Market* (Harmondsworth, Middlesex, Eng.: Penguin Books, 1970).

Restraints on International Competition

chapter thirteen

The international manager does his business in an environment that is widely regulated by various types of intergovernmental agreements. In Chapter 12, the focus was on agreements that were mainly devoted to reducing the barriers to trade. In this chapter, the focus is on arrangements that are designed to lay restraints on the international movement of goods.

In domestic markets, few nations are prepared to allow the marketplace to set the prices of all commodities; there are always certain products whose markets are thought to require some sort of control, state or private. Sometimes the commodities are pivotal items in the cost of living of the country concerned, such as wheat in Britain; sometimes they are key products in the maintenance of general price stability, such as steel in France; sometimes they acquire importance because they affect the income of a group of producers with political power, such as petroleum or sugar in the United States.

The products that are singled out for special concern tend to have certain common economic characteristics. In these products, as a rule, either demand or supply or both respond sluggishly to price changes. This, of course, is the familiar concept of low price elasticities, which the reader has encountered in other contexts.

On the demand side, low price elasticities are often explained by taste or habit, as in the case of coffee and tobacco; or by biological necessity, as in the case of wheat. Sometimes low price elasticities are the consequence of the phenomenon of *derived demand;* the demand for an exotic alloy that makes up a small part of the cost of a special steel is determined largely by the demand for the special steel and is little affected by the price of the alloy. On the supply side, a sluggish response to price change may be due to the length of the production cycle, as in the case of tree crops, or the unwillingness of producers to cut back production as long as marginal costs are being covered by the market price, as in the case of lead or zinc.

Concepts of this sort apply to all markets, whether domestic or international. Accordingly, this is not the place to explore them at any length. The reader who does not feel at home with concepts such as price and income elasticity of supply and demand, average and marginal cost, derived demand, the cobweb theorem, and similar price-related ideas can easily remedy the lack from standard texts on the economics of the firm.

Market stabilization is almost always difficult; international stabilization, particularly so. Consuming countries see their interests differently from producers; large dominant producers, differently from smaller ones; producers with expanding output, differently from those with declining production. Nevertheless, the manager is likely to encounter large-scale efforts at international stabilization in several different institutional forms.

COMMODITY AGREEMENTS

Man's recorded efforts to stabilize the prices of raw materials go back at least to the days of Joseph's extraordinary operation in Egypt. But modern efforts of this sort usually are thought of as beginning with the European agreement of 1902 regulating the international dumping of beet sugar. As transportation in Europe improved during the latter half of the nineteenth century, beet-sugar producers in a number of European countries had taken to dumping their excess supplies in the neighboring countries' markets. With the annual crop largely determined by weather conditions, sugar producers followed the practice of selling at high prices to their main markets at home and selling "surpluses" to foreign markets at any price that would cover harvest and transport costs. Given the low price elasticity of demand for sugar, this pricing pattern was thought by each producing group to generate more revenue than would a general price reduction to all consumers. But the strategy obviously failed when it was played by all countries; by dumping in neighbors' markets, each undermined the price structure of the other. Hence, to maintain the sugar price, an international antidumping agreement was necessary.

Price stabilization arrangements in raw materials did not become a common feature of the international economy, however, until after World War I. In the period between the two great wars, these arrangements proliferated until they covered many scores of products, including cocoa, meat, sugar, tea, wheat, copper, lead, mercury, nickel, tin, zinc, petroleum, potash, and rubber. The arrangements took many forms. Some, such as those that prevailed in the markets for copper ore and petroleum up to

World War II, were almost wholly in the hands of private producers. Other arrangements, such as those in diamonds, rubber, and quinine, involved very active participation on the part of exporting governments.

After World War II, there was a period in which governments sought to develop systematic rules that might govern the development and operation of international commodity agreements. Intergovernmental commodity agreements came to be thought of as joint actions of sovereign governments aimed at improving on the behavior of the marketplace in the common good. In principle, agreements would be developed with full publicity, they would provide for equal representation on the part of exporting and importing countries, and they would be legitimate only for certain specified purposes—purposes that came to include the management of situations of extreme glut and scarcity, and the management of commodities that were dogged with persistent price instability.

Under these procedural and philosophical guidelines, only four full-fledged agreements were successfully negotiated among governments during the first two decades of the postwar period; these covered tin, wheat, sugar, and coffee. (More limited intergovernmental efforts to regulate the world market in olive oil, tea, and cocoa also were tried from time to time in the period, but without much effect.)

The International Tin Agreement was first ratified in 1956 and renewed regularly thereafter. Most of the world's tin is mined in only a few countries, notably in Malaysia, Thailand, Indonesia, and Bolivia. Historically, production has been in "strong" hands; that is, it has been dominated by a few large tin smelters with their clusters of dependent mines. The problem of organizing international controls, therefore, has never been very difficult. Still, there have been problems. From time to time, sales from the U.S. government strategic stockpiles and sales from the USSR have threatened to shake the market's stability; but, on the whole, the organizers of the agreement have been able to maintain some control over the tin market. To that end, two techniques have been employed: (1) the imposition from time to time of export quotas, and (2) the operation of a buffer stock, with purchases and sales timed to iron out short-term fluctuations in the price of the metal.

A series of International Wheat Agreements has been in effect since 1949. These agreements have been wholly different in origin and purpose from those relating to tin. For several decades, wheat had been the subject of extensive national controls. The governments of the principal producers, including the United States, Canada, Australia, and Argentina, were deeply involved in influencing domestic output and prices. Besides, many countries conducted their foreign wheat trade through government agencies. International regulation, therefore, was only a small step beyond domestic regulation. The International Wheat Agreement, in effect, legitimized governmental interventions that were already widespread. In substance, the agreement provided that in periods of glut exporters would be guaranteed certain sales volumes and floor prices, and in periods of scarcity importers would be guaranteed certain supplies and ceiling prices. In addition, as the agreement's structure has evolved, provisions for emergency help to food-short nations have been linked to the stabilization purposes of the agreement.

The search for legitimacy also was a factor behind the U.S. government's support of an International Sugar Agreement in the early 1950s. As a result of extensive national restrictions, an international division of sugar markets along fairly rigid lines had been in existence for some time. The United Kingdom usually filled its import needs from the British Commonwealth and from colonial dependencies. The United States filled its needs, according to a rigid quota system, from its own high-priced domestic producers, from the Philippines, and from selected Latin American countries. France was drawing her imports from her associated overseas dependencies and colonies, principally in Africa. To the extent that a "free" market existed, its needs were filled from only a few sources, of which Cuba was the most prominent.

In effect, the International Sugar Agreement of 1954 legitimized the principle that the main preferential systems were to be allowed to continue, and that only the so-called "free market" was appropriately of international concern. In that market, a target price range was defined, and export quotas were applied and manipulated to keep the price from moving outside the range. Member importing countries were favored by member exporters at the expense of nonmembers. When the Cuban revolution upset the structure of the world sugar market, the International Sugar Agreement was allowed to lapse. This time the major holdouts were the members of the European Economic Community, who wanted to be free to break into world export markets in the event a European beet-sugar surplus developed. The International Sugar Agreement was finally renewed in 1968 for a five-year period, only to lapse again in 1973. The cause of the lapse this time was a shortage of sugar in world markets, not a surplus. The principal exporters were profiting so heavily from the shortage that they saw no purpose for the time being in restricting their freedom of action. Experience with sugar suggested how difficult it was to find the conditions under which both buyers and sellers saw some advantages in a balanced international agreement.

The International Coffee Agreement, described in more detail later in this chapter, was perhaps the most important of all. Its main beneficiaries were intended to be the less-developed countries, but from their viewpoint the approach embodied in the International Coffee Agreement was unsatisfactory. Accordingly, in the early 1970s, as the world's commodity markets were overcome by a series of acute shortages, various groups of less-developed countries seized the opportunity to reject the principles governing commodity agreements that had previously prevailed. The concept of equal representation for exporters and importers went by the board; so did the concept of open negotiation and publication. In its place, the less-developed countries substituted another fundamental set of ideas, on which they sought to organize the exports of oil, bananas, copper, bauxite, and various other products.

The basic ideas of the less-developed countries were these. First, as pointed out in Chapter 7, it was generally agreed among them that the prices of raw materials had been declining over the long run in relation to the prices of manufactured products, thereby favoring the industrialized countries. Second, it was agreed that even if this were not the case (the data on the point being ambiguous and indeterminate), the exporters of raw materials were in justice entitled to higher prices. The justification derived partly from the fact that, where nonrenewable resources were concerned, exports would be once-and-for-all transactions which could only go on as long as the resource existed. The justification was based also on the assumption that buyers of raw materials in the industrialized countries were as a rule powerful monopolies or oligopolies capable of setting a buying price unless confronted by a countervailing force in the form of a well-organized group of sellers.

The extraordinary market conditions that existed in many commodities in the early and middle 1970s created the possibility that this approach might displace earlier ideas about the nature and form of justifiable commodity agreements. Wherever a considerable proportion of the supply of some raw material lay under the control of a relatively small number of developing countries, the possibility seemed to exist that the world market in the product would be controlled by the joint action of these countries. Both the facts and the prospects, however, proved much more complex, as the succeeding sections will indicate.

RESTRICTIVE BUSINESS PRACTICES

The recent attempts of the less-developed countries to restrict the sale of their commodities in world markets are similar in some respects to the restrictive business practices that have occurred in international trade among individual enterprises. In the jargon of intergovernmental discussions, restrictive business practices are agreements among enterprises to fix prices, limit production, allocate markets, restrain the application of technology, or engage in similar restrictive schemes that adversely affect international trade.

APPROACHES TO CONTROL. Private restrictive business practices in the field of international trade have a lurid history. As a rule, arrangements of this sort have been cloaked in secrecy and have been framed for private ends, but they have not always been limited to wholly private membership. At times, such arrangements have been quite widespread, particularly in the decades between World War I and World War II.

These agreements have taken many different forms. When only a limited number of producers were involved, and when the threat of new entries into the industry was not a major problem, it was possible to envisage arrangements based simply on agreed production quotas and agreed prices. Other simple schemes involved a grant of rebates to buyers, the size of the rebate depending upon the size of the buyer's aggregate purchases from members of the cartel. When more producers and more products were involved, however, the arrangements had to be more complex; the International Steel Cartel, for example, was built upon an elaborate structure including eight national groups and about twelve international sales-coordinating entities that collectively managed a detailed scheme of prices, quotas, penalties, and premiums in the production and international sale of steel. International restrictive agreements also have been built at times on the exchange of patents and trademarks among potential competitors along lines that created a rigid division of markets.

Issues involving the structure of industry are likely to be prominent in national and international circles during the next decade. The probability has been enhanced by the speed of recent changes in such structures, especially in industries in which multinational enterprises are prominent. Practically every industrial country has been reporting a strong trend to greater national concentration in such industries, that is, a strong tendency for the national economy to have fewer and larger firms in the lines in which multinational enterprises are dominant.

Despite that fact, international markets characteristically include more selling firms, not less, as compared with a decade or two ago. The reason that national economies report fewer and larger firms in key industries is the prevalence of mergers. These mergers, however, have arisen partly as a reflex action to the increased penetration of national markets by foreign firms; and the national merger movements, in their turn, have been accompanied by an increase in counterpenetrations by the merged firms into distant markets. The result, therefore, has been that at the international level many markets have grown more diffused, not more concentrated. In the industrial sectors where multinational enterprises predominate, it is no longer three or five or seven huge firms that dominate international markets in any line; the number now tends to be closer to ten or fifteen.

As the number of firms in international markets has grown, the efforts of some of them to reduce the threat of instability in the markets has also grown. These efforts have taken a number of different forms. There has been a growth in transnational partnerships and even an occasional reappearance of cartels of the pre-World War II type. Because national policies on restrictive business practices are not very strong when applied to international trade, many restrictive arrangements have continued in force.

Of the various national philosophies on restrictive business practices, that of the United States is probably the most unequivocal. The Sherman Act lays down a general prohibition against both trade restraints and monopoly. Included in the scope of the general prohibition is "trade or commerce . . . with foreign nations." Even in the U.S. case, however, certain loopholes are applicable to restrictions on foreign trade, and some are explicit in the law. Of the statutory limitations, the most notable is the Webb Pomerene Export Trade Act, which exempts from the Sherman Act certain duly registered associations created "for the sole purpose of engaging in the export trade. . . ." The exemption does not provide an easy escape from the Sherman Act because it has been narrowly construed by the U.S. courts. Still, it reflects a common characteristic in the policies of most countries.

More important than the explicit statutory limitations, however, are the practical limitations of national jurisdiction. Whatever the national law may say, the jurisdiction of a government cannot always be applied effectively beyond the edges of its national boundaries. When the enforcement of law requires the serving of subpoenas, the collection of evidence, and the execution of decisions on enterprises located in a foreign country, a government cannot be sure of securing the necessary cooperation from its fellow sovereigns. Thus, the application of the Sherman Act to the international trade of the United States has been limited by jurisdictional issues.

Nevertheless, as the U.S. courts have interpreted the application of U.S. antitrust law to international commerce, the law has sometimes had a long reach. Agreements consummated outside of the United States have been included, as long as they have substantial impact on American commerce; this has been the case even when all the parties to the arrangement were foreigners. To be sure, the courts have generally qualified the sweeping prohibitions of the Sherman Act with a "rule of reason"; whereas price-fixing or production-control agreements have been regarded as illegal per se, other kinds of agreements have been gauged by surrounding factors and effects. Patent agreements that had the practical effect of extending a group of legal monopolies beyond their intended grant have been struck down; so have trademark arrangements with similar effect. And foreign subsidiaries jointly owned by potential competitors have been held illegal even in the absence of visible agreements between the competitors. United States antitrust policy, therefore, has been a tangible element in the international environment.

In the early 1960s, nearly a score of countries had statutes on the books dealing with restrictive business practices. As a general rule, the condemnation of restrictive business practices in these laws was more qualified than that in the Sherman Act. The presumption of wrongdoing was less automatic. Exemptions from the remedial provisions of the law were more extensive. When remedial provisions were applied, they were the result of a more eclectic evaluation of the individual case. In fact, apart from the United States, only the United Kingdom could be said to have developed a systematic body of case law that offered some reliable guideposts to the manager. Yet the number of instances in which remedies were applied by one country or another was not inconsiderable; and the Draconian nature of the remedies (as illustrated by the imposition of price ceilings in Norway) occasionally exceeded in impact any legal sanctions that might be likely in the United States.

On the other hand, there was a marked tendency to exclude export agreements from the remedial reach of the laws in most countries. Those nations that required the registration of restrictive business arrangements commonly exempted export agreements from the reporting requirements; and those that did not exempt such agreements from the reporting requirements commonly exempted them from the application of remedial measures. A few countries, such as the United Kingdom and Norway, retained a nominal power to apply corrective measures against export agreements detrimental to the domestic economy, but the application of corrective measures to the export trade tended to be quite uncommon everywhere.

Trade among the constituent countries of the European Economic Community, however, was subject to far-reaching antitrust regulation. Whether one cares to refer to trade among the countries of the EEC as "exports" and "imports" is a matter of taste. To the manager in the international economy, it is important to be aware that such transactions are subject to the provisions of the EEC's treaty and regulations.

The general rule of the EEC regarding restrictive agreements is sweeping in its formulation: agreements are prohibited and are void if they contain restrictions on prices, production, markets, investment, or technology, and have the object or result of restricting or distorting competition within the EEC. The appropriate authorities of the EEC are authorized to exempt certain agreements; but the exemptive power can only be exercised if the agreement improves production or distribution or contributes to technical progress, and only if the agreement does not eliminate competition in respect of a substantial proportion of the relevant market. The exemptive power has in fact been used sparingly.

The control of monopolies is always a more difficult field than that of restrictive business practices and one in which nations tend to move more slowly. Nevertheless, the EEC's treaty does attempt to deal with the subject. Even in the absence of a restrictive business agreement, enterprises are forbidden to take "improper advantage" of a dominant position in the EEC by devices such as undue limitations on production, discriminatory selling policies, or tied sales.

There are other provisions of the treaty and its related regulations that are of considerable operational importance. Enterprises that are uncertain as to whether an agreement might be infringing on the treaty's provisions can submit such agreements to the authorities for the purpose of getting a "negative clearance." Enterprises that are uncertain about the legality of their agreements can also choose not to file at all; but if they have chosen unwisely, they run the risk of being subject to fines that can run as high as 10 per cent of their gross sales during the period of infringement.

By the mid-1970s, the EEC's actions suggested that the restrictive business practice provisions of the treaty carried a real bite. To be sure, certain kinds of agreements that might otherwise have been considered subject to the prohibitions of the treaty were granted blanket exemptions, such as arrangements for sole agencies, grants of patent licenses, and arrangements for joint research by industrial firms. But in a rapidly growing number of cases, the EEC's commission directed the revision of agreements that had obvious restrictive effects of the kind contemplated by the treaty; particularly objectionable to the commission were arrangements that created a territorial division of markets among competitors within the EEC area. In addition to compelling some enterprises applying for exemption to modify their agreements as a condition of exemption, the commission also has taken action against a number of enterprises on its own initiative. In several landmark decisions, substantial fines have been levied on enterprises that were found in violation of the articles and regulations.

On the whole, it had begun to appear in the mid-1970s that the subject of international restrictive business practices might become more pressing and difficult for the manager in the international economy in the years ahead. One reason was the reappearance of a few restrictive arrangements in international trade. Indications of the reestablishment of a quinine agreement after World War II had appeared in U.S. congressional hearings and in EEC antitrust proceedings; various governmental bodies had remarked on the existence of restrictive arrangements in the international trade in refined sugar, wood products, and sulfur, as well as in building materials and sanitary ware. Indications of the return of international cartel activity in electrical and telephone cable, nitrogenous fertilizers, and artificial fibers had also appeared.

Even without such evidence, there seemed to be a certain inevitability in the return of this subject to international attention. For one thing, many U.S. firms with little prior experience in the field of international business had ventured abroad and had developed numerous ties with foreign firms, some of which were potential competitors. At some point, there was bound to be a testing of the consistency of the new arrangements with the tenets of U.S. antitrust laws. In the effort to determine the consistency of existing practices with U.S. statutes, it would be necessary to probe some particularly difficult and murky corners of U.S. law. To what extent would the law be applied in arrangements between parents and subsidiaries? To what extent would it be applied to arrangements that had the express or implied encouragement of foreign governments?

Quite apart from the application of U.S. law, there was the possibility of a more extensive application of the laws of other countries. The United Kingdom had already completed a decade or more of experimentation with the regulation of restrictive business practices. Other countries showed a disposition from time to time to do the same. Accordingly, the field of restrictive business practices was very much alive.

One vexing problem for the manager in the international economy as regards restrictive business practices is how to work in harmony with a number of different regimes, each applying somewhat different rules of the game. In some instances, the national rules could be flatly at loggerheads, as when the government of France demands the collaboration of businessmen regarding exports to the United States while the laws of the United States prohibit such collaboration with regard to imports from France. In other instances, the legal procedures of one country could command a defendant in an antitrust case to deliver up information to the state while the laws of another country prohibited the surrendering of that information. In one or two international forums, including especially the Organization for Economic Cooperation and Development in Paris, the problem was being identified and addressed. Still, for the manager, the threat of being caught in a clash among sovereigns is real.

AGREEMENTS BASED ON PATENTS

Agreements among large international enterprises based on patents have had a special place in the history of cartels and restrictive business practices. Authorities in the advanced countries usually approach the subject of patents with a presumption that the patent serves a useful social purpose. Authorities in some less-developed countries look on patents as suspect and exploitative. Restrictive agreements based on patents have frequently been flushed up in the advanced countries, especially in the more sophisticated industries such as chemicals and machinery. So the problem of securing the advantages that patents are capable of providing while at the same time avoiding harmful consequences has been very real.

A patent is a monopoly granted by a government to an inventor or to his assignee for some limited period. A monopoly of that sort, of course, applies only to the country of the government that granted it. So an inventor who acquires a patent monopoly in more than one country does so as a result of the separate grant of each country concerned.

Since every country is free to decide on its own patent laws, patent grants differ in their terms from one country to the next. In the United States, for example, the patent period is seventeen years. In other countries, grants may cover periods as short as five years and as long as twenty.

In most countries, a patent monopoly normally permits the patent holder to prevent others in the same country from making or selling the same product. Since a country can grant a monopoly only for the area that its jurisdiction covers, an inventor who wants to acquire a monopoly in many countries must promptly apply for a patent separately in each of them; his invention, if he does not apply, lies in the public domain, free to be used by everyone. In some cases, the inventor may find his patent application refused under national law; Italy, for instance, will not ordinarily grant a patent on drug products. In some cases, he may find that, because of differences in national laws, his patent extends for different periods in different countries.

Even if patents have been issued by a number of countries on a given invention, the inventor may discover that the courts of one country will uphold the monopoly grant as valid while the courts of another country will strike it down. If the monopoly right is challenged, the patent holder may be obliged to prove that others did not invent the product or process before him, or to demonstrate that the product or process contributed something novel to human knowledge. In some countries, his proof may be sufficient; in others, not. Moreover, in many countries, if the patent holder fails to produce the patented item domestically, or if he "abuses" his patent rights in some other defined way, he may be compelled to grant licenses to other producers or sellers in the country.

Despite the difficulties, inventors or their assignees do often manage to secure patents from many countries covering a given invention and to protect these patents successfully in the courts. They are helped in their efforts by the provisions of the International Convention for the Protection of Industrial Property, an agreement whose antecedents stretch back to the 1880s. Among other things, this agreement provides that, if an inventor files an application for a patent in any signatory country, that act does not disqualify him from receiving a patent in other signatory countries provided he files within a grace period of one year. This provision has proved an important source of protection for inventors.

Of the various international agreements on patents, those being developed among the European countries in the mid-1970s were of particular importance. Under the emerging system, inventors would soon be able to obtain patents in a dozen or more European countries (some of them members of the EEC, some not) by means of any single application-and-issuance procedure. The patents so acquired, dubbed European Patents and issued from a single European Patent Headquarters in Munich, would consist of a bundle of national patents, not a single unified patent, for the territories of the countries concerned. In their original terms and their subsequent enforcement each of the patents would still be subject to the laws and procedures of the respective countries.

In addition to the European Patent, but quite different in nature, was the impending creation of a Community Patent, applicable only to the area of the EEC. The Community Patent would cover the EEC area in a single patent grant, pursuant to a single set of provisions regarding issuance and enforcement. In this case, national governments and national courts would have no role in the life of the patent, which would be subject only to the administration of specially created European institutions. The realization of that undertaking, however, would require considerable alteration in national patent laws before it became a reality; so the concept was still some years from fruition.

The subject of patents and the subject of cartels touch shoulders because leading firms located in different countries have found it possible to pool their patent rights in such a way as to create an extremely effective division of international markets. Picture three large chemical firms, one dominant in the United States, one in the British Commonwealth, and a third on the European continent. Each of the three firms makes a practice of securing patents for all its inventions in all three areas. To divide the existing markets among them, the three enter into an agreement to exchange their rights. The U.S. firm then receives by assignment from the others all the patents that have been issued to them in the United States; the British Commonwealth firm is assigned all the patents issued in the Commonwealth; and the firm on the European continent takes control of all the European patents. With the regrouping, each firm has come to control all the monopoly rights in its own area, which otherwise would have been divided among the three. No one firm can be blocked by any of the others operating in its home territory; but none can venture outside its home territory without encountering a block from another. In practice, the possession of a dominant patent position accumulated in this way leads to an effective international market division among the cooperating firms. This was the main basis on which the world's leading chemical producers divided world markets in the interwar period.

How to secure the benefits that are sought through the grant of patent monopolies without their potential drawbacks is one of the unresolved problems of governments that the manager will encounter repeatedly in the international environment. Among less-developed countries, there is a growing tendency to curtail the rights granted under patents; the monopoly acquired is more conditional and more limited than that usually granted in the more industrialized countries. That tendency has been stimulated not so much because less-developed countries have any special aversion to making monopoly grants but because they are averse to granting monopolies to foreigners. In most of these countries, the majority of patent grants are issued to foreigners. Accordingly, as the patent grant is qualified, a foreign inventor's power over local producers and users is reduced.

MARKETS UNDER RESTRICTION

The objective of this section is to provide a sense of the complexities of markets that actually operate under conditions of restriction, public or private. The cases briefly reviewed here, oil and coffee, have been chosen mainly because of their importance in international trade.

THE CASE OF COFFEE. Coffee is the world's largest tropical crop. The world trade in coffee amounts to about 5 billion U.S. dollars annually. This amount is only a fraction of the net sales of General Motors, but it is still big business.

The principal producing areas in the mid-1970s were Brazil, which dominated the world market with slightly over 30 per cent of the output; Colombia, with another 12 per cent; the Central American republics, whose aggregate output was only a bit less than that of Colombia; and the African nations, which collectively produced another 25 per cent.

The conditions of supply suggest one reason why prices cannot be counted upon readily to "clear the market." Trees begin to yield five or six years after planting and continue to yield for many years thereafter. Short-run increases in yield are not easy to obtain, although variations in fertilizer use, cultivation practices, and picking techniques do affect output. The most powerful short-run force affecting output, however, is the weather, which can have drastic effects. And the major long-run force affecting output is probably agricultural technology plus prices; but the price effects are five or six years in showing themselves. Since the land used for coffee is generally not suitable for other agricultural purposes, the cross-elasticity of supply with other crops is probably not very high for most areas.

As for markets, the United States for many years has been far and away the dominant importer, accounting for about one third of the world's imports. The second most important market in the mid-1970s was Germany; but it was well behind the United States, with only 10 per cent of world imports.

From the buyer's viewpoint, the coffee bean is far from being a standardized product. It comes in many varieties and subvarieties; some of these are substitutable by taste while others are not. For the processor and roaster, the art of buying consists partly of shifting among the various varieties to exploit price differences while maintaining the taste characteristics desired for marketing purposes. With the appearance of soluble (or "instant") coffee in the late 1940s, the possibility of shifting among the various species of coffee increased dramatically. The flavor of soluble coffee can be manipulated more readily than that of the roasted bean. As a result, the demand for the relatively cheap African Robusta strains increased rapidly for a time and tended to displace Latin American varieties.

Although the relative prices of different types of coffee have a substantial effect on the demand of processors and roasters, the price level of coffee as a whole has little effect on consumers. Numerous studies of the price elasticity of demand for coffee indicate that when coffee prices are at their usual levels, such elasticities are generally below .40; that is, a 10 per cent increase in price would generally reduce purchases by less than 4 per cent. Once the price gets very high, however, the demand reactions begin to be stronger.

All the conditions seem to exist, therefore, for violent fluctuations in the price of coffee. And such expectations have frequently been realized. As a result, very early in the twentieth century, Brazil, as the world's principal producer, was already instituting schemes to control the supply of coffee. In the years prior to 1930, these schemes seemed to have marked success, producing high and stable prices for years at a stretch. But the very success of these efforts contributed in part to their ultimate collapse. Attracted by relatively stable prices, other countries, particularly Colombia, increased their production. With Brazil providing a price umbrella, Colombia and the Central American countries were able to sell their total production at attractive prices.

The year 1930 saw a sharp cut in demand for coffee at a time when production was beginning to increase rapidly. At first, Brazil burned large amounts of coffee in a desperate effort to maintain the price. Eventually, as Colombia's production kept expanding, Brazil decided to abandon its support policy. Only the Inter-American Coffee Agreement of 1940, the first in a series of international coffee agreements, put an end to the competitive battle between the two countries.

The 1940 agreement is the first instance of an international commodity agreement in which an importing nation, without significant production of its own, joined exporting countries to control the market. Fourteen Latin American exporting republics and one importer, the United States, participated. The agreement was originally for three years but was extended several times until it finally expired in 1948. Essentially, the agreement placed quotas on exports of the Latin American producer nations and quotas on imports by the United States. Since almost all Latin American coffee exports were shipped to the United States during the war, the two sets of quotas were substantially the same. Although the agreement itself did not mention prices explicitly, prices were strictly controlled by the United States through the Office of Price Administration.

After World War II, supply was unable to keep pace with demand and prices rose rapidly. Spurred by high prices, both Latin American and African countries increased their plantings greatly during the late 1940s and early 1950s. Because of the five- or six-year lag in getting a coffee crop from newly planted trees, prices continued to rise until 1955, when significant amounts of coffee were harvested from new trees.

By 1957, coffee prices were weak again and another round of stabilization efforts began. At first, seven Latin American countries alone attempted to stabilize the market; then fifteen. All to no avail. In September 1959, the Latin American accord was expanded into a worldwide International Coffee Agreement, including African producing territories for the first time. The hesitation of the producers to impose effective production controls continued to be apparent, so the agreement did not provide for such controls. Sales quotas were applied; but they were set quite high relative to demand, and no effective way was provided for policing the agreement. Accordingly, prices continued to decline slightly during the life of the agreement, although the agreement was generally credited with moderating the decline substantially.

The unending search for ways and means to stabilize the coffee market led next to an even more comprehensive agreement in 1962. For the first time, all the principal coffee-importing nations agreed to help the producing countries stabilize coffee prices. Prices would be supported through the use of export quotas, and the "traditional" importing nations would have the obligation of helping to enforce the quotas. They were expected to discriminate against those exporters who had not signed the agreement. This discriminatory action would go into effect whenever 5 per cent or more of world exports were not covered by the agreement.

The operation of the International Coffee Agreement was never smooth. Some exporting countries colluded with their own domestic producers and with foreign importers to violate its agreed provisions by exporting quantities above their quotas. Moreover, problems continually arose over changes in price relationships among the leading coffee types. Few countries showed any inclination to take active measures toward reducing their production. But despite all, the agreement seemed to work to some extent.

The 1968 renewal negotiations brought a new problem to the fore, a problem that reflected the changing character of the coffee-exporting countries. With the development of soluble coffee, exporting countries for the first time were in a position to sell the coffee bean in a processed state. The export of coffee in soluble form had been foreseen in the 1962 agreement, where such exports were counted against green bean quotas on a three-for-one basis by weight. The incentive to export the coffee bean in soluble form was increased by the fact that exporting countries imposed export taxes or equivalent measures upon the bean but not upon the soluble coffee. Accordingly, the domestic price of beans in producing countries was lower than that prevailing in world markets. Moreover, inferior grades of beans that were kept out of the export trade could be used in countries like Brazil quite satisfactorily for the manufacture of soluble coffee.

By 1969, Brazilian exports of soluble coffee to the United States had mounted to over 40 million pounds—about one fifth of the U.S. supply of soluble coffee—with every expectation of further increases. Some U.S.

coffee distributors, especially those using private brands in the sale of their instant coffee, were delighted. Those that had more widely known brands and that had established production facilities in the United States, however, saw the development as a threat. From their viewpoint, U.S. participation in the International Coffee Agreement was elevating the price of the raw material upon which their U.S. processing facilities relied. At the same time, as they saw it, the exporting countries that benefited from the high export price were encouraging their local processors to acquire the raw material at home at a lower price, thereby giving those processors a cost advantage when selling their product in the U.S. market. Efforts on the part of the U.S. and Brazilian governments to find a compromise on the issue, although briefly successful, broke down in the early 1970s, leaving Brazilian processors with a cost advantage.

By the end of 1972, the interests of the key countries had grown sufficiently complex and diverse that it proved impossible to continue the agreement. By that time, both Brazil and Colombia had managed to reduce their reliance on coffee exports to such a degree that the stability of their respective economies did not depend quite so much upon the stability of the coffee market; accordingly, both of them were in a position to assume the higher levels of risk that might be involved if the agreement were suspended. At the same time, the coffee-importing interests in the United States had no strong reasons to assume that an uncontrolled market would be hurtful to their interests. With significant amounts of coffee being produced in more than forty countries widely dispersed around the globe, the buyers did not see themselves as facing a strong threat from a well-organized sales organization.

Consistent with the general spirit that prevailed among the less-developed countries in the mid-1970s, however, some of the leading coffee-exporting countries were actively engaged in trying to keep up the international price of coffee, with or without the cooperation and concurrence of the major importers. One part of their effort was the creation of a coffee exporters' cartel, which included about twelve countries and accounted for four fifths of the world's coffee bean exports. The other part of this effort was the creation of a four-country marketing organization, with a mandate to buy coffee in the open market whenever the price was thought to be too low. As an indication of the mood of the period, it was reported that Venezuela would provide some of the financing out of its surplus oil revenues to permit the coffee pool to keep prices high. The prospects for the pool's success, however, were short-lived. The number and spread of the existing and prospective producers, coupled with consumer resistance to high coffee prices, caused coffee prices to sag. By the mid-1970s, coffee producers again were soliciting the support of the importing countries for the effective control of the international coffee market.

THE CASE OF PETROLEUM. The international trade in petroleum is larger than that of any other product, involving about 100 billion of U.S. dollars annually. From 1928 until World War II, the international petroleum market was organized on the classic lines of an international cartel. Thereafter, as the cartel structure crumbled, the market began a complex transition to a new structure, a transition still far from complete.

Mention of the international petroleum industry conjures up the well-known names of several giant enterprises, each controlling scores of subsidiaries in many different parts of the world. Ranked by their share of world oil production, the roster of these giant organizations is headed by Exxon, followed by Shell Oil, British Petroleum, Gulf Oil, Texas Oil, Standard Oil of California, and Mobil Oil. To complete the list of the prime participants in the international structure, one also would be obliged to include France's Compagnie Française des Pétroles (CFP) and Italy's Ente Nazionale Idrocarburi (ENI). The list covers four nationalities, the United States, Britain, France, and Italy. And it covers both privately owned enterprises and state-owned enterprises. All told, this group alone accounts for about 65 per cent of the world's oil production. Most of the rest is distributed among about twelve lesser companies that for the most part were not drawn into international markets until the 1950s or 1960s.

Each leading oil enterprise has a highly developed vertical structure. Each therefore represents to some extent a microcosm of the oil industry as a whole.

The first stage in the production process for each of these giants consists, of course, of the development of crude oil reserves and the lifting of crude oil from the ground. All the leaders have extensive operations of this sort located outside their own national territories. In most cases, the legal basis for their oil-producing operations is established in an agreement to which the local government and the foreign-owned company are parties. Companies are usually assigned an area for exploration and exploitation during a stated period. The provisions of the agreement usually require a minimum amount of exploration activity and usually return a part of the area to government control in the event oil is not discovered and produced.

The government is paid for these rights in various ways. In less-developed areas, companies build roads, houses, power stations, hospitals, and so on, with the agreement that the facilities are or will eventually become the property of the host country; they pay royalties, usually expressed as so much per barrel of oil produced or as a percentage of the value of that oil; they agree to deliver certain quantities of crude oil to the host government and at the government's option to buy back such oil for cash on the basis of an agreed-upon price formula. Most important of all, companies pay income taxes to host governments, the calculation of "income" for this purpose usually being defined in some detail.

This pattern has many variations. By the mid-1970s, the preferred pattern, especially in the less-developed areas, was one in which the foreign oil company appeared to have nothing more than a management contract, without any attributes of ownership; physical properties and physical output, according to this formula, never left the hands of the producing countries.

From the viewpoint of the companies, however, the substance of the relationship was more important than its form. In terms of cash-flow expectations, one form of contract could be as attractive as the other. Different legal forms might have implications for security of tenure. But events of the 1960s and 1970s had demonstrated that the traditional concession agreement was neither secure nor enforceable, and that the newer management contract was no less so. The strength of any oil company's position depended mainly on the host government's perception of how badly the company was needed, especially on the company's ability to provide access to technology and foreign markets.

The second major stage of the petroleum industry, that of refining, has developed in patterns that reflect the basic strategy of most crude oil companies, that is, the strategy of owning and controlling the refineries that consume the oil. Such ownership has an advantage in the eyes of each of the companies; it reduces the risk of competitive factors causing variations in its crude oil sales, according to the reasoning developed in Chapter 1.

The objective of balancing crude oil production with crude oil refining is not achieved by every company, however. Some companies, especially the newer and smaller ones in the international field, acquired crude oil before they had developed outlets for it. Some were in the reverse position. Partly to exploit these independent sources of crude oil, some countries insisted on owning their own refineries and importing from sources of their own choice; others obliged refineries in the country, whatever their ownership might be, to process oil from independent sources, such as oil from the Soviet Union. As a result, a large "free" crude oil market existed despite the efforts of many producers to achieve "balance." And with the increasing activities of state-owned companies in the oil-exporting countries, the prospects were that free oil would come to constitute an even larger share of the oil moving in international channels.

The final stage of the petroleum industry, that of distribution of the final products to the ultimate consumers, is too complex for easy description. In the search for stability, most oil producers made heroic efforts to develop a captive distribution system capable of absorbing the offtake from their captive refineries. This was the stage of the industry at which competition was keenest, however. Barriers to the entry of newcomers were low; no great amounts of capital and no profound grasp of technology were needed to open a chain of gas stations or fuel oil depots. What was mainly needed was access to a source of product. This was sometimes difficult; but many independent distributors overcame the obstacles. The distribution activity, when operated separately from the rest of the vertical chain, proved a relatively risky and unprofitable business.

In the 1960s and 1970s, another aspect of the business strategy of the industry was acquiring added importance. This was the tendency on the part of the larger oil firms to diversify in various directions: to move into coal and nuclear energy, as alternative sources for power-using customers, and to expand their commitments to the manufacture of petrochemicals. In terms of the concepts developed in Chapter 1, these could be seen as risk-reducing measures intended to lessen their earlier vulnerability as enterprises engaged primarily in the exploitation, refining, and distribution of oil and its basic products.

The mid-1970s was an especially challenging period for managers attempting to analyze the future of the international oil industry because of the extraordinary stresses that had surfaced in the industry during the Israeli–Arab war of 1973 and during its aftermath. The implications of these changes seemed profound; and it was hard to grasp their meaning without some comprehension of the international oil industry's rich and fascinating history.

From the very first, the evolution of the industry seemed—at least in retrospect—to be driven by a consistent and logical set of forces. But for our present purpose it is sufficient to go back to the early 1950s.

At that time, the seven leading oil firms mentioned earlier controlled about 90 per cent of the oil that moved in international trade. The possibility of an outbreak of price competition was held in check by a variety of factors. One was the fact that leading companies, operating in an accommodating and cooperative atmosphere, had gradually adjusted their pricing practices to a common set of norms. As early as the 1930s, all major sellers, irrespective of the source of their oil, calculated their delivered price to any market by reference to the price prevailing in the Texas Gulf port area. The "cost of transportation" from the Gulf port to the market in question (a figure based on published tanker rates) was added to the Gulf port f.o.b. price to produce the conventional delivered price. In this way, all parties quoted substantially identical rates on crude oil for delivery in any market, whatever the source of their crude oil might be.

As long as the world's oil exports came mainly from the Gulf ports and nearby Venezuela, the system was tolerable in the eyes of buyers. As Middle East exports began to grow, however, anomalies began to appear. These anomalies were epitomized by the British Navy's complaint during World War II. Buying their bunker oil in the Persian Gulf from wells within sight of the bunkering station, the British were nonetheless obliged to pay the price prevailing at the Gulf ports in the Western hemisphere plus "phantom freight" for the haulage of the oil across the world to the Persian Gulf. (Ironically, the British Navy's complaint at being overcharged was directed principally at a British oil company in which the British government owned a majority interest.)

The upshot of complaints such as these, when coupled with the rising supplies of Middle Eastern oil in search of a market, was the emergence of a Persian Gulf basing point. Thenceforth, a Persian Gulf f.o.b. price was quoted by the international oil companies; but the price was linked to the Gulf port price so that the two sources would not compete unduly. The Persian Gulf f.o.b. price was then calculated by (1) beginning with the Gulf port f.o.b. price, (2) adding the "cost of transportation" based on quoted freight rates from the Gulf ports to a watershed point in Europe, (3) subtracting the "cost of transportation," similarly computed, from the watershed point to the Middle East, and thus (4) generating the Persian Gulf f.o.b. price.

Given enough time, a system of this sort can eventually be adopted and adapted by an industry that has few actors, even if an explicit agreement does not exist. At first, the Persian Gulf f.o.b. price was fixed in such a way that the watershed was the mid-Mediterranean; here, the delivered price of Middle Eastern oil and the delivered price of Gulf port oil were equal. As long as this was the case, the oil companies could supply their Asian and eastern Mediterranean markets from the Persian Gulf, while supplying the rest from the Western Hemisphere. But as Middle East reserves continued to grow and as the cost advantages of expanding Middle East production became increasingly evident, it became necessary in effect to assign a larger market to the Middle East wells. In late 1947, to accommodate this necessity, the point of price equalization began to drift westward from the mid-Mediterranean to the United Kingdom. By 1949, the cost attractiveness of Middle East oil was beginning to result in substantial shipments to the New York market. When that happened, the price-equalization point was shifted farther west still, to New York itself.

Other factors shored up the stability of the industry. One was the existence of a series of oil-producing partnerships among the leading firms. These partnerships had various stabilizing effects. For one thing, the partners shared similar patterns of production costs. For another, they were obliged constantly to negotiate the levels of output that they found collectively tolerable. These ties still left plenty of room for suspicion and rivalry among some of the leaders, and even for outright competition in some markets. But, on the whole, the risks of large-scale competitive behavior were well contained.

Beginning in 1954, however, signs of change began to occur. Smaller oil companies, located mainly in the United States, had begun to develop increasing concern over the fact that their principal rivals in the U.S. market, the major oil companies, were drawing more and more heavily on their supplies of Middle East crude oil. That source of oil, as was well known, was the cheapest in the world by a considerable margin. The vulnerability of the smaller companies to hard competition from the majors was palpable.

Happily for the smaller companies, however, the barriers to entry into the Middle East and North Africa were declining. Travel and communication were growing easier. Officials in the oil-rich countries were growing more knowledgeable. When a new oil consortium was established in Iran in 1954, a few small U.S. firms were included in the structure. In addition to this group of newcomers, others soon appeared. In the late 1950s, Japanese producing companies were formed in both Saudi Arabia and Kuwait. In the late 1950s, Libya opened up her rich, low-cost reserves to about a score of companies, some of which were comparatively new to the international market. By the early 1960s, the Russians had returned to world markets on a large scale; although in general they accepted the price structure of the international oil companies in sales outside of the Communist countries, they were prepared to cut prices by 10 or 15 per cent if necessary to make sales to independent buyers. For that matter, the major oil companies themselves began to manifest an increasing willingness quietly to offer discounts from the formal Persian Gulf f.o.b. prices.

The entry of the smaller companies—the independents—weakened the position of the majors in still another way. From the viewpoint of the oil-exporting countries, one advantage of inviting an independent company to bid for exploration and exploitation rights was the fact that such companies were likely to be less inhibited than the majors in bidding for such rights. With a strong need for access to cheap oil and with a lesser stake in maintaining the stability of the existing pattern of agreements, the independents could readily offer improved terms. That factor appears to have been more responsible than any other for the gradual shifts in the agreements during the 1950s and 1960s, which involved repartitioning the profits in favor of the oil-exporting countries.

Indeed, the presence of the independents in the Middle East and North Africa weakened the negotiating position of the majors even further. The governments of the oil countries soon learned that an independent which had acquired only one source of cheap oil was especially vulnerable for renegotiation—much more vulnerable than a major with multiple sources. That realization was put to good advantage by governments in the Middle East and North Africa whenever an impasse was reached in negotiations over a division of the rewards.

By the late 1960s, the oil-exporting countries were already the senior partners in the international oil oligopoly, at least as measured by their share of the oligopoly profits; in general, the countries received about 65 per cent of the profits at the crude oil level, which was the level at which practically all the profits were earned. The oil-exporting countries' continued reliance on the international oil companies rested on the fact that it was the companies, not the countries, that had the needed access to foreign markets. Meanwhile, the majors had been obliged to share their leadership with around twelve independents, bringing the majors' share of the international crude oil market down below 70 per cent.

As long as the independents were a significant part of the market, the efforts of the major oil companies to arrest their position of declining power in relation to the oil countries would prove unavailing. In the early 1970s, the supply of oil showed signs of tightness. This was a seemingly fortuitous condition unrelated to the decline in the majors' market position. The introduction of pollution controls, coupled with a period of roaring growth all over the world, led to a tight supply situation. The period of tightness, however, simply accelerated the efforts of the smaller oil companies to develop their own sources of cheap oil. It also gave the oil-exporting countries a new sense of their bargaining power. When an oil embargo was announced during the 1973 war in the Middle East, frantic large-scale users of oil tried to bypass the oil companies and to make their purchases directly from oil-exporting government agencies. This development, another manifestation of the decline in entry barriers, led to unheard of prices of $8, $10, and even $17 a barrel. The process rapidly raised the oil countries' pricing goals and created a new price platform for their subsequent discussions with the oil companies.

The role of the Organization of Petroleum Exporting Countries (OPEC) in this process was on the whole a quite secondary one, at least up to the mid-1970s. Its capacity to accelerate exchanges of information among the countries was, of course, well established. That capacity helped the oil-exporting countries to respond more quickly to the opportunities that the extraordinary markets of the 1970s were providing them. But there had been no real test of the capacity of OPEC to promote a common course of action among exporters in circumstances in which a burden had to be distributed. In the conditions of slack demand and oversupply of the mid-1970s, it appeared that the test might not be long in appearing.

SUGGESTED READING

ADELMAN, MORRIS A., *The World Petroleum Market, 1946–1969* (Washington, D.C.: Resources for the Future, 1971).

BANKS, FERDINAND E., *The World Copper Industry: An Economic Analysis* (Cambridge, Mass.: Ballinger, 1974).

BROWN, MARTIN S., and JOHN BUTLER, *The Production, Marketing and Consumption of Copper and Aluminum* (New York: Praeger, 1968).

BRUN, SUSANNE, "Antitrust Policy in Europe: The Emergence of Strict Enforcement," *Journal of World Trade Law,* September–October 1974, pp. 475–492.

Daedalus, "The Oil Crisis: In Perspective," September 1975.

EDWARDS, CORWIN D., *Control of Cartels and Monopolies: An International Comparison* (Dobbs Ferry, N.Y.: Oceana Publications, 1967).

JACOBY, NEIL H., *Multinational Oil* (New York: Macmillan, 1974).

STEINER, HENRY J., and DETLEV F. VAGTS, *Transnational Legal Problems* (Mineola, N.Y.: Foundation Press, 1968), pp. 904–962.

STEWARDSON, BERNARD R., "Nature of Competition in the World Market for Refined Copper," *Economic Record,* June 1970, pp. 169–182.

VAGTS, DETLEV F., "The Multinational Enterprise: A New Challenge for Transnational Law," *Harvard Law Review,* February 1970, pp. 739–793.

Index